Class, Ethnicity, Gender and Latino Entrepreneurship

New Approaches in Sociology
Studies in Social Inequality, Social Change, and Social Justice

NANCY A. NAPLES, *General Editor*

Class, Ethnicity, Gender and Latino Entrepreneurship

María Eugenia Verdaguer

Routledge
Taylor & Francis Group
New York   London

First published 2009
by Routledge
270 Madison Ave, New York, NY 10016

Simultaneously published in the UK
by Routledge
2 Park Square, Milton Park, Abingdon, Oxon OX14 4RN

Routledge is an imprint of the Taylor & Francis Group, an informa business

Typeset in Sabon by IBT Global.
Printed and bound in the United States of America on acid-free paper by IBT Global.

Library of Congress Cataloging in Publication Data
Verdaguer, María Eugenia.
    Class, ethnicity, gender and Latino entrepreneurship / by María Eugenia Verdaguer.
        p. cm.—(New approaches in sociology)
    Includes bibliographical references and index.
    1. Equality.   2. Social change.   3. Social justice.   I. Title.
    HM821.V47 2009
    338'.0408968073—dc22
    2008043625

ISBN10: 0-415-99560-4 (hbk)
ISBN10: 0-203-87946-5 (ebk)

ISBN13: 978-0-415-99560-3 (hbk)
ISBN13: 978-0-203-87946-7 (ebk)

To my mother,
who provided the love and encouragement that
steered me in my quest for knowledge

And to my father,
who offered the best role model of
professionalism and determination

Contents

Tables

Abbreviations

BDAG	Business Development Assistance Group
CARECEN	Central American Refugee Centre
ECDC	Ethiopian Community Development Council
EDG	Enterprise Development Group
FINCA	Foundation for International Community Assistance
IRCA	Immigration Reform & Control Act of 1986
LEDC	Latino Economic Development Corporation
MBDA	U.S. Minority Business Development Agency
OLA	Washington Office of Latino Affairs
PRIME	Program for Investment in Microentrepreneurs
SBA	U.S. Small Business Administration
SBDC	Small Business Development Center
SDB	Small Disadvantaged Business
TPS	Temporary Protected Status
VLAC	Virginia Latino Advisory Commission

Foreword

According to the 2000 Census, for the first time, among the various racial and ethnic subgroups, Latinos outnumbered African-Americans as the largest minority group in America. In view of this demographic reality, María Eugenia Verdaguer's new volume on the social determinants of Latino entrepreneurship is a timely and welcomed addition to the existing literature on immigrant integration in contemporary America. Just as this book responds to the imperatives of the burgeoning Latino demographic—addressing cutting edge issues of immigrant labor incorporation into today's US economy—it also strives to throw light on a component of migrant research that has traditionally been overlooked: women's migratory and entrepreneurial experiences.

The United States has historically been considered a land of opportunity and freedom for millions of immigrants coming from different shores. Traditionally, the word migrant conjured the image of young, solitary men venturing into foreign lands in search of a better life, their dependents following later. Yet, despite the fact that the number of women migrating to the US has increased significantly over the past few decades—and that even back in the 1930s the number of women migrants already surpassed those of men—research on women migrants was generally neglected until the 1980s. This knowledge gap needs to be filled.

We know that in large and small ways, Latino women entrepreneurs remain autonomous actors, demonstrating their human agency by engaging in income-generating activities both for self-realization as well as for family survival. In fact, according to the Global Entrepreneurship Monitor[1], women remain key contributors to economic development in low and middle-income countries throughout Latin American and the Caribbean. Thus, following this self-employment trend, Latino women immigrants thrive in their US-based economic enterprises. According to the National Women's Business Council, as of 2002[2], Latina-owned firms represented eight percent of all privately-held, majority-owned, women-owned firms in the US. In fact, Latinas owned 39 per cent of women-of-color owned firms, growing in numbers at six times the rate of all US firms. As this study illustrates, Latino women leverage limited financial and human capital, utilize formal and informal social networks, and creatively combine Spanish and English language skills to integrate family members in business ventures. Their creation of new enterprises not only empowers them but galvanizes their capacity-building skills; it also strengthens the vitality of the Latino community, which plays a critical role in bringing market prosperity and economic growth to receiving localities. Therefore, Verdaguer's volume both fills the knowledge gap on women's agency in immigration research while responding to the demand for empirical data to inform the ongoing debate on newcomers' contributions to American society and economy.

Verdaguer's book documents, quantitatively and qualitatively, the labor force experiences of distinct groups of Latina and Latino entrepreneurs in the Washington Metropolitan area. Her empirical study goes beyond merely giving voice to Latino women and men entrepreneurs to underscore variations within and across groups, systematically comparing and contrasting Salvadoran and Peruvian experiences. In the process, it provides rich and meaningful evidence to examine the ways in which the intersectionality of ethnicity, class, and gender profoundly influences immigrant adaptation processes, resource mobilization strategies, social embeddedness dynamics, and actors' entrepreneurial behavior. By demonstrating ethnic variation and divergence in business strategies, including borrowing, labor, and management practices, Verdaguer challenges notions of Latino panethnicity and ethnic solidarity in the context of increasingly transnational social and economic practices. Hence, she cautions that the Latino population should not be treated as a homogenous group, but that their differential opportunity structures to start and develop small businesses are contingent on the socio-economic context of the local institutional and business regulatory environment where immigrant entrepreneurs are situated.

Most recently, the growing number of minority women-owned firms has attracted an incessant interest in entrepreneurship among academics, policy-makers, and practitioners. For academics, Verdaguer's insightful analysis intricately weaves theoretical threads that contribute to a better understanding of the social fabric of Latino economic life. In many aspects, it sets base-line data to explore Latino gender gaps in various types of enterprising activities, to identify factors that have led to Latinos' access to and success in entrepreneurship, to highlight determinants of their slow progress or even business failure, and to explore possible mechanisms to effectively foster their economic enterprises. Recognizing the need for continued scholarship on the subject, Verdaguer also identifies emergent key issues and suggests innovative ideas for further investigation.

For policy-makers, Verdaguer's study raises sensible questions of existing institutional barriers and opportunities, which could better inform policy and facilitate a healthier business environment for immigrant entrepreneurship, particularly for Latinos. For example, their general lack of trust in US financial institutions and their operating in a "cash" economy disadvantage them in terms of start-up capital, asset building, and cumulative investments.

For practitioners, Verdaguer points out pragmatic concerns of considering immigrant entrepreneurship to be a form of social and economic integration that reduces newcomers' vulnerability, increasing their sense of belonging as full citizens in their adopted homeland. She has thoughtfully offered sound advice to employ useful strategies for economic partnership, information, training, technical assistance, and other outreach programs to foster Latino men and women's economic empowerment.

In sum, a nuanced understanding of Latino entrepreneurs as differentiated social and economic actors necessitates a comparative framework that accounts for both the intersectionality of structures of differences (class, ethnicity, and gender) in immigrants' lives, as well as for their degree of resilience as they reshape the terms of their opportunity structures. Rooting our understanding in the comparative framework provided by this book enriches our social imagination by linking structure to the individual and to public policy.

Esther Ngan-ling Chow
American University

Acknowledgments

This book began as a doctoral dissertation I wrote at the Department of Sociology at American University, and it would not have been possible without the unstinting support of a number of people. At American University, Ken Kusterer guided the organization of my initial thinking on this subject. His theoretical insights, wisdom, and kindness continue to inspire me in ways that have shaped me both intellectually and personally. During my graduate studies, I was fortunate to have Esther Ngan-Ling Chow as my main academic adviser. Through the years she has been a mentor, a friend, and a role model of feminist scholarship and activism. Her substantive feedback and trenchant questions have indelibly influenced the arguments, methodology, and organization of this book. I also want to thank Nancy Naples, Routledge's series editor for her constructive thoughts and comments, which encouraged me to undertake the final revisions to the manuscript. I completed the data analysis and writing for this study while at Catholic University, where Michael Foley provided collegiality, sound advice, and insightful lessons on the application of social capital theories to the fluid realities of empirical research.

My friends have often served as my extended family, and have provided encouragement, affection, and assistance in more ways than one. I am thankful beyond words to my friends Milagros and Ivan Thorn for providing the luxury of time, space, and peace of mind so that I could devote myself to writing without the exigencies of childcare. I also owe a debt of gratitude to Gaspar Glusberg, Michael Howley, and Sherry Ampuero for their kindness and assistance at various stages of this project. Alex Antram read through the entire manuscript, offering editorial suggestions that have enhanced the text.

I am very appreciative of my family's love, patience, and understanding in the face of continued and extensive reclusions to complete this project. I want to thank my husband, Tony Homan, for his steady support, and stimulating discussions on immigration and economic sociology, and my son, Ian Homan, who never ceases to provide magical hours of joy.

I completed final revisions to the manuscript a few months into a position at the Bureau of Educational and Cultural Affairs at the US Department of State. Despite my present institutional affiliation, I am solely responsible for the views expressed in this book, which do not represent in any way those of the US Department of State or the US Government. Finally, I remain indebted to the many entrepreneurs across the Washington metropolitan area who allowed me into their lives, sharing with me their precious time and personal stories.

1 Latino Entrepreneurship Reconsidered

An Overview of the Study

Ever since classical economic sociologists embarked on an intellectual journey to elucidate the relationship between social structure and the economy, scholars have attempted to unveil the complex mechanisms through which cultural elements of a social system influence economic behavior. Thus, from Max Weber's classical study on Protestant religious values as the driving force behind the emergence of capitalism, to Mark Granovetter's theory on embeddedness, sociologists have attempted to understand the way in which social relations and institutions pattern economic action. Immigrant entrepreneurship is just one empirical manifestation of socially oriented economic behavior, but one of particular relevance given its far reaching implications for immigrant integration, social welfare, technological innovation, and economic development in 21st century America.

Thus, the immigrant entrepreneurship literature finds its intellectual roots in a tradition of scholarship that began over a century ago. Yet, it has retained, by and large, an elitist and culturalist flavor. In all, scholars have continued to glamorize the cultural traits that distinctively endow "successful" immigrant groups for entrepreneurship, enhancing their business practices and performance. In the process, they have primarily focused on entrepreneurial groups exhibiting high levels of commercial performance, thereby neglecting to examine those entrepreneurs less successful from an economic standpoint. As a result, in painting a celebratory portrait of immigrant entrepreneurial success, the literature has left behind the stories of those less visible, of whom little is known. In other words, beyond Cubans in Miami and/or Dominicans in New York, there is a dearth of knowledge on the entrepreneurial experiences of "Other" Latino newcomers, whose growth rate is faster than that of any other immigrant group in America.

Not only has the scholarship retained a culturalist lens, but, for the most part, it has also suffered from a myopic tendency to treat ethnicity as a monolithic construct, overlooking within group variation. In fact, members of a same ethnic group often harbor dissimilar values and face distinct opportunities due to class, gender, religious, racial, and/or other stratifying cleavages. This attempt at ethnic homogenization is perhaps nowhere as ubiquitous as in the use of panethnic labels. Often, panethnicity subsumes, under broad categories, divergent national experiences with little more in common than colonial legacies and/or close geographic proximity. This is certainly the case for recent Latino newcomers, who arrive to America from all walks of life, peasants and professionals, political refugees and economic migrants, women and men, young and old, documented and undocumented.

Likewise, and to the same extent that the ethnic entrepreneurship literature has tended to homogenize Latinos' entrepreneurial experiences, it has also remained androcentric, largely treating entrepreneurs as genderless actors. Nevertheless, the evidence gathered from the gender and migration scholarship invariably shows that gender, as main organizer of social life, profoundly shapes the immigrant experience. Therefore, neglecting to explore the gendered components of immigrant entrepreneurial behavior blinds us to important insights about the dynamics of Latino small businesses in particular, and of immigrant integration processes in general.

Beyond androcentric biases, the ethnic entrepreneurship literature has evolved, over the past couple of decades, from a dichotomous "class and ethnic resources" focus to an interactionist approach, where immigrant group traits interact with demand side factors in receiving communities to determine entrepreneurial outcomes. As a result, scholars now concede that the local business regulatory environment, immigration policy, and localized institutional factors in host communities also shape newcomers' economic experiences. Equally important—although far less explored—racial and ethnic relations, including the social structure of Latino immigrant communities in places of reception, remain paramount to the development of thriving entrepreneurial environments. Scholars agree that, underlining these contextual forces, social networks mediate the degree of agency individuals' exert, galvanizing or hampering their resource mobilization strategies. Ultimately, it is the social embeddedness of newcomers' networks that seems to play a critical role in conditioning immigrant mobility and integration into American society.

Although such a rich intellectual tradition has fundamentally advanced our understanding of contextual and group determinants of immigrant entrepreneurship, prevailing theories provide only a partial explanation of the Latino entrepreneurship phenomenon. Because Latinos are differentiated social and economic actors, unevenly positioned in a stratified hierarchy along interwoven structures of class, ethnic, and gender difference, their access to resources, including entrepreneurial opportunities, is uneven. Yet, immigrants exert various degrees of agency contingent on collective resources and an intrinsic sense of empowerment. Therefore, a nuanced understanding of Latino business experiences necessitates a theoretical framework that accounts for the intersectionality of structures of difference in entrepreneurs' lives as well as for their degree of resilience and agency at recasting the terms of their opportunity structure.

Responding to this void, this book examines the ways in which gender, class, nationality, and the local environment shape entrepreneurial experiences among dissimilar Latino immigrant groups. To this end, it focuses on Salvadoran and Peruvian immigrant entrepreneurs in the Greater Washington metropolitan area. The questions that drive this research are straightforward: Is there variation in Latino resource mobilization strategies within panethnic, national origin, and gender boundaries? Or what are the ways in which the intersectionality of structures of difference—class, ethnicity, and gender—shape mobilization and opportunity structures for distinct Latino newcomers? How does gender mediate access to business ownership and business development? Is the social embeddedness of Salvadoran and Peruvian men's and women's networks equally effective in facilitating entrepreneurial ventures? And how do informants and institutional gatekeepers perceive the policy environment for Latino immigrant business development across the Greater Washington metropolitan area?

To look at intra-ethnic variation within panethnic categories, this book compares the experiences of Salvadoran and Peruvian first generation immigrants. The reasons behind this choice, as chapter three will address, is that the Central and South American share of Latino immigrants—of which Salvadorans and Peruvians are a part—are the fastest growing segment of the US Latino population; they are also the majority of Latinos in the Washington region (US Census Bureau 2006; Singer 2007). Most important, Salvadoran and Peruvian socio-demographics differ significantly upon arrival. Thus, a comparison of Salvadorans and Peruvians provides an empirical illustration of the ways in which dissimilar pre-migration circumstances and levels of reception condition opportunity structures for different groups of Latino/a entrepreneurs. In the process, this study also contributes to a more nuanced understanding on the lesser known experiences of "Other" Latinos, that is Latinos other than Mexicans, Puerto Ricans, or Cubans (Rodriguez, Saenz, and Menjivar 2008).

The Greater Washington area provides the backdrop to this study because of its unique demographic characteristics. Having rapidly evolved from historically defined black and white dichotomies, the region has recently become an emerging immigrant gateway to countless Asian, African, and Latin American newcomers.[1] With counties where either non-Hispanic US whites or African-Americans predominate, the region allows for a rich examination of Latino entrepreneurial dynamics within multicultural contexts. Most recently, virulent anti-immigrant tensions have erupted across Washington suburban localities, bringing communities such as Manassas, Herndon, and Prince William County into the national limelight. Adding complexity to the picture, Washington Latinos draw from a more diverse group of nationalities than counterpart populations across the country. Notably, no Latino immigrant group dominates the Washington demographic landscape in the same way that Mexicans do in California or Cubans do in Miami. While Salvadorans constitute the largest Latino national origin group, followed by Mexicans and Peruvians, Washington Latinos remain fragmented precisely because of the lack of a massive numerical dominance from any one group.

Thus, focusing on a new immigrant receiving area and on Latino immigrant entrepreneurs we know little about, this book broadens the ethnic entrepreneurship debate from an empirical and theoretical standpoint. Empirically, it begins to disclose the untold story of less "successful" immigrant entrepreneurial groups in America. Not only those less visible and deemed less fit for such an undertaking, but those of more modest means, with businesses that have few or no employees. Such focus is strategic given that Latino immigrant entrepreneurship is primarily a non-employer phenomenon (Robles and Guzman 2007; Valdez 2008). Further, because of the breadth and wealth of Latinos' experiences, a greater understanding of their bifurcated trajectories, either as survivalist or upwardly mobile entrepreneurs, is paramount to better inform policies geared to develop their potential.

Theoretically, this book deglamorizes the ethnic solidarity thesis, largely premised upon the notion of harmonious and cohesive social relations among co-ethnics and co-nationals. In fact, the most recent scholarship argues that the solidarity of immigrant networks is not only a function of structural factors in places of reception (Menjivar 2000), but of specific pre-migration and demographic characteristics of immigrant communities. Thus, while some immigrant groups might show a higher degree of social solidarity with co-ethnics, others will have fragmented co-national networks stratified along class and racial lines. In sum, stories in this study highlight the limits of reactive ethnicity and social solidarity when class, racial, territorial, and gender hierarchies brought from the homeland shape immigrant identity formation (Paerregaard 2005).

Furthermore, in the process of unveiling within group variation, this book engenders the immigrant entrepreneurial experience. Because Salvadoran and Peruvian entrepreneurial options, practices, and decisions are largely shaped by patriarchal gender relations within the family and immigrant community, entrepreneurial strategies are inherently gendered. Chapter seven examines the ways in which men's and women's access to capital, labor, and information, as well as their marketing and business styles, are regulated by varying degrees of patriarchal gender ideology. Social stigmatization, sexual predation, sexual harassment, and other forms of social control differentially affect men's and women's mobility, options, and aspirations as they engage in economic life. Paradoxically, for men, patriarchal gender ideology not only carries privileges, but also significant burdens as many struggle with the need to reconcile rigid masculine roles as breadwinners with status incongruence and downward mobility in their new homelands. As stories will eloquently illustrate, gender, interwoven with structures of class and ethnic difference, conditions men's and women's entrepreneurial options in distinct and significant ways.

And yet, defying structural barriers, participants' narratives invariably suggest that their collective mobilization through ethnic, gender, and class-based networks often aid them in recasting the terms of their opportunity structure. For most study participants, entrepreneurship provided a strong source of personal empowerment that went beyond economic prosperity. Entrepreneurship allowed men and women study participants to develop a deeper sense of belonging to American society, nurturing hope, self-confidence, and motivation. Ultimately, in fostering their self-sufficiency and integration to America, entrepreneurship often unleashed a virtuous cycle of prosperity, well-being, social engagement, and productivity.

From a policy perspective, this book should be of relevance to policy-makers interested in fostering the development of ethnic small businesses. Small businesses are of considerable importance since many sources estimate they generate more job growth in contemporary America than big corporations. Given that immigrant (and ethnic) entrepreneurs occupy a strategic portion of the small business sector, a better understanding of their experiences is pivotal. As important, findings from this study will be relevant for immigrant integration, social welfare, and economic development discussions. With the current disturbing wave of anti-immigrant sentiments in America, it becomes more necessary than ever to realize that these sentiments constitute not only a political, but also an economic liability. Today's newcomers, following on their predecessors' footsteps, bring vitality to American society and economy; they engage in productive activities that generate jobs, offer services, produce tax revenue for federal and state governments and, ultimately, enable America to remain competitive in the global marketplace.

COLLECTING THE STORIES: RESEARCH DESIGN

To examine the research questions driving this study, I applied a multi-staged field research design, which allows for the collection and presentation of information in a way that provides rich context. Further, given the exploratory nature of the study, field research enabled me to capture nuances on the experiences of populations for which there is virtually little, if any, empirical information. In the process, qualitative research allowed me to incorporate both study participants' and other relevant actors' voices. Although the key units of analysis were men and women business owners, I also looked at their social networks, hence shifting the research focus from the micro to the meso-levels of analysis.

My presence as a "quasi-insider" in the field (Latina immigrant of Argentine origin) often enabled me to gain easier access to and rapport with prospective informants. Because of my Spanish-English bilingual and bicultural abilities, I was able to conduct all in-depth interviews in Spanish, capturing linguistic and cultural subtleties. As the data collection process evolved, I gained the confidence of many study participants, to whom I became a trusted friend. To protect their confidentiality, I have de-identified real names and relevant demographic information, slightly reconfiguring informants' backgrounds to protect them from social disclosure.

Finally, this study presents some theoretical and methodological limitations. First, I use national origin as an imperfect measure of ethnicity with the caveat that national labels often conceal significant regional, racial, and religious in-group variation. Second, my sample combines dissimilar self-employment categories and business sizes, including formal and informal economic ventures. Yet, approximately 60 per cent of businesses participating in the study are micro-enterprises with no more than five employees. This empirical combination of businesses at various stages of growth is congruent with broad theoretical definitions that aggregate a wide variety of entrepreneurial and self-employment practices. Therefore, I use entrepreneur and self-employment indistinctly throughout the book. Last, because of my non-probability sampling design, I do not intend to make generalizations from my findings to the entire Washington Salvadoran and Peruvian populations. Instead, this exploratory study attempts to throw light onto social phenomena that has traditionally been studied from other perspectives.

Data Collection

Over a three year period, the data collection methodology aimed to build knowledge from the general to the specific level of analysis. Following a "mixed method research" strategy (Creswell 2003), I moved from an initial review of census data to an exploratory qualitative research phase that paved the way for the final intensive interviews.

First Phase—Secondary Analysis of Census Data

The secondary data analysis entailed a cross-sectional demographic study of Latino small businesses, and of the Salvadoran and Peruvian immigrant populations in the United States, especially focusing on Washington Salvadorans and Peruvians. I framed this analysis in reference to broader Latino trends and demographics. I used both 1990 and 2000 US census data (Census of Population and Housing, The Foreign Born, Summary Tape Files 1, 3, and 4B), 2002 Economic Census data, and the 2006 American Community Survey. An important caveat to the usefulness of economic census data is that it does not disaggregate Latino small business owners by nationality, except for Mexicans, Cubans, and Puerto Ricans.[2] Furthermore, businesses for Peruvians and Salvadorans are collapsed into one single "South/Central American" category. Because of serious census data limitations to capture informal business practices (and their complex overlap with formal economic activities), this demographic analysis was only aimed at identifying descriptive patterns to be cross-validated through the subsequent qualitative methodology.

Second Phase—Exploratory Field Work

The second research phase was informed by an inductive approach and entailed: (1) twenty-five expert interviews with Latino business leaders and institutional gatekeepers; and (2) 107 initial survey interviews with Salvadoran and Peruvian men and women entrepreneurs. In addition, I conducted participant observation at federally and locally-sponsored business training courses, at Latino chambers of commerce-sponsored events, and at similar social functions bringing together the Latino business community. In addition, I gathered information from secondary sources, such as government reports, non-profit and community organization brochures, and small business assistance programs' publications.

The purpose of the expert interviews was to obtain information on policies affecting Latino immigrant small businesses, including licensing requirements, labor standard and zoning laws, funding levels for minority small business assistance programs, training opportunities, and outreach programs available for minority and immigrant entrepreneurs. In sum, the purpose of these interviews was to get a sense of the opportunities available to the groups under study, and to capture the impressions of gatekeepers and individuals who work closely with Washington Latinos.

Expert interviewees were drawn from institutions such as the Greater Washington Ibero-American Chamber of Commerce, the Hispanic Chamber of Commerce of Montgomery County, the Northern Virginia Peruvian-American Chamber of Commerce, Casa de Maryland, the Latino Economic Development Corporation (LEDC), Finca USA, the Spanish Catholic Centre, the Enterprise Development Group (ECDC), the Business Development Assistance Group, Inc., Mason Enterprise Center, the Small Business Administration (SBA), the Minority Business Development Agency at the US Department of Commerce, CARECEN, the Washington Office of Latino Affairs (OLA), and the various SBA-funded Small Business Development Centers (SBDCs) across the metropolitan area. In addition, I interviewed key Latino business and community leaders.

I also conducted 107 initial survey interviews of Peruvian and Salvadoran seasoned, nascent, and aspiring entrepreneurs. The table in Appendix B lists the types of business enterprises participating in the survey. These structured interviews collected standard socio-demographic data as well as grounded preliminary information on major themes shaping informants' lives. Most importantly, these initial interviews were critical to establish trust and rapport with potential informants for the subsequent phase of in-depth interviews. Further, this early fieldwork allowed for the identification of theoretically sound business industries for the snowball sampling design of the subsequent research stage.

To select survey participants, a non-probability sampling technique was used in light of the fact that there is no sampling frame of all Peruvian and/or Salvadoran small business owners across the Washington metropolitan area. I used dispersed referral snowball sampling to select survey informants from distinct neighborhoods given that there is no single research site for all Washington Salvadoran and Peruvian small businesses. Thus, I conducted fieldwork across the District of Columbia, Arlington, Fairfax, and the cities of Falls Church and Alexandria in Northern Virginia, and in Montgomery and Prince Georges' Counties in Maryland. In dispersed referral snowball sampling, the investigator selects relevant dimensions of units to be studied through a dispersion of initial referents at the beginning stage to ensure sample heterogeneity (Chavez 1998; Bernard 1988). My grounds for initial differentiation among referents were class background, nationality, sex, geographic location of business, and business industry.

Although I primarily used snowball sampling to recruit study participants, in the beginning stages of the fieldwork, I attempted to use organization-based networking sampling. Whereas snowball sampling uses a process of chain referral where members of the target population, once located, are asked to provide names and addresses of other members of the target population, chain referral sampling is often necessary to reach hidden populations, such as informal and/or undocumented entrepreneurs (Cornelius 1982; Mahler 1995). In contrast, in organization-based networking sampling the investigator makes presentations to social, educational, or commercial organizations and elicits volunteers for the study. Then, she assigns a code number to each volunteer and randomly selects subjects from each study site (Chavez 1995).

A couple of months into the fieldwork, as I was conducting participant observation at a small business assistance program agency in the District of Columbia, a change in senior management resulted in the incoming executive director banning my access to program participants. Although I was interviewed and provided extensive information on my research, I was not further allowed to conduct research on their premises. Thus, I had to resort to a combination of snowball and targeting sampling. To recruit participants, I placed advertisements on Latino stores, restaurants and churches, and on various Latino newspapers, including some exclusively serving the Peruvian and Salvadoran communities. Further, in exchange for participation in the survey, I offered participants both an informational package in Spanish on sources of assistance for aspiring entrepreneurs, as well as monetary compensation for participation in the study.[3] The newspaper advertisements ran for three weeks and elicited 44 phone calls, of which nine were of individuals ineligible to participate in the study.

I conducted face-to-face or phone interviews contingent on informants' level of trust and comfort in answering questions in a more or less personal setting. To minimize biases because of this fluctuation in methodology, I strictly adhered to the instrument and avoided digressions during the administration of the survey. Of the 107 surveys completed, 36 per cent were conducted face-to-face, 31 per cent were phone surveys, and 33 per cent were phone surveys in response to postings and newsletter advertisements. What became clear through these initial efforts was that different Latino populations required different recruitment techniques. Therefore, to recruit Salvadorans, I had to either go to the field and tour Latino-populated commercial neighborhoods or rely on chain referral sampling to gain informants' trust. Peruvians were often easier to recruit, and seemed less apprehensive and distrustful of researchers and public inquiries in general.

Third Phase—In-Depth Interviews

Drawing from information obtained during previous stages, I designed the interview protocol and conducted 45 in-depth interviews with selected Peruvian and Salvadoran men and women small business owners. Appendix B and Tables 1, 4, and 5 in chapter three present demographic profiles of survey and in-depth interviewees. The length of the interviews oscillated between an hour and a half and three hours, and interviews were conducted in business premises and/or in public places. With the exception of four interviews, all conversations were audiotaped and notes were taken verbatim. The purpose of these intensive conversations was to obtain content-rich data on informants' resource mobilization strategies, on the operation of their social networks, and on their perceptions of local opportunities and barriers to their entrepreneurial pursuits.

In this final phase, to select informants, I used a combination of theoretical and targeted sampling. Whereas I used theoretical sampling along dimensions of interest—such as national origin, sex, business location, degree of business formality, and business industry—targeted sampling ensured dispersion and heterogeneity in the snowball sample. Theoretical sampling (Glasser and Strauss 1967) is a non-probability sampling strategy that allows to sample broad analytical categories that facilitate the development of theoretical insights (Singleton, Straits, and Straits 1993: 329). The targeted sampling process involved: 1) identifying research sites with a high concentration of potential informants; 2) selecting potential informants after careful observation and interviews with people at these sites; and 3) developing specific plans for recruitment at each site (Watters and Biernacki 1989).

Data Analysis

Before initiating the second research phase, I conducted ten pilot survey interviews with individuals sharing similar characteristics to the population under study to ensure that the instrument was clearly understood and accurately interpreted. This aimed at improving survey data measurement and reliability. Further, the survey data were checked for inconsistencies during the analysis of the in-depth interviews since participants were drawn from the larger initial interview sample.

A couple of Spanish-speaking assistants were hired to transcribe the in-depth interviews and the resulting transcriptions were carefully checked for accuracy against the recorded data. This verification process was instrumental in the conceptualization and classification of information through "categorical aggregation" (key themes/codes) and in establishing patterns of categories to look for correspondence between them. Further, I developed nested coding categories with different levels of specificity ranging from descriptive to detailed pattern codes (Coffey and Atkinson 1996; Miles and Huberman 1994). I ensured that the qualitative data adhered to scientific validity and reliability by constantly probing informants and by regularly providing verification of information and interpretation. In line with this approach, I made use of a mixed method design throughout the bulk of the data analysis.

The qualitative analysis entailed extensive reading through transcripts and field notes as well as detailed memoing. Only relevant passages cited to illustrate informants' themes and narratives were translated into English. Finally, the analysis benefited extensively from the application of a computer software package, NVivo, which greatly enhanced the storing, retrieval, representation, and visualization of data from multiple sources, expediting cross-comparisons (matrixes) among themes and cases.

Definition of Terms

Business size: this study focuses on Salvadoran and Peruvian-owned small businesses with anywhere from zero to 30 employees. Individual proprietorships, partnerships, and corporations were included in this study.

Individual proprietorship: an unincorporated business owned by an individual. Self-employed persons are included in this category (consistent with census data). The business may be the only occupation of an individual or the secondary activity of an individual who performs wage work for an employer.

Partnership: an unincorporated business owned by two or more persons having a financial interest in the business.

Entrepreneur: the terms "entrepreneur" and "small business owner" will be used interchangeably throughout this study.

Immigrant: this category will include only first generation immigrants or those not born in the US.

Latin American or Latino: the terms will be used interchangeably, although they are slightly different. "Latin American" exclusively refers to the Latin American foreign born, whereas "Latino/a" is the US Census category for all individuals of Latin American, Spanish, or Hispanic descent.

ORGANIZATION OF THE BOOK

The book is organized into nine chapters, including this initial overview, a review of related research, a socio-demographic analysis of census data on Salvadoran and Peruvian immigrants, five substantive empirical chapters, and a conclusion. Although each empirical chapter tackles a particular line of inquiry, this study is predicated on the concept that, in everyday life, class, ethnicity, and gender constantly intersect to shape entrepreneurial behavior. Yet, for purposes of clarity, I have addressed each variable and its effect on separate chapters, with the exception of the chapter on social networks. Thus, chapter eight presents an intersectional analysis of the simultaneous ways in which structures of difference shape participants' lives. The following summary of substantive chapters lays out their content.

Chapter three provides a contextual overview of Salvadoran and Peruvian immigrants in the United States, including a brief description of the political, economic, and social forces that fueled their migration, and their distinct demographic characteristics and settlement patterns. It situates Latino-owned small businesses in the national economy, including their embeddedness in various geographic regions, and their position vis à vis other ethnic minorities. Next, it outlines the economic and social changes that have affected the Washington area in the last three decades, attracting a growing contingent of Salvadorans and Peruvians.

Chapter four presents a demand side analysis of Washington Salvadoran and Peruvian entrepreneurship. Reviewing the US institutional framework, it first considers government policies affecting immigrant small business development in general. Next, it focuses on the Washington economic, social, and institutional landscape, discussing its repercussions for Salvadoran and Peruvian entrepreneurial performance. As important, it examines gatekeepers' and informants' perceptions of the opportunity structure, including attitudes about blocked mobility and about the effectiveness of business assistance programs.

Chapter five introduces a supply side analysis of immigrant entrepreneurship, advancing the theoretical proposition that social relations based upon class and/or ethnic ties mediate Salvadoran and Peruvian business ventures. It reviews the factors that have contributed to Salvadorans' stronger group cohesion, including socio-demographic, transnational, and reception dynamics. Further, it presents an overview of participants' resources, including human, financial, and class-based social and cultural capital. Last, it examines Salvadoran and Peruvian class-based business strategies.

Continuing with a supply perspective, chapter six examines the economic value of ethnicity and the mechanism through which it mediates Salvadoran and Peruvian entrepreneurship. It compares Salvadoran and Peruvian ethnic-based resources, and highlights the strategic value of family and extended kin in the running and management of immigrant businesses. Finally, it reviews Salvadorans' and Peruvians' business strategies, demonstrating that ethnicity significantly patterns their financing, labor, marketing, and management practices.

Chapter seven brings a gender analysis approach to the study of Washington Salvadoran and Peruvian entrepreneurs. It examines how gender, as main organizing category, interacts with class and ethnicity to mediate informants' access both to resources and to concomitant business strategies. It looks at gender stratification in the immigrant economy, and discusses how gender socialization processes differentially shape men's and women's motivations for migration and self-employment. As important, it engenders Salvadorans' and Peruvians' cultural, ethnic, and social capital in the context of enduring patriarchal gender relations within the family and community. Last, it reviews gendered strategies in informants' deployment of familial resources, labor, and marketing strategies.

Chapter eight explores how Washington Salvadoran and Peruvian class, ethnic, and gender-based networks mediate their entrepreneurial ventures. It discusses the distinct types of informal and formal networks to which study participants had access, the types of social capital these networks accrue, and how their social embeddedness grants members uneven access to opportunity structures.

Finally, chapter nine summarizes the empirical and theoretical contributions of this study, synthesizing main empirical findings, and exploring their theoretical and policy implications for immigrant integration, social welfare, and economic development in the US. In so doing, the chapter also identifies areas for future research, particularly relevant in the current post 9/11 immigration environment.

2 Theorizing Immigrant Entrepreneurship

This chapter reviews the rich corpus of literature that informs the theoretical framework of this study. Specifically, I draw from four bodies of work to address the research questions outlined in the previous chapter: 1) economic sociology; 2) the sociology of immigration; 3) the ethnic entrepreneurship literature; and 4) the gender and migration literature. In drawing from and engaging with these scholarships, some conceptual and thematic convergences emerge. I turn to a discussion of each intellectual tradition next.

ECONOMIC SOCIOLOGY

The Classical and the New Economic Sociology

Classical economic sociology traces its origin back to the turn of the twentieth century when its founding thinkers sought to explain the economy as an historical social system. Underlying this grand theoretical project, focused on unveiling the origin and nature of modern capitalism, laid the assumption that any economic model was a reflection of its social system. In other words, the economic structure had been significantly shaped by culturally based elements of the social system. Variations of such lines of thought were most notably advanced by Weber (1958, 1978), Marx (1956, 1965), Sombart (1951), and Schumpeter (1934, 1988) who believed that modern capitalism emerged from and superseded a primitive ethnic ancestor. Classical economic sociologists, thus, were among the first ethnic entrepreneurship scholars.

In his 1957 essay "The Economy as Instituted Process," economic anthropologist Karl Polanyi provided the theoretical insight that would fuel the latest iteration of economic sociology studies. Challenging the ahistorical and universalistic approach of economics—which conflated economy, markets, society and polity—Polanyi argued that the understanding of economic systems necessitated a conceptual shift. Such reconceptualization, he sustained, entailed a comprehension of the "human economy as an instituted process . . . embedded and enmeshed in economic and non-economic institutions such as religion and government" (Polanyi 1957: 250). Like Weber, Sombart, and Schumpeter, Polanyi's work also suggested that, with the advance of modernization, economic exchanges would eventually be freed from constraining social relations.

Decades later, in the 1980s, a new economic sociology body of work emerged to contest the influence of neoclassical economics in the social sciences. Despite their common intellectual tradition, the classical and new economic sociology differ in that the latter does not seek to advance a grand theory of economic development within a historical social system. Instead, the new economic sociology attempts to unveil the relationship between social structures and economic behavior. In fact, responding to Polanyi's argument, Granovetter (1990) postulated that modernization, on the contrary, would lead to a proliferation of sociability in economic transactions. Hence, Granovetter's spin on Polanyi's model paved the way for what now amounts to a copious body of literature on the effect of social relations on economic action (Smelser and Swedberg 1994; Swedberg 2002, 2003; Guillen et al. 2002; Granovetter 1985, 1990, 1995, 2002). Three key theoretical and methodological concepts are the cornerstone of the new economic sociology: social embeddedness, social networks, and social capital.

Social Embeddedness and Social Networks

Polanyi's concept of embeddedness, rediscovered by Granovetter decades later, has become a central conceptual framework in studying the role of social expectations in market transactions within firms. Paramount to the concept of embeddedness is the notion that social expectations play a key role in determining market (as well as non-contractual) transactions (Granovetter 1985). Granovetter distinguishes between "relational" and "structural" embeddedness and gives primacy to the latter since it is the "larger social world of which all transactions are a part which becomes the prime source of expectations guiding individual action" (1995: 8). Relational embeddedness refers to behavior induced by reciprocity expectations arising from economic actors' personal relations with one another, while structural embeddedness refers to the broader network of social relations to which economic actors belong. Embedded transactions, therefore, encompass qualitatively distinct economic exchanges which, in turn, are inserted into overarching social structures (networks).

Therefore, for economic sociology scholars, the relationship between sociability and economic behavior is mediated through social networks. As I will examine later, the focus on social networks has also become increasingly salient in immigration research. Social networks bridge the gap between the dyadic relationship and the larger social structure, thus constituting an intermediate level of analysis. Further, network theory scholars emphasize that social actors have differential access to valued resources (information, power, favors, money, etc.), thus giving place to stratified social systems with shifting patterns of coalition and conflict among networks of the social structure (Wellman and Berkowitz 1988; Burt 1992; Freeman, White, and Romney 1989).

There are various network features that can shape the degree to which a social group accesses opportunity structures. These include size, density, centrality, clustering, and multiplexity[1]. Among these, internal class differentiation or multiplexity can be of strategic importance (Boissevian 1974; Fernandez-Kelly and Schauffler 1996; Granovetter 1973, 1985; Portes 1995; Portes and Sensenbrenner 1993). Scholars sustain that relatively large and dense networks, with high levels of internal class differentiation, are the most effective at generating normative regulations, reciprocity expectations, and attitudes within a group. In Granovetter's formulation, networks characterized by strategic "weak and strong ties" remain the most efficient since they maximize the array of opportunities available to its members. As individuals successfully interact with others who belong to different institutional circles, they increase the flow of information and resources available to the network and the community as a whole (Granovetter 1973).

Social network analysis draws from two intellectual sources: social anthropological studies and Simmel's formal sociology. On the one hand, based on the early work of British anthropologists, network scholars argue that an individual's position within a network largely determines his or her decisions and actions (Barth 1963; Bott 1957; Boissevain 1974). Further, social network analysis has built on Simmel's emphasis on the form over the content of social interaction. Thus, the structural organization of a network, rather than members' personal attributes, can grant members privileges and opportunities. Other studies focus on "deep structures" in the pattern of ties linking both individual and collective members of society, primarily because "actors and behaviors are seen as constrained by these structures" (Wellman 1983: 267). Echoing Granovetter's "weak and strong" ties proposition, Burt (1992) has similarly advanced that structural holes, or relationships of non-redundance, provide better sources of information than relationships with close friends, whose knowledge base is not very distinct from that of the central actor.

Social Capital

Social capital emerges as a direct product of embeddedness (Granovetter 1985; Portes 1995). First theorized by Bourdieu (1977) and Coleman (1988), social capital has become the focus of substantial theoretical debate among sociologists and political scientists (Edwards, Foley, and Diani 2001; Putnam 1993). More intangible than other types of resources, social capital does not inhere in the individual, but accrues to him/her by virtue of his/her set of relationships with others. In other words, it accrues to individuals through their membership in particular social networks.

While Coleman's analysis emphasized the rational, facilitative, and positive effect of social capital, recent studies note that it can also exert negative effects on members of a social network (Portes and Landolt 1996). Although scarce resources obtained through social capital seem free to recipients from a market standpoint, they entail tacit expectations of reciprocity in the long run. Thus, social capital can entail collective constraints on individual innovation and behavior (Nee and Nee 1974), exclusion of out-group members from valuable opportunities (Waldinger 1995), or social obligations that prevent capital accumulation (Portes 1995).

Given the recent popularity of social capital and its widespread application across a range of academic disciplines, there has been some confusion about its actual meaning. Often, it has been misconceived as an individual's ability to access quality resources. Yet, as scholars (Fernandez-Kelly 1994, 1995; Fernandez-Kelly and Schauffler 1996) eloquently argue, social capital is a resource inherent to all collective settings. Individuals are able to mobilize resources (information, financial assistance, personal favors, etc.) whether they are rich or poor; the difference is that while the social capital of certain networks advances individuals' goal-seeking behaviors, that of others' might constrain, derail, or impede members' access to opportunity structures of high quality.

In line with this perspective, scholars have recently elaborated a typology that differentiates between bonding and bridging types of social capital (Foley, McCarthy, and Chavez 2001; Edwards, Foley, and Diani 2001). While bonding social capital promotes feelings of social belonging, trust, and reciprocity within a closed circle of family and friends, bridging social capital facilitates members' connections to groups and institutions beyond their closest circles. In so doing, the latter may facilitate access to valuable resources outside the immediate community, including information about jobs, services, and other assets. Similar to Granovetter's concept of "weak and strong" social ties, "bonding" and "bridging" social capital represent distinct but complementary network assets. Despite its insular character, bonding social capital remains instrumental in strengthening social cohesion, group trust and collective identity. Further, both types of social capital are directly related to the level of internal class differentiation within a network (multiplexity) and the type of purposive action its members seek to advance.

Related to individuals' purposive action and the type of social capital that best serves personal networks, Lin (2001) argues that networks seeking to promote members' expressive action, or the maintenance of collective resources, are best served by strong ties or bonding social capital. Whereas those seeking to advance members' instrumental action—that is aspiring to gain access to new resources—are best served by weak ties or bridging social capital. Yet, beyond this distinction, most scholars coincide that networks that want to improve their members' socioeconomic standing are best served by both their ability to maintain group cohesion, solidarity, and internal trust, as well as by capitalizing on bridging connections to others who control valuable assets (Edwards et al. 2001; Granovetter 1985; Light and Gold 2000; Portes 1998).

Finally, Portes and Sensenbrenner (1993) distinguish between altruistic and instrumental motivations on the part of donors in non-contractual transactions. They identify various sources of social capital differentiated by their embeddedness (or lack thereof) in overarching structures that define the character of the exchange. Building on this work, Portes (1998) further elaborates on these motivations, arguing that there are two altruistic sources of social capital: moral obligations and bounded solidarity. While the former refers to actions inspired by values introjected by individuals during the process of socialization (i.e. charity, family assistance), the latter applies to actions borne out of solidarity with members of the same territorial, religious, racial, or ethnic community. Further, Portes identifies two kinds of instrumental motivations: simple reciprocity and enforceable trust. The former refers to interpersonal transactions that entail reciprocity expectations, while the latter points to transactions embedded in larger social structures that serve as social collateral to donors, either on behalf of the benefited party or the community at large.

SOCIOLOGY OF IMMIGRATION

In contrast to economic sociology, the sociology of immigration is far less abstract and more empirically driven. One of its key focus is immigrant settlement processes, including their social and economic adaptation to the host society. Beginning in the 1970s, immigration scholars began to focus on the role of social networks, immigrant social capital, and the differential social embeddedness of various immigrant groups. Parallely, during the same period, a copious body of literature on ethnic/immigrant entrepreneurship emerged as a particular variant of immigrant economic incorporation. I examine these subfields next.

Immigrant Social Networks

Similar to new economic sociologists, immigration scholars assign primacy to social networks and their various resource mobilization strategies as they mediate immigrant economic and social incorporation to host societies. Such focus, predicated upon the salience of social embeddedness, challenges neo-classical individualist theories of immigrant socioeconomic attainment because it emphasizes the overarching structures in which social relations are situated (Fernandez-Kelly and Schauffler 1996; Portes and Sensenbrenner 1993). As Portes (1995) argues, immigrant economic transactions are said to be socially embedded in structures from which values, norms, criteria for social approval, and reciprocity expectations stem.

As a middle ground between individual and structural forces, social networks differentially mediate the adaptation of immigrant groups (Light and Bhachu 1993; Portes and Borocz 1988; Aldrich et al. 1990; Menjivar 2000; Massey el at. 1987). Networks remain resources for the acquisition of scarce means and effectively constrain the purely instrumental behavior of its members. In fact, scholars conclude that immigrants' options in the host country largely "depend on their spatial location, their contact with specific social networks and their access to political and economic resources" (Fernandez-Kelly and Schauffler 1996: 34).

Traditionally, the immigrant network literature sustained that the presence of relatives and friends at the place of destination lowered the costs, both monetary and psychological, of immigration (Boyd 1989; Lomnitz 1975; Taylor 1986). Following this logic, social networks based on kinship and friendship allowed immigrants to draw upon obligations implicit in these relationships in order to gain assistance at the point of destination, substantially reducing the costs of migration (Massey et al. 1987; Tilly and Brown 1967). Newcomers relied on these social relations for material and emotional needs, even for a few years after arrival (Portes and Bach 1985).

However, Mahler (1995, 1996) and Menjivar (1997, 2000) have more recently placed under scrutiny this celebratory view, exposing the problematic features of localized immigrant networks. Menjivar's and Mahler's research concluded that the commodification of Salvadorans' social relations upon arrival to the San Francisco and Long Island suburban areas acted in detriment to their group cohesion. It destabilized home-based networks and altered home-established rules of social relations among co-nationals. Consequently, the receiving context has acquired more prominence as a determining factor that strengthens or weakens social mores and network ties. Given that networks do not exist separately from their physical locations—that is that localized economic, social, and political institutions shape immigrant networks—it is important to look at the structures in the context of reception as a key factor in understanding network dynamics (Fernandez-Kelly 1994) and immigrant integration, or what scholars have recently coined as the "the politics of place" (Singer et al. 2008:157).

Immigrant Adaptation

A number of theoretical frameworks focus on both the organization of migrant labor in industrialized nations and immigrants' economic and social adaptation to the host society. These include the assimilation model, the ethnic-resilience perspective, the dual economy literature, and the middleman minorities (Bonacich 1973; Bonacich and Light 1977) and economic enclave literatures (Portes and Manning 1986). In fact, the ethnic entrepreneurship literature emerged as an alternative conceptualization of immigrant economic incorporation, as well as an empirical ground to test some of the tenets of economic sociology. I now turn to a brief description of the perspectives that inform the ethnic entrepreneurship literature.

First, the assimilation model argues that the settlement process entails a series of progressive stages that culminate in the assimilation of newcomers into the core of society or one of its segments. The immigrant adaptation experience involves a tension between immigrants' cultural values and beliefs and those of the receiving majority in the host society. From this perspective, immigrants gradually and irreversibly absorb the cultural norms of the core as the initial step towards structural, attitudinal, and identificational assimilation (Glazer and Moynihan 1970; Gordon 1964).

Second, in contrast, the ethnic-resilience perspective (Portes and Bach 1985) does not portray immigrants' socio-cultural adaptation to the host society in unilinear terms. Adaptation involves an initial stage of rejection, followed by immigrants' subsequent reaction. As immigrants attempt to assimilate to mainstream society and experience discrimination, racism, and xenophobia they are indirectly forced to reconstitute their national identity as a mechanism to maintain their self-worth and status. They then transform their national identity into an ethnic identity by combining values and norms from their original culture with elements from the host culture. This reactive ethnicity (Light and Rosenstein 1995b), as opposed to primordial ethnicity brought from the homeland, facilitates immigrant group cohesion and resource mobilization strategies. Yet, focusing exclusively on Peruvian immigrants in Miami, Los Angeles, and New Jersey, Paerregaard (2005) examined the ways in which newcomers construct notions of Peruvianness, concluding that such reactive ethnicity was not always conducive to group cohesion and trust. In fact, while Peruvians' reconstituted ethnic identity allowed them to effectively distinguish themselves from other co-ethnics, it also reproduced class and racially-based hierarchies brought from the homeland.

Third, focusing on immigrants' occupational attainment, labor market theorists (Sassen-Koob 1980, 1984; Piore 1979) argue that under advanced capitalism, social relations of production undergo segmentation. Such bifurcation in the economy allows for a segment characterized by capital-intensive bureaucracies where promotion, advancement, and fringe benefits for employees are possible. In the remaining segment, however, workers enjoy none of these advantages, relegated to dead-end jobs. Immigrant workers, argue dual economy theorists, are concentrated in this second segment of the economy. Also drawing from the concept of differential strata, segmented assimilation theorists argue that newcomers can attain intergenerational mobility in either of two ways: by conforming to mainstream cultural norms and/or by retaining their ethnic customs and traditions (Portes and Zhou 1993). Thus, while some members of certain immigrant groups (those with racial/ethnic phenotypical markers) assimilate to disadvantaged segments of mainstream society, others smoothly integrate into more advantageous social strata.

Finally, the late 1980s saw the emergence of a transnational perspective to migration, coming from the pioneer work of anthropologists. Addressing the unrelenting intensity of globalizing forces in modern society, scholars argued that immigrants adapted to destination societies without severing ties to their homelands. Thus, they challenged the linear nature of traditional assimilation theories, exploring the ways in which today's international flows of capital, technology, and information intensified world connectedness and transnational identity formation. Unlike earlier immigrant flows, they argued, today's newcomers create fluid social fields that cross national boundaries through their daily life activities and social, economic, and political relations. In so doing, they exercise dual citizenship rights, contribute to their home economies through remittances, and engage in various types of activities that constantly connect them to their sending communities (Glick Schiller et al. 1992; Basch et al. 1994).

Ethnic Entrepreneurship

As examined above, entrepreneurship is but one variant of immigrant economic adaptation and scholars define it broadly with a wide range of applications. Some refer to entrepreneurs as managers or innovators; others include in the definition the self-employed (those who work for themselves without employees); and others also include business owners who hire workers and work for themselves on a part-time basis (Schumpeter 1943: 131–2; Steinmetz and Wright 1989: 979; Aldrich et al. 1990: 17). These definitions encompass part-time, full-time, low-skilled, marginal, and highly skilled self-employment. Nevertheless, among most ethnic entrepreneurship scholars, the main focus is on any member of an ethnic/immigrant group who owns and operates a business (Auster and Aldrich 1984: 39; Light and Bonacich 1988; Light and Gold 2000; Rath 2000; Aldrich et al. 1990). Despite these broad definitional criteria, however, scholars have historically tended to focus on highly entrepreneurial immigrant groups such as Koreans, Chinese, or Cubans. In fact, recent studies have criticized such an elitist focus, arguing that a broader research scope should include transnational and survivalist micro entrepreneurs—including day laborers, petty-traders, domestics and others in the informal economy—who also merit close examination given their entrepreneurial characteristics and differential mobility outcomes (Valenzuela 2000; Light and Gold 2000; Morawska 2004; Robles and Cordero-Guzman 2007; Valdez 2008; Zhou 2004).

The classical economic sociologists' predictions on the demise of traditional capitalism implied that small businesses and entrepreneurs, on whom traditional capitalism relied, would also vanish into oblivion. This school of thought had such intellectual weight that it would take until the mid-1970s for research on immigrant entrepreneurship to eventually reemerge. The combination of the restructuring of industrialized economies and the massive increase in immigration after the 1960s account, in part, for this shift. Thus, scholars rekindled their interest in ethnic entrepreneurship and sought to elucidate the reasons why the foreign-born were over-represented in small businesses, even surpassing the native born in self-employment only after ten years in the US (Light 1972; Waldinger 1986b; Aldrich et al. 1990).

Attempting to answer this dilemma, labor market theorists argued that blocked mobility—the discriminatory practice of employers to limit access to opportunities for advancement and promotion among immigrants, minorities, and women—explained ethnic group entry into self-employment (Chiswick 1974; Sanders and Nee 1987; Portes and Zhou 1992). They claimed that racial discrimination, limited English language skills, and few opportunities for wage employment conspired to push immigrants towards self-employment. Yet, while blocked mobility could successfully account for the participation of highly entrepreneurial immigrant groups in small businesses, it failed to explain the situation of groups with low entrepreneurship rates, such as Salvadorans or Mexicans.

From a different perspective, neo-classical economists claimed that individual human capital attainment, captured through education and work experience, determined self-employment outcomes (Becker 1975; Borjas 1990; Chiswick 1985). Given that many immigrants brought technological, managerial, and professional skills acquired in the homeland, they were in a better position than those groups without these assets to start a business. Thus, this framework explained immigrants' self-employment rates primarily on individualist grounds.

Therefore, in response to neo-classical theories of immigrant human capital attainment, immigrant entrepreneurship scholars developed alternative conceptual frameworks that moved the focus away from individual self-employment determinants towards group and contextual factors. The main immigrant entrepreneurship perspectives include: the resources theory of entrepreneurship, the middleman minorities and enclave literatures, and the interactionist frameworks.

RESOURCES THEORY OF ENTREPRENEURSHIP: CLASS AND ETHNIC ENDOWMENTS

Pioneered by Light (1972), the resources theory perspective posited that the survival and success of immigrant business ventures largely depended upon group resources. Focusing on the social structure of immigrant groups, Light and Bonacich argued that class and ethnic-based resources determined access to business ownership since they differentially endow immigrant groups for the entrepreneurial challenge (Light and Bonacich 1988; Light 1972). Thus, they defined ethnic resources as "social features of a group which co-ethnic business owners utilize in business or from which their business passively benefits . . . values, knowledge, skills, information, attitudes, leadership, solidarity . . . sojourning, and institutions" (Light and Bonacich 1988:18–19).

Thus, Light and Bonacich claimed that bounded solidarity and enforceable trust were key features of ethnic-based resources. Likewise, ethnic solidarity was the outcome of being foreign and being treated prejudicially by the dominant society. This induced seclusion created a natural ethnic market that fostered an ethnic identity and community, often held together by social sanctions against those who attempt to leave or who break the ethnic group trust (Bonacich 1973; Bonacich and Modell 1980; Light 1972). Later, Sanders and Nee contributed to the debate, highlighting that the immigrant family, by definition an ethnic resource, also constituted a source of social capital since it "acts as a social base for the organization of group resources in the pursuit of economic gain" (1996: 246).

On the other hand, in Light and Bonacich's formulation, class resources encompassed "private property . . . personal wealth, and investments in human capital . . . bourgeois values, attitudes, knowledge and skills transmitted intergenerationally in the course of primary socialization" (Light and Bonacich 1988:19; Light and Gold 2000). While they argued that class and ethnic resources were different phenomena, they acknowledged that the definitions overlapped since class-derived cultural and social capital was class specific rather than common to an entire immigrant group. Instead, ethnic endowments were social features ascribed to the entire ethnic group, regardless of class background. Therefore, they explained immigrants' participation in small businesses to inherent-specific and class-specific attributes.

Further, building on Bourdieu's notion of cultural capital, Light and Gold later refined the resources theory of entrepreneurship perspective to include class-derived "bourgeois occupational culture" or the occupational culture of entrepreneurship. A form of class-based cultural capital, they define it as "the skills, knowledge, attitudes and values that bourgeoisies need to run the market economy" (Light and Gold 2000: 92–3). Likewise, they differentiate class-derived social capital from ethnic-derived social capital. Whereas the former entails "ownership of class-derived social relationships that facilitate entrepreneurship" (2000: 94), the latter consists of ownership of ethnic-derived social relationships, that is relationships acquired through common membership in ethnic groups.

In line with his theory of class and ethnic-derived resources, Light developed a typology of immigrant entrepreneurs, which distinguished between "individualist" versus "collectivist" entrepreneurs. He claimed that entrepreneurial groups endowed with class-preponderant resources tend to exhibit individualistic attitudes and values whereas those endowed with ethnic-preponderant resources tend to be more collectively oriented. Individualistic entrepreneurs "think and act independently, albeit in utilization of class-linked resources" (1984: 205) and collectivist entrepreneurs tend to more actively participate in community life and collective projects.

Despite widespread popularity, however, the ethnic solidarity thesis has been the subject of great academic debate. Scholars have criticized the celebratory tone of the ethnic solidarity perspective, emphasizing that employment in the ethnic economy does not necessarily give place to solidarity among co-ethnics, but to exploitation and oppression (Anthias 1992; Bonacich 1993; Sanders and Nee 1987; Pessar 1995). In fact, a study on the Washington DC Latino business community concluded that ethnic solidarity remained elusive given crosscutting class and nationality cleavages among community members (Pessar 1995). This fragmentation, in turn, prevented the consolidation of an ethnic enclave. Such findings echo scholars' recent claim that panethnicity often conceals important internal differences among national origin groups (Rodriguez et al. 2008; Robles and Guzman 2007; Valdez 2008), critical in conditioning collective social cohesion and solidarity (Espiritu 1996).

Ultimately, these critiques underscore the need to refine our understanding of immigrants' adaptation and entrepreneurship outcomes. Beyond monolithic perspectives on class and ethnic-based group endowments[2], to best capture nuances in the experiences of various immigrant groups, the immigrant entrepreneurship scholarship necessitates a theoretical framework that accounts for the intersectionality of multiple group identities on immigrants' business practices and strategies. Given the salience of the local opportunity structure, immigrant entrepreneurship remains a highly localized phenomenon.

Ethnic Enclave, Middleman Minorities, and Occupational Niches

The concepts of "ethnic enclave" and "middleman minorities" provide another alternative structural approach to understand immigrant economic performance in the host society. Once immigrant enterprises have become a principal employer, the immigrant economy is likely to have evolved into an "ethnic enclave," where immigrants provide cheap labor accessed through ethnic networks. Ethnic enclave theorists sustain that while immigrants provide cheap labor, they benefit in the patron-client relationship, enjoying flexible work conditions, learning the business as they work, and maximizing their opportunities for upward mobility and business ownership (Portes and Manning 1986; Portes and Rumbaut 1990; Portes and Zhou 1992). Scholars define ethnic enclaves as immigrant concentrations where ethnic-owned businesses market to co-nationals and where three conditions are met: 1) a substantial presence of immigrants with business expertise acquired in the homeland; 2) sources of financial capital readily available; and 3) access to cheap co-national pools of labor.

For the most part, enclave theorists underscore the vitality of the immigrant economy, which they believe enhances and accelerates newcomers' upward mobility and stimulates community networks. In contrast to the assimilation model which postulates that immigrant economic mobility only follows after structural and symbolic acculturation to American norms and values (Gordon 1964), the enclave theoretical framework allows immigrants both to retain their ethnicity and to thrive economically, precisely, because of it. Further, unlike dual economy predictions which relegate newcomers to perpetual dead-end jobs in the secondary labor market (Piore 1979), enclave theory allows immigrants access to better opportunity structures, highlighting the role of social embeddedness in determining economic mobility.

Middleman minorities, on the other hand, is the term used to describe immigrant groups that may be closely knit, but whose businesses are not geographically clustered and do not cater to co-ethnics. Instead, these groups tend to take over businesses catering to low-income groups, often in the inner cities (Bonacich 1973; Bonacich and Light 1977; Light and Gold 2000; Portes and Rumbaut 1996). Although middleman minority theorists originally applied this label to describe ethnic minorities specializing in market trading such as Jews, their repertoire later expanded to include trading people all over the world. Koreans in California and Cubans in Puerto Rico are prime examples. Scholars contend that middleman minorities have developed unique group resources that enhance and maximize their business success. Bonacich (1973), for example, has argued that their expatriate condition, that is their sojourning orientation, made them more likely to intensify their social solidarity, which in turn enhanced their business practices.

Finally, scholars argue that ethnic succession is the primary means used by immigrants to access available niches (Waldinger 1996; Aldrich et al. 1990). Once immigrants establish themselves in a new industry, they create social networks and ethnic bonds much as in an ethnic enclave. Therefore, the middleman minorities, ethnic enclaves, and immigrants' occupational niches affirm the centrality of networks in promoting ethnic solidarity, ethnic mobilization, and enforceable trust within community boundaries (Bonacich and Modell 1980; Hechter 1987; Light 1984; Olzak 1983; Portes and Manning 1986; Portes and Zhou, 1992; Sassen-Koob 1979; Aldrich et al. 1990). Immigrant enterprise remains key to the success of immigrant groups, who pursue business opportunities strictly as a reaction to a hostile environment which gives them fewer options to upward mobility than natives. In this process, according to these frameworks, immigrants create sheltered economic spaces divorced from the mainstream.

Interactionism

Responding to traditional culturalist approaches, Waldinger (1986b) pioneered a theoretical reconceptualization of the determinants of immigrant entrepreneurship. Offering an interactive approach, he sustained that ethnic entrepreneurship rested on the interaction between the "opportunity structure of the host society and the social structure" of the ethnic group

(Waldinger 1986b: 250). In a later work, collaborating with Aldrich and Ward (1990), he argued that ethnic group characteristics are unique and that they allow distinct groups to exploit non-ethnic niches in the greater economy. Once ethnicity became well established within the immigrant community (reactive as opposed to primordial ethnicity), groups used personal, familial, or community networks and the interlacing of these ties with positions in the economy to develop their own business strategies.

Waldinger and his colleagues presented three sets of characteristics which explained variations in immigrant self-employment: pre-migration characteristics, circumstances of migration, and postmigration characteristics. Premigration characteristics consisted of skills immigrants bring from the homeland, including human capital. Circumstances of migration entailed factors such as legal status, whereas postmigration characteristics referred to the occupational position of the immigrant group upon entry to the host society. These group characteristics interacted both with the opportunity structure of the host society and ethnic group strategies to explain immigrant entrepreneurship. He concluded, however, that despite unique endowments, immigrant groups tend to adopt relatively similar strategies that position them in selected niches of the economy.

Despite its more comprehensive treatment of the various factors involved in entrepreneurial outcomes, Waldinger's model continued to treat ethnicity as monolithic. In other words, in his logic, ethnic resources are equally available to the entire group with all members possessing similar ethnic characteristics, social capital, and ascribed resources. Thus, his argument does not entertain the possibility that members of an entire ethnic group face different opportunities. He does not account for class, gender, nationality, religion, and other crosscutting cleavages. Further, his conceptualization of opportunity structures in the host environment remains underdeveloped with only cosmetic references to the salience of local market conditions and governmental policies.

In a different formulation, Portes and Rumbaut (1990, 1996) present a similar argument positing that contextual effects account for variations in immigrant entrepreneurship. Like Waldinger, they identify a series of individual, cultural, and structural factors that help explain differences in immigrant social and economic adaptation. The various combinations of these factors produce differential "modes of incorporation" for particular immigrant groups. As Portes and Rumbaut argue,

> The extent to which migrants' human capital is productively used and increased is determined by three contextual effects or reception levels including: (1) the government's policy toward the immigrant group; (2) the 'social reception' or attitudes of civil society and public opinion [. . .] conditioned in part by the phenotypical and cultural characteristics of the immigrant group; and (3) the situation of the ethnic community to which the migrant belongs, including the size of the community and the

prior existence of a large entrepreneurial or professional presence (1996: 85–90)

Therefore, Waldinger's interactive model and Portes and Rumbaut's concept of "modes of incorporation" shift the focus of analysis away from individual and cultural factors toward contextual factors that interact with immigrants' human capital to determine differential settlement patterns. Yet, the underlying assumption is that an immigrant group's ethnicity alone, conceived as monolithic without intra group variation, interacts with contextual effects to determine immigrant economic and social outcomes, an assumption that becomes more problematic when extrapolated to broad panethnic categories such as Latinos. Some scholars have criticized Waldinger's interactive approach for paying little attention to gender (Morokvasic 1993), and class antagonisms (Bonacich 1993), and for virtually leaving unexplored the politico-institutional framework of the local environment from where immigrant entrepreneurs operate (Rath 2000).

Further, responding to interactionist claims, Light and Rosenstein (1995a, 1995b) eventually conceded that variations in immigrant entrepreneurship respond to specific combinations of class and ethnic resources and local economic characteristics. Thus, they expanded their previous class and ethnic resources framework to account for more complex configurations contingent on the interaction between concrete groups and spaces. In the case of Latino entrepreneurship in particular, immigrant entrepreneurial diversity is magnified by the fact that over eighty per cent of their businesses are small ventures without employees and small receipts (Robles and Guzman 2007; Valdez 2008). This begs an exploration of the ways in which the interaction of simultaneous stratifying forces, mediated through localized social networks, unevenly shape entrepreneurial practices, especially of less studied Latino immigrant groups such as Salvadorans and Peruvians.

GENDER AND THE IMMIGRANT EXPERIENCE

As has been the case in most disciplines, androcentric biases have permeated immigration research until quite recently. Up to the mid-1960s, women remained completely absent from immigration research with stereotypes of economically active young male migrants inundating the literature and theoretical paradigms (Lee 1966; Massey 1987; Piore 1979; Portes and Bach 1985; Portes et al. 1977). Across most of the social sciences, actors remained genderless. The following decade, however, witnessed a major turning point as feminist scholars sought to unveil women's experiences to remedy their previous exclusion from empirical and theoretical studies. This valuable body of literature, while providing a most needed baseline of data to supplement the existing knowledge, presented a major blind spot.

In looking at women exclusively, it neglected the other side of the coin. Because gender is a relational construct, engendering women's experiences necessitates engendering men's.

Therefore, starting in the early 1990s, immigration research began to incorporate gender as main organizing concept that included both male and female migrants' experiences. Scholars underscored that gender played an important role in the process of migration decision-making and settlement outcomes, and as a central building block of institutions (Pedraza 1991; Pessar and Mahler 2003; Honganeu-Sotelo 1994, 2001; Mahler and Pessar 2006). Equally important, gender theorists argued that gender was historically, culturally, and socially constructed, thus opening the possibility that men's and women's experiences differed not only from each other, but also amongst each other. As many scholars concluded, not all men and women were created equally since social actors belonged to different hierarchies of masculinities and femininities contingent on the intersection of gender with other axes of power such as race, class, ethnicity, nationality, and sexual orientation (Cantu 2002; Chow 1996; Young and Dickerson 1994; Kimmel and Messner 2001; Messner 1990; Noon 2001).

A glance at the gender and migration literature produced during the last couple of decades reveals that, for the most part, studies engendered immigrants' settlement and adaptation processes in the United States, including gendered accounts of community and family dynamics (Hondagneu-Sotelo 1994; Kibria 1993), processes of political (Hagan 1998), civic or religious incorporation (Ebaugh and Chafetz 1999), and labor recruitment practices (Repak 1995; Hondagneu-Sotelo 2001; Brennan 2004; Parreñas 2003; Espiritu 2003). Yet, except for a few notable studies (Gilbertson 1995; Espiritu 1997; Sanders and Nee 1987; Zhou and Logan 1989; Portes and Zhou 1992; Zuiker et al. 2003; Morawska 2004; Livingston 2006), the literature on immigrant entrepreneurship, and Latino experiences in particular, has remained, by and large, gender blind.

For the most part, the immigrant social capital literature has also remained genderless. Among the few exceptions is Grasmuck and Grosfoguel's (1997) study on Cuban, Dominican, Puerto Rican, Haitian, and Jamaican immigrants in New York. After looking at the interaction of local opportunity structures and culturally specific gender and kin relations affecting the social capital of their communities, they concluded that social capital was gendered. Because Haitian and Jamaican women possessed higher educational levels, better English language skills, and a stronger tradition of female employment in their homelands, these women had access to better non-manufacturing employment opportunities outside the declining neighborhoods where Puerto Ricans and Dominicans settled. Therefore, Grasmuck and Grosfoguel argue that gender dynamics interact with the opportunity structure of the local environment, resulting in highly localized and gendered immigrant adaptation outcomes.

Further, recent studies have shown the gendering of social capital as immigrant men and women use distinct networks to obtain jobs (Livingston 2006), to ameliorate the costs of adaptation and settlement in destination countries, and to access family resources that, in turn, collectively condition immigrant entrepreneurial success (Sanders and Nee 1996). Invariably, studies show that gender, as main stratifying force, shapes the quality of migrant social capital, manifesting itself in differential work experiences, patterns of remittances and visits home, and obstacles and/ or facilitators to migration. As scholars conclude, neglecting to explore the gender content of social capital blinds us to important insights about the dynamics of the migration process (Curran and Saguy 2001; Curran and Rivero-Fuentes 2003).

In all, the past few years have proved fruitful for the gender and migration literature, including important strides in scholars' engendering of transnational migration theory. Pioneering this effort, Mahler and Pessar developed a conceptual framework to explore the malleability of "gendered identities and relations when conducted and negotiated across international borders, as they relate to multiple axes of differences, and as they operate along and across many sociospatial scales" (2006: 42). Their theoretical model, coined "gendered geographies of power," includes four main components that systematically examine the ways in which gender, intertwined with other stratifying forces (i.e. class, ethnicity, race), organizes social, economic, and political life for both individuals and institutions across national and transnational spaces. By looking both at gender as a fluid, spatial, and multi-dimensional socio-cultural construct, as well as the degree of agency individuals exert, they have provided a solid analytical tool to grasp the complex nuances of transnational gendered contexts, and their effects on those who engage in border-crossing activities and long term migration (Pessar and Mahler 2003; Mahler and Pessar 2006).

Women's Work and their Participation in the Immigrant Economy

Most notably, there is an abundance of studies on the impact of ethnic women's wage work on gender relations. Unequivocally, these conclude that diverse women groups experience diametrically opposed trajectories. While some women perceive work as an opportunity to raise the family's living standard compatible with enforcement of patriarchal ideology (Fernandez-Kelly and Garcia 1990), others are thrust into positions of financial vulnerability that, paradoxically, endow them with increased ideological autonomy as a result of men's inability to fulfill their socially assigned role.

Women's wage work, thus, can hold distinct meanings for different groups, highlighting the interaction of class and ethnic background on gender ideology (Fernandez-Kelly and Garcia 1990; Repak 1995). Accordingly, it can either increase the potential for greater personal and financial autonomy, or it can translate into severe economic need and vulnerability in the home and the labor market. Likewise, immigrant women's labor in family businesses can be perceived as either an extension of domestic responsibilities or as a career path to self-fulfillment (Espiritu 1997; Mobasher 2003). So while men's new dependence on the economic and social resources of women seems to, indeed, shift some of the decision-making power to women, this shift often leads to frictions among household members (Espiritu 1997; Grasmuck and Pessar 1996; Hondagneu-Sotelo 1994; Kibria 1993).

Given that the division of labor in the immigrant economy is as gendered[3] as in the general economy, a look at the role of family, personal, and community ties in the operation of immigrant businesses reveals the persistence of a gender division of labor which remains critical for their success. For example, focusing on Asian American families, Espiritu (1997) examined the impact of ethnic self employment on gender relations and family dynamics. She concluded that, in most instances, immigrant entrepreneurs accrued low gross earnings and ran high risks of failure. Most of the meager profits of these labor-intensive small businesses came at the expense of the minimally paid labor of spouses, children, and relatives and of excessive work hours or what scholars call "self-exploitation" (Light and Gold 2000). The wife's status as co-owner of the family business, Espiritu concluded, remains ambiguous "being at the same time the co-owner of the business working for self and for the family and unpaid family labor, working as unpaid employee for her husband" (1997: 80).

Therefore, through the non-remunerated labor donated by female relatives to family businesses, or through the accumulation of start-up capital juggling formal and informal economic activities, immigrant women represent a flexible and cheap source of labor that directly benefits the entrepreneurial experience of immigrant communities (Boyd 1989; Zhou and Logan 1989; Pedraza 1991; Phizacklea 1983).

Immigrant Gendered Networks

Feminist scholars have also examined how gender organizes social relations through networks, which unevenly circulate information, resources, and belief systems that can give way to newfound aspirations among men and women. In her pioneering study of Central Americans in Washington DC, Repak (1995) showed how an informal gendered labor recruitment cycle brought thousands of Salvadoran women to the United States to fill childcare, cleaning, and other social reproduction jobs since the 1960s. In fact, the Washington Salvadoran female-led migration flow illustrated how group characteristics (class, gender, and ethnicity) interacted with employment opportunities in the local economy to determine who migrates where and why.

It was, however, Hondagneu-Sotelo's (1994) groundbreaking study on Mexican men and women migrants in the San Francisco Bay area that clearly engendered the immigrant experience. Her research demonstrated that gender significantly shaped immigrants' settlement and family dynamics. Men and women, she argued, were readier to renegotiate traditional gender roles in the host society according to particular types of migration patterns. Ultimately, Hondagneu-Sotelo's research not only engendered immigrants' experiences, but also gave intellectual validity to a gender analytical framework in the migration literature.

Later, building on Hondagneu-Sotelo's work, Hagan (1998) examined gendered networks among Mayan immigrants in Houston, and their role in mediating social and political incorporation outcomes. In looking at how immigrant networks facilitated and/or impeded men's and women's access to legalization opportunities, Hagan argued that social networks fluctuated over time, changing differentially for different segments of the immigrant community. Whereas men's networks expanded through their participation in more formal types of work, women's contracted as they became secluded in private homes doing domestic work. Ultimately, this isolation from information sources prevented Mayan women to find out and apply for legalization under the Immigration Reform and Control Act of 1986 (IRCA) program.

Further advancing our understanding of immigrant network dynamics, Menjivar (2000) studied Salvadoran men and women in the San Francisco Bay area. As noted earlier, her research focused on localized conditions under which immigrant networks eroded. After an initial stage when immigrant networks facilitated members' migration and settlement projects, she argued that the lack of material resources in the immigrant community weakened such networks' effectiveness. Menjivar explored the differential effect of gendered networks among Salvadorans, concluding that whereas men's networks granted members access to larger financial resources, women's gained access to more diversified sources of information beyond the immigrant community. Because women were primarily involved in children's schooling and other social reproduction duties, they relied on social service agencies and had larger contact with mainstream representatives than men. This bridging out beyond their immediate social circles benefited women's networks' effectiveness, as they became more multiplex than men's.

Throughout the following chapters, insights from all these intellectual traditions will throw light on distinct dimensions of the Latino entrepreneurial experiences captured in this study. Let's move on next to an examination of empirical diversity in Latino entrepreneurship as we look at the contrasting cases of Salvadorans and Peruvians in America.

3 Divergent Latino Immigrant Stories
Salvadorans and Peruvians in America

This chapter provides a contextual overview of Salvadoran and Peruvian immigrants in the United States, including a brief description of their distinct demographic, economic, and settlement patterns. Equally important, it offers a snapshot of Latino small businesses in the Greater Washington and national economy.

The chapter is organized in three parts. First, it explores nationwide population demographics for Salvadorans and Peruvians, including divergent socioeconomic indicators and self-employment rates. Next, it provides a close up look at Washington Salvadorans and Peruvians, including the social, political, and economic forces that have fueled their migration to the area. Last, it explores Washington's unique features as a new immigrant receiving gateway, outlining the economic and social changes that have affected the region over the last three decades.

NATIONAL DEMOGRAPHIC OVERVIEW

Salvadorans and Peruvians in the United States

Salvadorans constitute the fourth largest Latino population in the United States after Mexicans, Puerto Ricans and Cubans.[1] According to 2000 Census data, there are 655,000 Salvadorans in the US, which shows a modest increase of 100,000 above the 1990 census figure of 565,081. More realistically, the recent 2006 American Community Survey estimates the national Salvadoran population as high as 1,371,666. Underlying these disparate figures is the fact that Latinos have been, and still remain, historically undercounted by the census,[2] a situation which is particularly acute for undocumented migrants who are reluctant to participate for fear of deportation. Thus, an accurate number is clouded by thousands of Salvadorans awaiting approval of their applications for legal permanent residency under various US immigration programs.

The US Salvadoran community is popularly referred to as Salvador's "15th Department"[3] given that over 15 per cent of the total Salvadoran population of seven million now reside in US territory. Salvadorans are concentrated geographically in metropolitan areas such as Los Angeles, Washington DC / Northern Virginia, Houston, Phoenix and the Greater New York region. These Salvadoran settlements, however, differ in important ways. While the Los Angeles metropolitan area has a larger concentration of Salvadorans in absolute terms, Washington Salvadorans constitute a much larger percentage of the Latino population in the metropolitan area. In fact, with the exception of the Washington region, most Salvadoran settlements are embedded in areas characterized by different racial and ethnic landscapes where either Mexicans, Puerto Ricans or Cubans predominate among Latinos.

Peruvians also tend to settle in a few select metropolitan areas. By 2000, the vast majority was concentrated in the Greater New York area, including New Jersey and its suburbs (US Census Bureau 2006). With the exception of a handful of recent studies, there is a dearth of research on Peruvians in the US, and none at all on Washington Peruvians. Although we know that they are the third largest South American national origin group in the US after Colombians and Ecuadorians, their precise numbers are, again, debatable given the historical undercount of Latinos in censuses. According to 2006 American Community Survey data, there are currently 435,368 Peruvians in the United States. Yet, Peruvian official sources claim there are over a million Peruvians in the United States, which is the top country of destination for emigrants from that country (US Census Bureau 2006; Organización Internacional para las Migraciones 2008).

Table 1 shows notable socioeconomic differences among both groups. In fact, one of the few early studies of Peruvian and Salvadoran migration to the New York / New Jersey area confirms a class divide between Peruvians and Salvadorans (Mahler 1995). Although both Salvadorans and Peruvians are newcomers with as many as 82 per cent of their total US population being foreign born, Peruvians include more recent arrivals given that 61 per cent of their newcomers arrived to US shores over the past two decades. Instead, over half of the Salvadoran immigrant population arrived to the US before 1990. Salvadorans are also younger than Peruvians, and least likely to have attained high school education and beyond (41 per cent). Furthermore, Table 1 shows Salvadoran median household income is lower than that of their Peruvian counterparts (US Census Bureau 2004). Conversely, Peruvians are one of the Latino national origin groups most likely to have attained high school education and beyond (89 per cent), showing one of the highest median household incomes among Latinos in the US.

Everywhere Salvadorans have settled, they have concentrated in the low-wage service sector of the urban and suburban economy. In fact, a disproportionate number of Salvadorans are concentrated in private service occupations such as maids, domestics, and babysitters (99 per cent of whom are females), sewing operators, construction workers, gardeners, and painters (primarily male occupations). Further, a sizable share of the

Salvadoran population resorts to self-employment in the informal and/or formal economy either as primary or secondary sources of income.

Table 2 shows that Peruvians' occupational distribution in the United States is less concentrated in the low-wage service sector than that of Salvadorans'. Recent American Community Survey data indicate that as many as 22.7 per cent of Peruvians are in the managerial and professional specialty categories, 25 per cent in the technicians, sales, and administrative support occupations, 26.5 per cent in service categories, 11.9 per cent in construction trades, and only 0.2 per cent in agricultural occupations (US Census Bureau 2004). Salvadorans, instead, have as much as 73.8 per cent of their population (over 16 years old) concentrated in the service and manual labor categories; only 9.8 per cent are in the managerial and professional specialty occupations.

Based on recent census data and on my personal observations, surveys, and interviews, it is clear that the Washington Peruvian community has as much as a fourth of its population in higher-wage professional occupations, particularly in service and high tech industries such as communications, marketing, and information technology. Simultaneously, however, they can be found in the low tech and lower wage sector of the formal and informal economy. Males are concentrated in construction and service industries in areas such as home remodeling, residential and commercial painting, janitorial services, restaurants, and professional specialty occupations.

Women, instead, work as childcare providers, hairdressers, caterers, and secretaries, as well as in professional categories. Very much like Salvadorans, Peruvians resort to self-employment in formal and informal settings and there is a growing entrepreneurial class among both populations. Yet, neither group reaches the level of economic dynamism, job generation, and co-ethnic employment that are pre-requisites to become an economic ethnic enclave. Miami Cubans' or Los Angeles Koreans' are the quintessential models of successful ethnic enclaves where ethnic-owned businesses that employ and market to co-nationals are salient features of the immigrant community (Portes and Manning 1986).

In contrast to Salvadorans, Peruvian immigrants have fewer peasants or poor among them; this fact that can be easily explained because poor Peruvians migrate primarily from the Peruvian countryside to the cities. The Peruvian upper and lower middle classes, and most recently some segments of the working class, seem to be those most likely to engage in international migration. Instead, Salvadoran migrants, because of their closer proximity to the US, the push effect of the civil war at home, and the momentum reached by the chain migration process that started in the 1970s, have a more heterogeneous class base, including the upper-middle and middle segments of society, the urban poor, and rural peasants. Salvadoran migration networks to the Washington DC area are younger than those of other Salvadoran settlements and have been largely restricted to the unregulated service sector. As will be examined later on, this

Table 1 Social Characteristics of Salvadorans and Peruvians in the United States, 2004 (National Average Values, Survey and Interview Data).

	Salvadorans			Peruvians		
	2004 ACS	Survey Population N= 49	Interviews N= 23	2004 ACS	Survey Population N= 58	Interviews N= 22
Male/Female ratio(adults, age 16+)	51/49	53/47	45/54	49/51	58/42	47/52
Median Age	29	40	39	35	44	43
Median Family Income	$36,789	—	—	$42,956	—	—
Per cent Foreign Born	67.7%	100%	100%	72.2%	100%	100%
Education(over age 25)						
% less than high school	58.7%	34.9%	22.7%	10.9%	03.4%	00.0%
% high school graduate or more	41.3%	59.1%	63.6%	89.1%	34.5%	36.9%
% bachelor's degree or more	06.2%	06.0%	09.0%	30.0%	46.5%	47.5%

Source: US Department of Commerce, Bureau of the Census, 2004 American Community Survey, Selected Population Profiles; survey and in-depth interview study participants.

Table 2 Occupational Distribution of Peruvians and Salvadorans in the United States, 2004.

Occupations	Peruvian	Salvadoran
Managerial and professional specialty	22.7%	9.8%
Technical, sales, and office occupations	24.9%	16.4%
Service occupations[a]	26.5%	33.5%
Construction, extraction and maintenance[b]	11.9%	16.1%
Production, transportation, and material moving	13.7%	23.7%
Agricultural, farm-related[c]	0.2%	0.5%

Source: US Department of Commerce, Bureau of the Census, 2004 American Community Survey, Selected Population Profiles, S0201.
Notes:
a This category includes workers in personal service, private household service, food preparation, restaurants, cleaning, building and protective services, and in childcare.
b This category includes mechanics, repairers and workers in construction trades, such as carpenters, electricians, and painters.
c This category includes workers in farming and in forestry, including groundskeepers and gardeners.

together with the fact that Washington Salvadorans are less educated than both Salvadoran national averages and other Salvadoran-American communities suggests that, as a whole, Washington Salvadorans are less diverse and heterogeneous in their class composition.

Latino Small Businesses

A great deal of research has been conducted on the success stories of Cuban and Dominican businesses in Miami and New York, while there is virtually no data on the entrepreneurial activities of Salvadorans and Peruvians. Captured in the census aggregate category of "Other Spanish/Hispanic/ Latino," they have the second largest share of Hispanic -owned small businesses in the US.[4] This lack of data is even more striking considering that, from 1992 to 2002, the only Latino ethnic groups that have increased their share of Hispanic-owned business have been "Other Spanish/Hispanic/ Latino"(US Census Bureau 1992, 1997, 2006).[5] Because of the lack of national origin disaggregated economic data beyond Cubans, Mexicans, and Puerto Rican-owned businesses, official figures fail to capture nuances among South and Central Americans' business experiences.

During the 1990s, Latino small businesses became the nations' fastest growing business population, after enjoying a phenomenal growth rate of 83 per cent from 1985 to 1992 (US Small Business Administration 1998). This figure is particularly striking when compared to the average small business growth rate of 26 per cent during that same period. By 2002, there were 1.6 million Latino small businesses in the US, up from 1.2 million only a decade earlier. Mexican, Mexican-American, and Chicano-owned businesses were at the lead, constituting 43.8 per cent of all Latino businesses, followed by Other Spanish/Hispanic/Latino businesses, which included Salvadoran and Peruvian-owned firms, and made up 37.2 per cent of all Latino businesses. Cuban and Puerto Rican businesses followed respectively with 9.4 and 6.8 per cent of all Latino businesses (US Census Bureau 2006).

Nationwide Hispanic-owned businesses operate primarily in the retail, construction, administrative and support services, concentrating disproportionately in business and personal services. Most of them operate as individual proprietorships and, although they own the largest share of firms owned by US minorities, Asian-owned businesses reap the largest share of minority-owned business revenues. This is indicative of the relatively lower profit margin of most Hispanic small businesses, a fact which is confirmed by their underrepresentation in the more profitable wholesale trade and manufacturing industries (US Census Bureau 2006).

During the 1990–2000 decade, the growing presence of Latinos other than Mexican, Cuban, and Puerto Rican in southern states strikingly diversified the Latino immigrant population across a wider range of American communities. Census data show that, during this time period, the proportion of Central and South Americans living in the Northeast decreased from 30 per cent to 25 per cent whereas that of those living in the South (including Washington DC and Miami and Orlando metropolitan areas) rose from 17.6 per cent to 18.5 per cent. In northern Virginia, in particular, by 2000, "Other" Latinos (Central and South Americans) accounted for 62.5 per cent of all Latino residents in the region (Vazquez et al. 2008).

Naturally, this new pattern of immigrant dispersion beyond traditional destinations reshaped the geographic concentration of Hispanic-owned businesses in traditional immigrant receiving states. Thus, by 2002, it was not only California, New York, Florida, and Texas that had the largest numbers of Latino owned firms. Urban areas across the Washington DC region, North and South Carolina, Nevada, and the New York-New Jersey corridor welcomed important concentrations of Other Spanish/Hispanic/Latino-owned small businesses. Most notably, in all other geographical settings where there is an important concentration of Central and South American businesses, Other Spanish/Hispanic/Latino are second in numbers to more numerous Latino national origin groups such as Mexicans in California or Cubans in Florida. Only in the greater Washington DC and New Jersey areas do Hispanic Latin American-owned businesses acquire numerical prominence without being eclipsed by other Latinos.

Salvadoran and Peruvian Self-Employment

Because the foreign-born have been traditionally over-represented in US small businesses since the 1880s, it has long been perceived that immigrants are distinctly entrepreneurial. Scholars largely attribute the survival and success of ethnic business ventures to group specific resources and, to determine which immigrant groups are more or less entrepreneurial than others, they have computed immigrants' self-employment rates. As with census data, exact self-employment rates for Salvadorans and Peruvians are elusive and figures vary from one source to the next. Yet, while there are discrepancies in the various figures used, the differential national and gender patterns remain the same.[6]

In analyzing 1990 census data on the foreign born, Light and Gold (2000) argue that even the smallest ethnic economies of American ethnic groups—which they define as the sum of co-ethnic self-employed, employers and their co-ethnic employees—merit more attention than what they have received thus far. Table 3 presents some of their sex disaggregated data on self-employment rates[7] of selected immigrant groups categorized by the level of significance of their ethnic economies. To evaluate the importance of individual ethnic economies, they establish that threshold significance is reached when an ethnic economy occupies 5 per cent or more of any group's civilian labor force, high significance when it occupies 10 to 19 per cent, and extreme significance when it occupies 20 per cent or more. Men, women, total self-employed, and unpaid family workers of each national group are shown as a percentage of that group's labor force in 1990. Adding the ethnic economy's co-ethnic employees at one half the self-employed, they arrive at an estimate of individual ethnic economies in 1990. Their analysis yields an immigrant median ethnic economy of 10.4 per cent of the total labor force.

Thus, the data in Table 3 shows that Peruvian's ethnic economy not only coincides with the median ethnic economy for all foreign born but reaches high significance since it occupies over 10 per cent of Peruvians' labor force. Meanwhile, Salvadoran's 7.4 per cent ethnic economy falls below the median but easily surpasses Light and Gold's 5 per cent threshold of significance. Hence, while Peruvians seem to be more entrepreneurial than Salvadorans, both groups have ethnic economies important enough to merit attention. Remarkably, Salvadoran women exhibit much higher rates of self-employment than men. In contrast, Peruvian women show rates of self-employment lower than their men but almost as high as Salvadoran women. As we will see in chapter eight, the dynamics of Washington Salvadoran women's networks might help explain their higher levels of entrepreneurship relative to Salvadoran men.

WASHINGTON SALVADORANS AND PERUVIANS: A NEW LATINO PRESENCE

Salvadorans and Peruvians are certainly newcomers to the Washington area, although their presence in other regions of the United States traces back many generations. Salvadoran migration to the Bay area, for example, was fueled by the commercial trade between San Francisco and Central America in the early 1900s. California's burgeoning shipping industry attracted a pioneer wave of Salvadorans to the area in the 1940s, which paved the way for subsequent migration networks heading to the West coast (Menjivar 2000). Similarly, Peruvian presence in the US traces as far back as 1848, when experienced miners and Andean women migrated to California for the gold rush (Julca 2001; Monaghan 1973). Almost a century later, beginning in the 1930s and 1940s, both working class Peruvians and members of the elite settled in the New York and New Jersey areas (Altamirano 2003). It would take until the second half of the 20th century for either Salvadorans or Peruvians to establish a presence in the Greater Washington region.

Salvadoran's first significant contingent arrived to Washington during the 1960s, when an informal gendered labor recruitment cycle brought thousands of Salvadoran women to work in the houses of international civil servants to fill childcare, cleaning and other social reproduction jobs (Repak 1995). This first wave of pioneer immigrants built the initial network that would attract the subsequent chain migration (spouses, children, relatives,

Table 3   Self-Employment Rates and Ethnic Economies for Selected Immigrant Populations, Census 1990.

Self-employed and unpaid family workers

Birthplace	Men	Women	Total	Estimated Employees	Ethnic Economy
Extreme Significance					
Korea	23.5	18.3	20.9	10.5	31.4
High Significance					
Cuba	10.1	4.5	7.7	3.9	11.6
Peru	7.2	6.5	6.9	3.5	10.4
Significant					
Vietnam	6.1	7.1	6.5	3.3	9.9
Dominican Republic	7.1	3.7	5.6	2.8	8.5
El Salvador	4.1	6.2	4.9	2.5	7.4
Below Significance					
Guyana	3.4	2.6	3.0	1.5	4.5

Source: This table was published in Ethnic Economies, Ivan Light and Steven J. Gold, Table 2.4, 34-35, Copyright Academic Press (2000). Data computed from 1990 Census of Population and Housing, The Foreign-Born Population in the United States.

friends and acquaintances) that would follow. Thus, the Greater Washington area contains the nation's largest Salvadoran community outside of Los Angeles. Official counts estimate 168,119 Washington Salvadorans, however, officials of the Embassy of El Salvador and others say the number of Salvadoran immigrants in the region may be as high as 600,000.[8]

Also recent newcomers, Peruvians comprise the largest South American population in the area.[9] Peruvians first significant contingents arrived, together with a sizable population of Bolivians, during the early 1970s when severe Andean droughts expelled many of them from their homelands. Back in 2000, census figures estimated that roughly 30,000 Peruvians lived in the Washington D.C metro area. Yet, according to the Peruvian Consulate, there are roughly 300,000 Peruvians in the Washington DC metropolitan area alone.

As discussed earlier, Washington Salvadorans differ substantially from their Peruvian counterparts. Most Washington Salvadorans trace their roots to the country's eastern provinces of La Unión, San Miguel, and Usulután, coming either from secondary cities or small rural towns. Incidentally, the Intipucá-Washington DC route is one of the oldest and most publicized Salvadoran 'transnational migrant circuit' (Rouse 1991), linking that small town at the southern tip of La Unión Department with migrant settlements in specific neighborhoods across Washington DC and suburban Maryland and Virginia. Over 20 per cent of Salvadorans from Intipucá have resettled in the Washington metropolitan area, moving back and forth between the town and the nation's capital since the 1960s (Levitt 2001; Pedersen 2001).[10]

Instead, exceedingly large numbers of Washington Peruvians come from Peru's capital city of Lima, where they had always lived or temporarily settled after migrating from the countryside. An exception is the less ubiquitous migrant circuit between the Andean town of Cabanaconde, in the Peruvian Andes south of Arequipa, and the Washington DC region. Since the early 1970s, roughly 400 Cabaneños have settled in the area, regularly traveling back to their hometown to partake in religious and cultural celebrations (Gelles and Martinez 1992). In general, Peruvians predominantly come from Lima or secondary cities like Trujillo and Arequipa.

Likewise, the largest Salvadoran influx arrived to the Washington metropolitan area after the 1970s, when Central American migration escalated as a result of political and economic turmoil back home. Despite the fact that most Salvadorans were fleeing from persecution and violence amidst the bloodshed of civil war, US immigration policy did not recognize them as political refugees. Hence, their "official" categorization as economic rather than political migrants made them ineligible to receive state-sponsored resettlement assistance, including programs to support and strengthen community building and social service efforts.

The following decade provided the backdrop for the migration of thousands of Peruvians to European and North American destinations as the

Maoist guerrillas-based Sendero Luminoso (Shining Path) unleashed a fierce terrorist campaign against the government. Guerrilla warfare, the violence resulting from State efforts to combat the insurgency, and the economic downfall that ensued during Alan Garcia's presidency fueled the migration of large numbers of Peruvians to the United States. Such was the economic chaos during those years that hyperinflation reached 2,350 per cent in 1989 (Julca 2001). Fleeing primarily from economic recession and, to a lesser degree, from political chaos, the Peruvian's exodus was nowhere as dramatic or as massive as that of Salvadoran refugees. While Peruvians did not enjoy the welcoming reception Cubans were given either, US immigration policies proved coldly neutral towards them and far less hostile as towards Salvadorans.

Reflecting national occupational patterns, Washington Salvadorans are mostly employed in construction, landscaping, restaurants, cleaning and maintenance, and as domestic workers (Repak 1995). Many of them also make ends meet in the informal economy as survivalist micro-entrepreneurs. It has been estimated that approximately 10 per cent of the Salvadoran population in the DC metro area receives its primary income from self-employment (Landolt 2000).

In contrast, Peruvians show a bimodal occupational distribution with a considerable share of its population in higher-wage professional occupations in service industries, most notably in communications and marketing. At the other end of the spectrum, Washington Peruvians concentrate in the low tech and lower wage sector of the formal and informal economy in the construction and retail industries. In fact, Peruvian entrepreneurs have a strong presence across the Washington area Latino immigrant business landscape together with Salvadorans and smaller number of Bolivians.

In terms of educational achievement levels, Table 4 presents socio-demographic census data for Washington Salvadorans. These figures highlight their lower levels of educational attainment since 61 per cent of its population has not completed high school studies, just 32.3 per cent having completed high school or more, and only 6.5 per cent reporting completion of college and beyond. Notably, a quick glance at demographic indicators of other populous Salvadoran communities across the country reveals that Washington Salvadorans show lower educational levels relative to fellow Salvadorans in Los Angeles or New York. This confirms that the Washington metro area has received a larger proportion of Salvadorans of lower working class and/or peasant background than might be the case in other Salvadoran settlements.

In contrast, Washington Peruvians show higher levels of educational attainment. Accordingly, 10 per cent of Washington Peruvians have not completed high school studies, 52.6 per cent have graduated from high school and beyond, and 37.4 per cent have completed college and a graduate or professional degree. In fact, findings from a poll conducted across the Washington metropolitan area in 2000 confirmed the differential human capital endowments of both populations.[11]

Table 4   Social Characteristics of Salvadorans, Census Figures 2006.

	Greater Washington	Greater Los Angeles	Greater New York	Survey Population (N=49)
Median age	28.0	30.9	28.4	40
Male	54.7%	48.1%	55.0%	53%
Female	45.3%	51.9%	45.0%	47%
Median household income	$54,637	$39,131	$49,724	—
Educational Attainment (age 25 +)				
Less than high school	61.5%	52.1%	51.5%	34.9%
High school graduate or more	32.3%	41.2%	41.2%	59.1%
Bachelor's degree or more	6.5%	6.8%	7.4%	6.0%

Source: US Department of Commerce, Bureau of the Census, 2006 American Community Survey; survey study.

Furthermore, it showed that one in four Latino immigrants in the region was of South American descent, making the Washington metro area one of the few American cities with a large concentration of South American residents. The data also showed that most South American families came from urban middle-class origins, thus being better educated and more prosperous than other Latino immigrants in the area. Finally, findings corroborated that large portions of particular Salvadoran rural villages resettled in the Washington metro area, thereby confirming that Washington Salvadorans include a disproportionate number of peasants among their population.

In contrast to traditional immigrant receiving destinations, Washington immigrants do not tend to cluster in immigrant neighborhoods in the city, but are scattered throughout suburban areas (Singer et al. 2008). Notwithstanding, there are key urban and suburban neighborhoods where Salvadorans and Peruvians settle selectively. While Salvadorans are likely to reside in both urban and suburban areas, Peruvians tend to settle almost exclusively in the suburbs. In fact, there are populous Salvadoran settlements in the areas of Mount Pleasant, Petworth / Brightwood Park and Columbia Heights in the Northwest quadrant of the District of Columbia, in South Arlington, Culmore, Arlandria[12] and Landmark in Northern Virginia, in the Langley Park / Hyattesville area of Prince George's County and in the Silver Spring / Takoma Park area of Montgomery County.

Conversely, Peruvians settle in largest numbers across Northern Virginia suburbs such as Annandale, South Arlington, Bailey Crossroads, and Landmark. A study based on INS data for legal immigration to the

Table 5 Social Characteristics of Peruvians, Census Figures 2006.

	Greater Washington	Greater New York	Survey Population (N=58)
Median age	33	35.4	44
Male	49%	48.7%	58%
Female	51%	51.3%	42%
Median household income	$62,033	$50,712	—
Educational Attainment (age 25 +)			
Less than high school	10.0%	10.3%	3.4%
High school graduate or more	52.6%	65.4%	34.5%
Bachelor's degree or more	37.4%	24.2%	46.5%

Source: US Department of Commerce, Bureau of the Census, 2006 American Community Survey, Selected Population Profiles; survey study.

Washington region between 1990–98 showed that 51 per cent of Washington Peruvians lived outside the Capital Beltway[13] whereas only 33 per cent of Salvadorans resided in the outer suburbs (Singer et al. 2001). These differential settlement patterns further suggest that Peruvians come to the area endowed with more financial resources and transferable skills than their Salvadoran counterparts. Regardless of differentiated residential settlement patterns, Salvadoran and Peruvian small businesses can be found across a wide array of urban and suburban locations in the Washington metropolitan area.

Latino Small Businesses in the Greater Washington Area

Over the last couple of decades, Latino small businesses have experienced a boom across the Greater Washington region, which is now listed among the top metropolitan areas with largest number of Hispanic-owned firms, ranking 7th among a total of fifty (US Census Bureau 2006). From an estimated 3,000 Latino-owned businesses in 1988, the number skyrocketed to 12,703 by 1992, to 27,000 by 1997, and to 32,419 by 2002 (US Hispanic Chamber of Commerce 1988; US Census Bureau 1996, 2001, 2006). Specifically, Washington "Central and South Americans" (including Salvadorans and Peruvians) own more firms than Mexicans, Cubans, and Puerto Ricans, and those of European Spanish descent (Economic Census 2002). In fact, in 2002, 67 per cent of all Hispanic-owned businesses were Central and South American-owned.[14]

As described earlier, the flux of Central and South American immigrants to the area in the 1970s fueled the reconfiguration of its Latino commercial landscape which, until then, had been dominated by Cubans and Dominicans. Thus, a dynamic Salvadoran, Peruvian, and Bolivian business community quickly emerged to respond to the market needs of co-ethnics, who painstakingly attempted to recreate a familiar environment in their new surroundings. A host of ethnic stores carrying a wide variety of Latino products and offering a variety of services, from translation and international couriers, to notaries and apparel retail, mushroomed throughout the area.

Simultaneously, a different but complementary type of Latino business emerged, formally or informally, to cater to the needs of Washington American and international clients: home-remodeling contractors, family childcare providers, construction and janitorial sub-contractors, and ethnic restaurants located in gentrified upscale neighborhoods. In fact, a close look at Central and South American-owned firms in the area reveals that they are primarily concentrated in service industries, followed by construction and retail. Such polarized Latino commercial landscape with immigrant business owners at both ends of the spectrum well fits the Washington metro area post-industrial economy with dual demand for higher tech/skilled and lower wage/skilled workers.

The racially and ethnically diverse demographic profile of the Washington region translates into a small business metroscape where Latino businesses are uniquely embedded in urban and suburban neighborhoods with distinct racial and ethnic configurations (Singer et al. 2008). Clearly, Washington Salvadoran and Peruvian small businesses respond to local structural forces such as active market competition from non-Hispanic white, minority, and other immigrant entrepreneurs, discriminatory practices that curtail Latino business creation and development, and marginalization from institutional mainstream agencies.

Table 6 presents findings from the latest economic census. Prince William and Arlington Counties in Northern Virginia have the largest concentration of Latino owned firms, whereas Maryland's Prince George's County and the District of Columbia have the highest concentration of African-American businesses. In fact, during the last decade, Latino small business growth has been modest in Prince George's County relative to growth in either Prince William, Fairfax, or Montgomery Counties. Notwithstanding, Virginia has become fertile terrain for Latino-owned businesses, ranking 10 among states with the largest numbers of Hispanic-owned businesses. As important, the data show that, without exceptions, Asian-American small businesses are a growing force in the area's minority commercial landscape, primarily concentrated in Fairfax and Montgomery Counties (US Census Bureau 2006). Therefore, Latino immigrant settlements and small businesses in the Washington metro area remain uniquely embedded in settings with distinct racial and ethnic landscapes.

Greater Washington as a New Immigrant Gateway

The Greater Washington area provides a strikingly distinct economic and social landscape than other Latino immigrant receiving US metropolitan areas. This is so because, historically, the Washington economy has been dominated by federal government services, and not by an industrial sector which rapidly absorbs immigrant workers in garment factories such as those in New York or Los Angeles. Because of this, most immigrants to the area did not have access to the local labor market until the beginning of the 1970s (Manning 1998). The most important exception to this exclusion were international civil servants employed by multilateral institutions such as the International Monetary Fund, the World Bank, and others, who started settling in the area after the 1950s.

Beginning in the 1960s and 1970s, the region underwent a major transformation as small businesses proliferated, and a growth of service industries, biomedical firms, research-and-development, defense, and consulting companies skyrocketed. As professionals and government technocrats settled in the area, Washington DC underwent a simultaneous and complementary process of gentrification. Thus its labor market expanded with a growing demand for low-wage personal services such as child-care and domestic

Table 6 Small Businesses across the Washington D.C. Metro Area by Ethnicity, 2002.

	Non-Minority Owned	Latino-Owned	African-American Owned	Asian-American Owned
District of Columbia	64.0%	4.6%	25.8%	5.1%
Alexandria, VA	71.8%	7.3%	12.4%	8.3%
Arlington County, VA	73.0%	9.9%	6.3%	9.9%
Fairfax County, VA	71.6%	7.7%	5.4%	15.2%
Loudoun County, VA	83.0%	5.6%	4.6%	6.2%
Prince William County, VA	71.3%	12.0%	9.4%	7.1%
Montgomery County, MD	69.7%	7.5%	11.5%	11.0%
Prince George's County, MD	40.2%	5.5%	47.7%	6.3%

Source: US Department of Commerce, Bureau of the Census, 2002 Economic Census, Survey of Business Owners.

workers for the two-career families residing in the area (Repak 1995). This economic growth peaked during the 1980s with the employment growth rate ranking the 6th most rapid among the nation's 25 largest metropolitan areas (Kingsley et al. 1998). Such expansion was largely driven by the dynamic creation of jobs in high-end service industries, such as information technology, biomedical industries, and business services. In fact, between 1980 and 1996 employment in information technology in private industries grew by 178 per cent in the metro area (Henry 2000; Friedman 2000).

Socially, the ethnic and racial composition of the Washington area has traditionally included a large presence of African-Americans and non-Hispanic whites at the expense of other ethnic groups. Further, since the 1970s, the region has had a strong African-American working and middle-class dominating government institutions both in the District of Columbia and Prince George's County. Starting in the 1990s, however, such dichotomous racial and ethnic landscape began to diversify as the area's increasing minority population, including Latino immigrants, accounted for most of the region's 16 per cent growth. Table 7 shows 2000 census data on population demographics in the Greater Washington area.

It is a well known fact that the region is racially segregated and the District itself has been traditionally perceived as a southern city. Sixteen Street, NW marks the racial divide with most whites living in western neighborhoods and most blacks living on the east side of the city, only recently separated by a growing belt of Hispanic newcomers. Precisely because of this black and white dichotomous landscape, Latino immigration to the area went largely unnoticed during the fifties and sixties when a few Cubans and Dominicans opened the first Latino businesses in the neighborhood of Adams Morgan in the District. Therefore, the changes in the local economy throughout much of the seventies and eighties coincided with a massive population gain in the area that included documented and undocumented immigrants from developing countries.

Following this trend, by the mid-1980s, the area had become home to one of the largest concentrations of Central Americans, the fourth largest settlement of Koreans in the US, and the largest Ethiopian community outside of Africa (Landolt 2000). Such massive population growth translated into a dramatic increase of Latinos. In fact, during the 1980s and 1990s, Washington Latinos grew by 96 and 90 per cent respectively (US Census Bureau 1990, 2000). As highlighted earlier, Central and South Americans remain the fastest growing segment of Latinos nationwide, and they are major contributors to the Washington metro area growth. Approximately 70 per cent of all Washington Latinos are of South and/or Central American origin and Salvadorans, Peruvians, and Bolivians show numerical dominance with the largest numbers of businesses in the area (US Census Bureau 2006; Economic Census 2002; Pessar 1995).[15] In fact, certain suburban areas show exceedingly high proportions of Central and South Americans. Such is the case of Langley Park in Maryland, or Culmore, Arlington, and

Alexandria in Northern Virginia, where Central and South Americans predominate within the Latino population.[16]

Strikingly, most of the population growth in the region has taken place in the suburbs. From 1950 to date, the District of Columbia has been consistently loosing residents while the suburbs have been expanding at an unabated pace. From 1970 to 2007 the area's population has almost tripled, increasing from nearly 3 million to over 8 million residents with the suburbs experiencing all of the area's growth. Official estimates show that nine out of ten immigrants choose to settle in the suburbs first and not in the city, and that over 85 per cent of Latino businesses concentrate in the Northern Virginia and Maryland suburbs (US Census Bureau 2006).

Undisputedly, over the past two decades, the Greater Washington region has acquired prominence as an "emerging immigrant gateway"; a term that Singer et al. have coined to describe metropolitan areas which, over the past twenty-five years, have shown rapidly growing immigrant populations (2008). According to 2005 ACS data, Greater Washington ranks seven in the number of foreign born residents with a total of 1,016,221 immigrants. Specifically, the area is home to a highly diverse immigrant population, partly because of refugee resettlement in the region starting in the 1980s. Thus, this wide range of immigrant diversity gives place to pockets of Latino settlements and businesses embedded in multi-ethnic/racial urban and suburban neighborhoods.

Adding complexity to the picture, Greater Washington also presents a uniquely "fragmented" Latino community with many national origin groups despite the numerical preponderance of Salvadorans. Likewise, because of its decentralized suburban/urban metropolitan landscape, including its fragmented governance structure, the region presents special challenges for, and uneven responses to, immigrant integration. Social tensions and uneven responses towards immigrants has become increasingly noticeable after the 9/11 terrorist attacks. The following chapter will examine the opportunity structure and business environment the region offers to Latino entrepreneurs.

Table 7 Racial and Ethnic Composition of the Population in the Washington Metro Area, 2000.

	Non-Hispanic Whites	Latinos	African-Americans	Asian-Americans
District of Columbia	30%	8%	61%	1%
Virginia	70%	5%	20%	4%
Fairfax County	64%	11%	9%	14%
Arlington County	60%	19%	9%	10%
City of Alexandria	58%	15%	22%	6%
Loudoun County	80%	6%	7%	6%
Prince William County	65%	10%	19%	5%
Maryland	64%	4%	28%	4%
Montgomery County	63%	11%	15%	11%
Prince George's County	27%	7%	62%	4%

Source: US Department of Commerce, Bureau of the Census, 2000 Census of Population and Housing, Summary File 1 (SF1).

4 The Washington Area Opportunity Structure and Latino Entrepreneurs

Continuing with an in-depth exploration of the Greater Washington environment, this chapter examines the demand side of Salvadoran and Peruvian entrepreneurship. First, it reviews the US institutional framework, including resources available and government policies affecting immigrant small business development. Next, it describes the local social and institutional environment, and the ways in which it shapes opportunities for Salvadoran and Peruvian entrepreneurial performance. Finally, it discusses informants' own perception of the opportunity structure, including attitudes about blocked mobility and effectiveness of business assistance programs.

THE DEMAND SIDE OF IMMIGRANT ENTREPRENEURSHIP

As discussed in chapter two, the literature on ethnic entrepreneurship has rapidly evolved from a historically-exclusive focus on the cultural characteristics of immigrant groups to a recent emphasis on localized features of the environment in which entrepreneurs operate. To recall, scholars conceive entrepreneurship as a good with a supply (entrepreneurs' intrinsic characteristics) and demand side (market features in the receiving context) (Light and Rosenstein 1995a; Thornton 1999; Waldinger 1985). Aldrich, Ward and Waldinger's interactive model (1990) further elaborated this concept when they postulated that the entrepreneurial capacity of every group emerges from the interaction of its resources and demand. In other words, the entrepreneurial performance of groups, immigrants or ethnics, depends simultaneously upon the fit between what they have to offer and what customers want. The better the fit, the larger the number of immigrant entrepreneurs in a given locality. Consequently, the entrepreneurial performance of groups can vary according to the location in which they are embedded. Responding to interactionist claims, Light and Rosenstein (1995a) similarly concluded that the answer to immigrant entrepreneurial performance lays in the intricate interaction between group-specific combinations of class and ethnic resources and local economic characteristics.

In a similar vein, Kloosterman and Rath (2003) expanded the demand side analysis to include factors beyond general economic markets and government policies. In giving primacy to the "economic, politico-institutional and social environment" in which entrepreneurs are embedded, they draw attention to national, state, county, and neighborhood levels of analysis. Moreover, they flesh out, in greater detail, specific factors that influence the number and performance of immigrant businesses. For example, they highlight the dynamics of the regional economy, the types of industries and markets it supports, local business and immigration regulations, and specific types of incentives and disincentives present for immigrant entrepreneurs.

Beyond institutional regulations to operate businesses and mechanisms to enforce them, racial and ethnic relations in the receiving context—including the political and economic clout of resident groups—remain a critical factor. This is perhaps more true than ever in post 9/11 America. After the terrorist attacks, as the protracted backlash against immigrants has intensified, fueled by the war in Iraq and a widespread economic slowdown, the social dynamics of receiving communities have become key determinants of immigrant integration outcomes. As scholars point out, the Greater Washington region offers an interesting case given uneven community responses to the immigrant presence, which range from outright nativism in localities such as Manassas or Herndon, to more welcoming responses across Arlington and Montgomery Counties (Price and Singer 2008).

Immigrant Entrepreneurs and the US Institutional Framework

Scholars agree that, relative to European institutional frameworks, American markets and their business regulatory environments are highly conducive to the development of immigrant entrepreneurship (Rath 2000; Aldrich et al. 1990). New businesses can only flourish in markets with certain characteristics, including remaining open to newcomers, and free of high entry barriers so that no extensive economies of scale or business closures take place due to government policies. As Kloosterman (2000) explains, the American economic model pulls individuals into entrepreneurship because it simultaneously generates low wage jobs (incentive to try out self-employment) as well as room for small-scale, low-tech businesses in personal, producer, and manufacturing businesses. Given the diversity of personal services in the American economy, and the fact that they require small capital investments, this sector presents ample opportunities for immigrant entrepreneurs. Thus, the American economic model is fertile ground for a wide scope of small businesses relying on low and semi-skilled immigrant labor in the growing service and sweatshop-type manufacturing sectors.

Small Businesses, Minority Business Development Efforts, and Immigration Policy

At the national level, the US federal government provides small business assistance through two main agencies: the Small Business Administration (SBA) and the Department of Commerce's Minority Business Development Agency (MBDA). Aldrich et al. note that, although the creation of the SBA in 1954 symbolized "the institutionalization of small business interests in Washington," the allocations made to the SBA have always been significantly lower than what had ever been available to small business assistance efforts when these were scattered among numerous agencies (1990: 187). Therefore, governmental commitments to the small business sector in general—and to minority entrepreneurs in particular—they emphasize, have historically represented more lip service than meaningful financial support.[1] In fact, many of my informal interviews with non-profit organizational representatives echo this view.

SBA funds are channeled through Small Business Development Centers (SBDCs) across the country which, in partnership with local private and/ or academic institutions, provide information and technical assistance to aspiring and novice entrepreneurs. Moreover, the SBA administers two business assistance programs exclusively for minority businesses: the 8(a) Business Development Program and the Small Disadvantaged Business (SDB) Certification Program. Created in 1969 to help small businesses owned by "socially and economically disadvantaged"[2] individuals compete in the mainstream economy, the 8(a) program offers participants management training, technical assistance and federal contracting opportunities. To be eligible to participate, minority business owners need to have acquired US citizenship before applying to the program. Instead, the SDB certification strictly relates to benefits in federal procurement.

The SBA offers a wide array of guaranteed loans to small businesses. Its most popular loan, the 7(a) Loan Program is designed to help small businesses that otherwise would be unable to obtain a conventional bank loan. The SBA minimizes the risk to lenders by guaranteeing a portion of the loan, which can be used to purchase equipment, machinery, business acquisitions, and expand or renovate business facilities (Small Business Administration 2006). Hence, the SBA does not provide direct loans to individuals, but acts through private lenders who, ultimately, make the final lending decisions.

Further, the SBA offers a Microloan Program with very small loans to start-up, newly established, or growing small businesses. Under this program, SBA makes funds available to nonprofit community based lenders (intermediaries) which, in turn, make loans to eligible borrowers in amounts up to a maximum of $35,000. Applications are submitted to the local intermediary and all credit decisions are made on the local level. Each non-governmental intermediary lender has its own lending and credit requirements, including some type of collateral, and the personal guarantee of the business owner, who needs be a legal permanent resident to qualify for a loan. Further, each community non-profit intermediary is required to provide business training and technical assistance to its micro-borrowers.

Under the Clinton administration, the SBA launched the Program for Investments in Microentrepreneurs (PRIME) to establish a microenterprise technical assistance and capacity building program. In contrast to its traditional microloan package, PRIME focused on providing training and technical assistance to low and very low-income entrepreneurs, regardless of whether they borrowed money. Thus, PRIME targeted a population distinct from SBA's traditional microloan program.

Instead, the Minority Business Development Agency (MBDA), created in 1969 under the Nixon presidency, has a coordinating role in the articulation of minority business interests vis à vis other agencies and the private sector. The MBDA's infrastructure includes national headquarters in Washington DC, regional offices in Atlanta, Chicago, Dallas, New York, and San Francisco, and district offices in Miami, Boston, Philadelphia, and Los Angeles. MBDA provides funding for Minority Business Development Centers located throughout the nation, which offer business services to minority entrepreneurs, including assistance in drafting business plans, financial and marketing planning, as well as management and general technical advice. Although agency representatives explained that regional centers were located in areas with the largest concentration of minority populations and firms, the DC metro regional center was closed under the Reagan administration and has never been re-opened since.

Despite this impressive federal bureaucracy, after the Nixon administration, governmental policy towards small businesses, including minority business development efforts, has come full circle. From lukewarm support during the Ford and Carter eras, it evolved into outright hostility under the Reagan administration, warmed up during the Clinton presidency, only to freeze back under the Bush administration. Most notably, the PRIME program, authorized and funded under Clinton at 15 million in 2001, only received 5 million from 2002 to 2005 and 2 million from 2006 to 2007 under the Bush administration. Although in 2008 PRIME received its first budget increase ever (one million dollars), the Bush administration has recommended eliminating the program every single year since taking office. Obviously, these budget cuts have adversely affected social service organizations providing business training and technical assistance to prospective minority and immigrant entrepreneurs.

This fiscal austerity has been further exacerbated by a growing decline in federal contracting for small businesses in general, and minority businesses in particular. In fact, federal agencies are currently spending less with 8(a) companies, even as overall government contracting increases. For the past decade, contract dollars awarded to 8(a) firms have dropped, from $64 billion in fiscal 1998 to $12.47 billion in 2006. Further, the 8(a) share of total federal contracts has remained generally stagnant with only an increase from 3.4 to 3.8 per cent from 1999 to 2006 (SBA Office of Advocacy 2002; Association for Enterprise Opportunity 2007).

Over the past few years, SBA minority business development efforts have also been under harsh scrutiny for allowing a few 8(a) minority businesses to dominate federal procurement programs, with SBA loans often geared towards business lines where African-Americans have historically been concentrated (Aldrich et al. 1990). As scholars note, minority business development programs largely emerged in response to political mobilization, namely as an extension of civil rights and affirmative action policies from the originally targeted group, African-Americans, to a broader group of minorities, including Latinos (Browning, Marshall, and Tabb 1984; Aldrich et al. 1990). As a representative from the US Hispanic Chamber of Commerce succinctly put it: "You know, the MBDA and the SBA are primarily oriented towards the needs of African-Americans and that's why we are here, to advocate and lobby the government for Latino business interests."

Complaining about diminishing funds, most of the interviews I conducted with institutional representatives emphasized that community organizations provided the backbone to minority business development efforts. In the words of a program officer for an Arlington-based microcredit organization,

> Resources are scant, there are no resources really. There's much lip service. At least in Northern Virginia, there's no real commitment to minority enterprise development. What the government says does not match with the resources allocated to this task. The problem is that resources are scattered across all the districts, which is politically efficient because all representatives want a piece of the pie. But this is also technically inefficient because scant resources are spread so thin. Then, SBA programs are not very useful to us since the loan guarantee does not benefit the type of client we have here. First generation immigrants rely on investment pools and family savings, not on bank loans since they aren't acculturated to the institutions and resources of the American system. What we really need are technical assistance programs".

And another microcredit institutional representative says,

> From the viewpoint of community organizations, yes, I would say there is a definite commitment to the development of minority businesses. From a mainstream viewpoint, though, no. There are racial and ethnic issues at stake. Virginia and Maryland are still largely white so there is a limited amount of commitment to the empowerment of these (Latino and other immigrant) groups.

As important, because most federal and state mandates restrict participation in minority business development programs to entrepreneurs who have at least obtained legal permanent residency, such eligibility requirements leave a whole segment of immigrant entrepreneurs underserved. As noted, the SBA 8(a) program requires participants to be American citizens. Likewise, the MBDA business assistance services and SBA microloan intermediary organizations require legal residency status from micro-borrowers. Thus, only those with legal immigration status have access to these resources, the most critical of which is technical assistance. Frustrated at this regulatory roadblock, a program officer for FINCA, one such non-governmental microlender, explains,

> You see, with the cut of funding for PRIME [SBA's program], we are being squeezed. This was the channel to provide training and assistance to all those Latino microentrepreneurs who have good ideas and need technical assistance to get off the ground. With the other programs, you know, the microloans, borrowers have to prove legal immigrant status here. And we have tons of Latinos who come to us who are in nebulous conditions like TPS status, work permits and so on. And we simply can't help them because we can only assist those who borrow from us, who have to be documented. PRIME would have provided us the funds to deliver more programs to these populations. There's a whole underground economy out there of undocumented entrepreneurs!

Eligibility criteria for participation in minority business development programs highlight the critical role of immigration policy in conditioning Latino immigrant entrepreneurs' access to resources. Immigration policy, closely aligned to foreign policy interests, sets the tone for the reception granted to newcomers. In the case of Salvadoran immigrants, their categorization as economic migrants granted them an initial hostile reception. It denied them refugee status, which, in turn, made them ineligible to receive federal assistance resources, including access to microcredit and technical assistance. By channeling them through various special visa programs such as Temporary Protected Status (TPS), government policies have kept them in a legal limbo that disqualifies them from benefiting from MBDA and SBA funded programs. Peruvians, with a substantially smaller immigrant population and a neutral reception relative to Salvadorans, have also been affected by restrictive immigration policies. In Gladys, a Peruvian informant's own words,

> We are talking about different scenarios here. For the Cubans who came here, you know, with papers, and refugee status and what not, that's a lot. When you arrive here with all your papers, you can blend right in. You can get insurance, you can get benefits, you enter through

the main door. We, Latinos, many of us, come here as tourists. We have to hide away, buy false identity cards, and I'm talking about most of us. Legalizing ourselves can take as long as 10 years! We come here to dance somebody else's song and we spend most of our time trying to survive.

In sum, federal minority business development programs primarily target ethnic minorities, and less so first generation Latino immigrant entrepreneurs, many of whom are recent newcomers. While many potential clients are, at best, in the process of securing legal residency status, others are, at worst, stalled within the ranks of the undocumented and/or temporary residents. Unfortunately, the PRIME program, which held the most promise as assistance vehicle for Latino micro-entrepreneurs, never really got off the ground given continuous underfunding.

THE GREATER WASHINGTON INSTITUTIONAL LANDSCAPE

Teasing out the local dynamics of the receiving context provides a nuanced picture of the social, economic and institutional forces at play in immigrant entrepreneurs' lives. Beyond federally sponsored minority business development efforts, states and local municipalities run similar type programs, although there is practically no research on their effectiveness. In the case of the Washington region in particular, program evaluation can be daunting given the complexity of a metropolitan area that encompasses counties across distinct states and a federal district. As newcomers primarily settle in suburban Washington, boundaries between Northern Virginia, Maryland, and the District have turned increasingly porous.

Economic Markets and Reception Levels

To recall from chapter three, the Greater Washington economic environment offers attractive markets for immigrant entrepreneurs. Despite its lack of manufacturing sweatshop-type opportunities, the region has a high demand for personal services, subcontracting, and high-tech know-how. Thus, it offers immigrant entrepreneurial groups markets with low entry costs, high demand for exotic goods, and a sizable and growing contingent workforce. In this context, both Peruvians and Salvadorans find alternative economic niches to exploit, at similar or different ends of the entrepreneurial spectrum. As noted earlier, a few Peruvian informants ran businesses in information technology and/or similar high-tech industries.

Just as it occurred at the national level, the politics of local reception for most Salvadorans, soon after arrival to the region, entailed both uneasiness and solidarity. The US government's hostile disposition towards them, expressed in their refusal to grant them refugee status and the benefits that come with it, was counterbalanced with sympathetic efforts by progressive sectors of civil society. In fact, the civil war in El Salvador and the refugee crisis constituted catalytic forces that fueled pro-Salvadoran activism during the 1980s. As Landolt summarizes, civil society's response to Salvadorans' arrival entailed both "hostile rejection and welcome reception" (2001: 93).

On the one hand, primarily influenced by mainstream discourse and mass media, a broad segment of the population rejected Salvadorans. In opposition, a coalition of grassroots local and national organizations, known as the "Central American Solidarity Movement," set out to change the government's foreign policy in Central America and its discriminatory immigration policy towards Salvadorans. What became known as the Sanctuary Movement, led by church congregations across the country, constituted just one branch of this broader organizational movement, and focused exclusively on the plight of Central American refugees arriving to US soil (Landolt 2001).

Churches in the Washington metro area joined the Sanctuary Movement early in the 1980s, significantly extending their provision of social services thereafter. For example, after joining the Movement in 1983, Luther Place of Washington DC founded a congregation called 'Casa del Pueblo' [People's House] at the edge of the Adams Morgan / Mt. Pleasant neighborhood. 'Casa del Pueblo' provided, in the early days when Salvadorans were first arriving, as it does to date, social services to Central American immigrants including daycare, English as a Second Language classes, domestic violence counseling, and an emergency relief program for the destitute. Likewise, 'Casa de Maryland' [House of Maryland], located in Takoma Park, Maryland, shares a similar story. Further, the Washington area also housed partisan organizations such as the FMLN-created Central American Refugee Centre (CARECEN), whose original purpose was to maintain the Salvadoran population informed of the political situation back home.[3]

In contrast, Peruvians arrival was far less dramatic, spurring less hostility but also less solidarity. Peruvians were not refugee claimants who had been unfairly denied asylum and resettlement assistance, nor did they arrive en masse. Although US government reception was coldly neutral towards them, and in that sense favored them over Salvadorans, Peruvians with scant resources failed to evoke the sympathy of civil society because their story was not as compelling. Such differential reception will have profound repercussions for Salvadoran and Peruvian levels of reactive ethnicity, the magnitude and breadth of community networks within and beyond their immediate circles and, ultimately, their entrepreneurial performance. By providing the organizational framework necessary to lobby for Salvadoran interests, local community organizations provided and developed a baseline of community resources that would galvanize Salvadorans' organizational capacity.

Local Social and Political Dynamics

Despite distinct levels of reception, Salvadoran and Peruvians unequivocally shared a main commonality: both were Latino newcomers in an area that had seen little, if any, international migration. More recently, the social climate in the aftermath of the 9/11 terrorist attacks have brought them closer together as Latinos now equally face increased nativism and scapegoating in the context of heightened national security concerns and a deepening economic slowdown.

As described in chapter three, the region had received a few Peruvians and Salvadorans in the late 1960s and 1970s with their immigrant flows dramatically increasing after the 1980s. Around this time, refugee resettlement in the area added complexity to the demographic diversity. As a result, in only a matter of a few decades, immigrants have dramatically reconfigured the demographic composition of long-established communities across the metropolitan area. Consequently, some immigrant receiving communities have found themselves unprepared, grappling with inadequate social and institutional systems in place to respond to the challenges of integration. Struggling with growing school and social service demand for limited English proficient populations, an expanding presence of day laborers across suburban areas, and residential overcrowding due to a shortage of affordable low cost housing, social tensions, nativism and immigrant marginalization have become painfully evident.

The rapid nature of these demographic changes—in the absence of an overarching immigrant integration policy at the federal level—resulted in insufficient resources, especially at the state and municipal levels, geared at facilitating Latinos' initial adaptation to the Greater Washington community. Ironically, the 1980s and early 1990s, although economically prosperous for the region's high-tech and biotechnology industries, brought diminishing resources for community development programs. For example, a representative for the Washington-based Foundation for International Community Assistance (FINCA) described the 1990s as an era of shrinking resources, despite the growing presence and needs of newly arrived Latino residents. Talking about the role of the DC Mayor's Office of Latino Affairs (OLA), she explains,

> OLA's original mission was to be a clearinghouse of health, employment, housing, and small business opportunities for the Latino community. It was supposed to help other NGOs. But, what to expect? Its budget went from $1,000,000 dollars to $200,000 since Mayor Pratt Kelly took power in the District. Marion Barry also took a stab at it. So we were given a mandate but scarce resources to serve the Latino population, including resources to identify Latino markets.

Actually, this early neglect of Washington Latinos would provide the backdrop for the 1991 Salvadoran-led youth riots in the Mount Pleasant

neighborhood of Washington DC.[4] As various other institutional representatives confirmed, it was not until the riots that the municipality started to
address the needs of Latinos in the District. Yet, rather than involve Latino
representatives in mainstream municipal agencies and committees—as a
representative of the Latino Economic Development Corporation (LEDC)
explained—the Mayor's office granted funds to create a whole set of autonomous non-governmental organizations to serve Latino needs exclusively.
Consequently, in 1991, the Latino Civil Rights Task Force[5] and the Latino
Economic Development Corporation were established, and a Latino was
appointed to head the Office of Latino Affairs (OLA). The task force won
some victories, established branches in the suburbs and, most important,
persuaded the US Commission on Civil Rights to investigate what it alleged
were the underlying causes of the 1991 riots: police abuse, discriminatory
hiring by District government, and the city's failure to provide services to
Latino residents. In 1993, the commission concluded that Latinos suffered
an appalling lack of civil rights and it called on the city to change the way
in which it hired and served Latinos.

These advances were short-lived as, by 1998, both the OLA and the
Latino Civil Rights Task Force faced severe budget cuts because of the District government financial crisis. In fact, the Office of Latino Affairs' staff
shrunk from thirteen to two during the 1990s. By the early 2000s, recover-
ing from the spending cuts of the previous decade, OLA received a slight
budget increase that allowed it to regain some of its staff. As for the task
force, by 2000, after its director stepped down from office, the organization lost community and foundation support and, in dire financial straits,
it was finally evicted from its Adams Morgan offices. In 2001, responding
to mounting pressure from Latino community advocates, critical of the
Williams administration's lack of Latino representation in municipal bodies, the DC government launched the Latino Community Education Grant
Program. This initiative awarded one million dollars to the OLA to provide
grants to community groups offering educational services to the District's
burgeoning Latino population.

In 2002, the Washington Lawyers' Committee for Civil Rights and
Urban Affairs, consisting of nine major Washington law firms and a civil
rights review panel of local and national Latino advocates, released a series
of reports on the status of the Washington Latino community. The reports
concluded that "eleven years after the riots, many of the same problems
identified after the 1991 disturbances continue to plague the Latino community" (Council of Latino Agencies 2002). The reports address police
abuses and police / community relations, discrimination in the criminal
justice system, health care, education, employment, rental housing, and
homeownership. Drawing conclusions based on census data and secondary
sources, they make a series of recommendations that range from additional
bilingual immersion programs in the public school system to establishing
a Latino credit union. Further, the employment report argues that the District's failure to track how many of its thousands of government workers

are Latinos, as recommended after the riots, "calls into question the city's commitment to a goal of incorporating more Latinos into the public workforce" (Moreno 2002).

After the terrorist attacks of September 11, 2001, the collective perception of heightened vulnerability in the context of national security concerns significantly exacerbated social tensions in America, putting pressure on state and local legislators to assuage, at whatever costs, anxieties about undocumented immigration. At the national level, this has increased Latino immigrants' vulnerability, adversely affecting their access to resources. Over the past few months, state and local police have been charged with broader enforcement duties to control undocumented immigration. In some northern Virginia localities, the anti-immigrant backlash that followed the terrorist attacks has been particularly fueled by the fact that Virginia was one of three states that issued drivers licenses to some of the plane hijackers. Consequently, the post 9/11 era has dramatically politicized the immigration debate with concomitant immigration policy changes that have unfairly targeted Latinos, further scapegoating and marginalizing them.

Because Latinos comprise the majority of the undocumented, they have borne the brunt of the political backlash. For many Latino advocates and civil right groups, the anti-immigrant backlash has become a more generalized attack on Latino residents, driven by anxieties over demographic changes across long-established communities. Throughout the Northern Virginia region, escalating social tensions have taken the form of anti-immigrant legislation aimed at discouraging undocumented Latinos from living or working in the region. In Herndon, for example, a protracted controversy over the construction and administration of a day laborers site placed the town at the heart of the national immigration debate.

Similarly, over the past few months, anti-immigrant bill proposals have emerged from localities such as Manassas, Culpeper, Loudoun and Prince William County. As many Northern Virginia residents show a heightened sense of anxiety about demographic changes and national security concerns, they are determined to deter illegal immigration through indirect tactics, including stricter enforcement of residential overcrowding zoning laws, amendments of zoning definitions to allow for the eviction of extended family members from single-family homes,[6] English-only proposals, and the commissioning of impact studies to assess the effects of illegal immigration in local communities.

Notwithstanding, Latinos have found collective mechanisms to resist the political backlash, becoming mobilized through a variety of organizations that actively oppose legislation demonizing immigrants. In Virginia, Governor Mark R. Warner appointed the Virginia Latino Advisory Committee[7] (VLAC) in 2003 to serve as an advisory body on issues facing Latino constituents, and to advocate for their interests. In a similar move, soon after coming to office in 2007, Mayor Adrian Fenty appointed five Latinos to the District's Cabinet, also creating a Commission on Latino

Community Development. That same year, Maryland's Governor Martin O'Malley relocated the Hispanic Affairs Commission from the Department of Human resources to the Governor's Office of Community Initiatives. Yet, despite these organizing efforts, Washington Latinos still suffer from disarticulated political leadership across the Greater Washington region.

Demographics, suburban settlement patterns across a decentralized metropolitan area, the local economic structure, racial tensions among ethnic groups, and Latinos' miniscule power at the ballot box all conspire to prevent an effective political presence. What are some of the concrete factors preventing Latinos' enfranchisement? First, unlike Mexicans in California or Cubans in Miami, Washington Latinos are more fragmented along national lines, precisely because of the lack of a numerical dominance on any one national group. Second, as the Washington region attracts newcomers to suburban locations (Singer et al. 2008), Latinos remain scattered across Northern Virginia, Maryland, and the District, rather than concentrated in more traditional immigrant enclaves in core city neighborhoods. As a result, their community organizing efforts become, often times, uncoordinated. Third, the Washington regional economic structure does not offer Latino immigrant entrepreneurs opportunities in industries that allow for high growth and capital accumulation such as, for example, the Los Angeles or Miami manufacturing industries.

Focusing on Washington Salvadorans, Landolt partly attributes their lack of insertion in mainstream American institutions to the dynamics of the local power structure, including African-Americans' demographic and political dominance in the District (2001: 202). The fact of the matter is that Salvadorans, Peruvians, and Latinos at large, remain disenfranchised across the region despite their burgeoning numbers. Table 7 shows how non-Hispanic whites control a large share of business opportunities in the Washington area. In both Prince George's County and the District, African-American small business interests dominate the minority business landscape, while Asian entrepreneurs are a growing force across Fairfax, Montgomery, and Arlington Counties, all heavily Latino populated suburban areas.

Washington Latinos' lack of political clout stems from both intrinsic community dynamics, including their socio-demographics and legal status, as well as from the political clout of non-minority and other minority groups in the area. Most poignantly, many of my interviews with institutional representatives stressed that Latinos' most pressing need was to secure representation in political and economic decision-making at the municipal and state levels. As the Executive Director of a well-known social service agency serving Central American immigrants summed it up,

> We're at a point where we still need to address these concerns [discrimination, prejudice] and issues with a task force. But not in the community, but in the city council with the participation of the mayor's

office. We still need to . . . come up with a set of solutions to make sure Latinos are included in the governance of the city.

In a similar vein, the Director of the Montgomery Hispanic Chamber of Commerce and a representative for the Arlington-based Small Business Development Center commented on Latinos' severe underrepresentation at various municipal, state, and federal small business assistance programs. As the latter explains,

> Latinos in this area need political clout so they can force their inter-
> ests. They are fragmented and cannot organize themselves under an
> umbrella label that might help them. That's why you don't see any Sal-
> vadoran [Chamber of Commerce] . . . or a strong Latino Chamber of
> Commerce in the area. One of their biggest problems is the issue of
> legal status and access to assistance programs. In order to get munici-
> pal and state small business loans, they need at least to be green card
> holders [legal residents].

The lack of a stronger collectively organized commercial presence among Washington Salvadorans and Peruvians seems striking when contrasted to similar immigrant communities across the country. In Los Angeles, Miami, and New York, for example, both Salvadorans and Peruvians seem to have attained a modicum of commercial visibility, even with thriving chambers of commerce of their own. In Salvadorans' case, for example, Landolt (2001) concludes that Los Angeles Salvadorans' institu-tional networks, including its business ties, have a better embeddedness than those of Washington Salvadorans.

Institutional Resources

As examined in the previous section, a host of social service programs tar-geting Washington Latino immigrants emerged in response to the 1991 riots and the political mobilization that ensued. As the Nation's Capital, the District of Columbia is the seat to both the Minority Business Devel-opment Agency (MBDA) and the Small Business Administration (SBA) headquarters. Nevertheless, neither work directly with entrepreneurs, but channel funding through intermediary organizations such as Small Busi-ness Development Centers and MBDA regional centers.

The SBA, instead, interfaces more with small business owners. Their Wash-ington District Office houses both the Office of Women Business Ownership and a Business Resource Center. There, aspiring entrepreneurs can research market opportunities, use computers, and become familiar with SBA pro-grams and regulations. Yet, among the District Office's staff, including the 8(a) Business Development Program staff, there are few Latinos or even Span-ish-speaking Business Specialists to assist program participants.

In the Greater Washington region, Latino entrepreneurs have a few assistance organizations they can resort to. The include both SBA-funded Small Business Development Centers, such as the Frank Reeves Municipal Center at the Howard University Center for Urban Progress, as well as community development corporations (CDCs) and not-for-profit microcredit institutions, such as the Latino Economic Development Center (LEDC) in Adams Morgan and the Foundation for International Community Assistance (FINCA) among others. LEDC provides business training in both Spanish and English, technical assistance, merchant association development and support, commercial property development, community needs assessment, tenant and coop organization, peer group lending, and microcredit programs for low and moderate income neighborhoods with significant Latino populations. LEDC does not target Latinos, exclusively, but provides services to District residents of all ethnic and racial backgrounds.

FINCA, on the other hand, focuses exclusively on providing individual microloans to low-income entrepreneurs in the area, offering minimal business training (in Spanish and English), and technical assistance. To participate in both programs, individuals need to present a valid passport or identification card but they do not need to be green card holders or American citizens as required by SBA programs.

In Northern Virginia, entrepreneurs can resort to several SBDCs scattered across Alexandria, Arlington, Fairfax, and Loudoun. Of these, the South Fairfax SBDC provides access to microcredit and business training, albeit exclusively in English. The other SBDCs are run in partnership with local universities, and provide information and general assistance primarily to English speakers. In addition, aspiring entrepreneurs can seek assistance at the Arlington-based Enterprise Development Group (ECDC), at the Business Development Assistance Group (BDAG), and at the Hispanic Committee of Virginia's Microenterprise Program. Whereas ECDC runs a comprehensive microloan business training and technical assistance program, the BDAG exclusively focuses on business training and technical assistance. Sporadically, they run training sessions in Spanish, English, Korean, and Vietnamese, also providing technical assistance to startups. Most recently, in 2007, Latino-owned One Security Bank opened its doors in Bailey's Crossroads to better serve the Latino community. Similar to LEDC and other CDCs, to participate in assistance programs, micro entrepreneurs do not need to be American citizens or green card holders, but do need legal proof of residency.

Finally, in Maryland's Montgomery and Prince George's Counties, prospective entrepreneurs can obtain general information from the SBA-funded SBDC at the University of Maryland in College Park. In addition, Montgomery College, in conjunction with the Economic Development Office and the Hispanic Chamber of Commerce of Montgomery County, hosts the Hispanic Business Institute, which offers yearlong business training courses in English to prospective entrepreneurs. Further, the Hispanic Catholic

Centre, with offices across both counties, and Casa de Maryland in Montgomery County, also offer basic business training workshops to Spanish-speakers throughout the year.

Although minority business assistance programs in the Greater Washington area emerged in response to political mobilization, conflicting agendas between economic developers and economic revitalization advocates have often stalled the flourishing of immigrant businesses in neighborhoods that have undergone gentrification under soaring housing and commercial real estate markets.[8]

A general environment of dwindling resources and anti-immigrant sentiment in the context of a national economic slowdown further exacerbates Latino immigrants' disempowerment as programs such as SBA's PRIME have struggled for bare survival over the past eight years. As several institutional representatives explained, the region suffers from a widespread lack of institutional coordination across counties and municipalities in different states. This compounded to the cannibalistic competition for scarce funding, and the ever diminishing funding for technical assistance and training programs adversely affects a large segment of Washington Latino immigrant entrepreneurs. I turn now to my informants' own perceptions of the opportunities available to them.

INFORMANTS' PERCEPTION OF THE LOCAL OPPORTUNITY STRUCTURE

My survey and in-depth interview data indicate that informants' perceptions of the Washington business regulatory and institutional environment were split along nationality and gender lines.[9] Salvadoran men had the most negative perceptions while Peruvian men had the most positive outlook. Women's narratives, on the other hand, at times unveiled ambiguity about regulations affecting their businesses. Notwithstanding, most informants wholeheartedly believed that the Washington area afforded abundant opportunities to exploit, if willing to apply oneself and work hard.

Hurdles: Discrimination and Ineffective Programs

Looking at national origin, Salvadorans' comments emphasized, to a larger extent than Peruvians, the many hurdles they had had to overcome, and continued to face, to run their businesses. Seventy per cent of all Salvadorans and forty five per cent of Peruvians interviewed described various types of barriers they had come against during their commercial undertakings. Related to this, approximately half of all Salvadoran and one third of all Peruvian in-depth interviewees perceived they had been discriminated against by mainstream institutions and/or other minority groups.

In many instances, Salvadoran informants complained about being the target of discriminatory practices that had hurt their businesses, an occurrence that they felt had become more routine in the wake of 9/11. For example, Reina, who owns a restaurant in suburban Maryland, bitterly described how a series of INS raids in her store had scared away many of her habitual customers. She says,

> I'd tell you, though, the one thing that did hurt our business were those 'migra' raids in the restaurant. They would come into our place and search around. And, you know, that scares people away! They did that a few times and we lost plenty customers because of that. It's very inconvenient to have something like that going on. I don't see them [the INS] doing these things in other people's restaurants.

Others complained about the difficulty in obtaining accurate information on business licenses, permits, and general regulations. They described poor customer service and disrespect from institutional representatives. Rocibel, for example, owner of several businesses across the District of Columbia and Prince George's County, described how she had had to return many times to complete zoning and permit paperwork, as she had been provided erroneous information. She states,

> It's not that the process to start the business was difficult. The hardest thing was that those who are in charge of dealing with the public, well . . . they are people who are not really skilled at doing customer service. They are not professionals; they don't know what they are doing. They feel superior and are in a position where they can take advantage of those who need information. They see that one needs to find out this or that, and they leave you waiting, just like that. They tell you: 'Go here, go there." Sometimes they would send me to one office, then to another one. It wasn't there. The person there would send me somewhere else . . . A very difficult process from that perspective. Then, as one learns the system, it becomes easier.

Likewise, other informants perceived differential treatment when it came to enforcing zoning laws and ordinances. Jose, for example, explained how difficult it had been to secure all the necessary approvals and paperwork that eventually allowed him to open his restaurant. He says,

> I don't know but I feel that these people [institutional officers] give us more problems than they give anybody else. Everything is a struggle, from getting the permit to paying the taxes, everything. Many of these people don't have any respect for us, and that is the real problem. But in spite of this, we apply ourselves and we get ahead.

Finally, other informants described antagonisms with commercial retail managers and administrators, many of whom belonged to other minority groups. Roberto, for example, commented on frictions he had had with the manager of the commercial mall where his business was located. Although he attributed these to the manager's fluctuating temper, he also suggested that his business had been singled out because of its commercial sign in Spanish. He explains,

> When I had the sign done, I had some problems with the property manager. I had it made in a store in our same mall. Then, when I put it in, the manager came to complain and told me that, because it was in Spanish, I had to take it down. "Why didn't you tell me before?" I told him. "And why didn't the people I had it made with didn't say anything either? They knew the rules and regulations of this mall." So he then told me that, if the other tenants didn't say anything, he would let it go. But if one of the other stores made a complaint, then I would have to take it down.

Instead, many Peruvians were quick to volunteer that they had never experienced discrimination, personally or commercially. For example, Elsa, having received a $200,000 dollar SBA loan to expand her restaurant, immediately made it clear she had never perceived discrimination of any sort. Likewise, Francisco, owner of a communications and marketing business, explained that Latinos' victim mentality proved a definite liability. He says,

> As for obstacles, I think that many times, we Latinos, as well as other minorities, including African-Americans, we walk with an imaginary cloud over our heads. Not me, I always feel the sun is shinning. I have never, or very rarely, come across that type of prejudice and, when I have, I have felt sorry for the other person. It's just ignorance and I don't waste my time with it. I know that many Latinos think: "Because I'm Latino I won't get this." Personally, I believe this is like a scapegoat; people use it as an excuse so if they fail they can always say that it was because they were Latinos.

Consistent with a recent study on Peruvians in New Jersey, my informants' narratives highlighted class and racial tensions within their own community (Paerregaard 2005). In that sense, they focused on internal discrimination and less on discrimination from mainstream institutions or from other minority groups. The one instance where a few informants expressed a profound sense of discrimination from American society was when referring to blocked mobility because of status incongruence between home and host country occupations.

My data also suggests that men and women's perception of hurdles varied according to informants' gender and class background. For example, while many Salvadoran and Peruvian women of modest class origin emphasized that lack of technical assistance had adversely affected them at the beginning of their startups, women with higher class endowments denounced pervasive gender discrimination in the business world. Thus, these women rarely perceived institutional discrimination from mainstream society, but felt at a disadvantage because of being women; a disadvantage that was particularly acute within their own immigrant communities.

Similarly, men with modest class backgrounds, mostly Salvadorans, tended to have an overly negative perception of business regulations and institutions in charge of monitoring them. In contrast, although aware of instances of exploitation and discrimination, most Salvadoran women's narratives did not emphasize mainstream institutional discrimination. The following chapters will show how feasible explanations for this might revolve around their more fluid linkages to social service agencies, including community development and microcredit programs, which reduce their sense of isolation from mainstream society.

A considerable number of both Salvadorans and Peruvians coincided that many of the existing small business development programs available were inefficient, at least in terms of meeting their needs. Both emphasized that many technical assistance programs available lacked cultural knowledge relevant to the dynamics of Latino markets and consumer practices. For example, Arturo, a Peruvian informant, and Carlos, a Salvadoran, both complained about the lack of effective technical assistance when they first launched their businesses. They agreed that the SBA volunteer counselors they had spoken to had been unable to provide the type of guidance they were seeking, given that these were not Latinos nor familiar with the Latino market.[10]

As important, most Salvadoran informants were unfamiliar with institutional resources available, including federal, state, and/or municipal programs. The few who did know about them explained that such programs were not geared to their needs since SBA loans, for example, were only given to businesses with substantial collateral and business histories. As Samuel explains,

> That's the problem. For the SBA, for example, you have to have been two years in business before applying to any of their programs. So what's the purpose? [He laughs]. Why do I need them after the first two years, when it actually was the time I needed them the most! The 8(a) program and the certification program . . . they are good for established businesses. In six months I'll have two years in business, I'll become a US citizen, and then I might be able to apply for SBA programs!

On the other hand, Peruvians familiar with federal assistance programs did not complain about being unable to access them, but about internal monopolies within established programs. For example, Jose, who runs an information technology firm and participates in the SBA 8(a) Business Development Program, expressed frustration at internal favoritism that awards a large proportion of contracts to a few companies. He says,

> I don't agree with the fact that the [federal] government allows companies like UNISYS [information technology consultants] to participate in their 8(a) Business Development program. They are rather large and do a lot of sub-contracting. Like UNYSIS, there are many other companies that receive the bulk of the federal procurement contracts. Why, then, should they have access to protected markets through the 8(a)?

Facilitators

As mentioned before, informants' perception of hurdles did not prevent them from seeing the opportunities around them. Half of all Peruvians and Salvadorans highlighted many factors that had facilitated their business startups. Salvadorans primarily emphasized the critical assistance provided by social networks, including clients and acquaintances who came to their rescue on several occasions. Blanca, for example, explained how an inspector, who eventually became one of her best customers, had helped her process the paperwork for the alcohol license and occupancy permit.

Further, some Salvadoran informants acknowledged the help of non-governmental or municipal programs that had come to their assistance. For example, Mercedes, who owns a childcare business, attributed a great part of her success to the help she had received from the Fairfax County Office for Children and Families. Not only had she received training, but materials and business referrals. Likewise, Yolanda, also felt that she had received substantial help from FINCA's staff, including a small loan to launch her hair salon.

Peruvians, on the other hand, felt they had received help from institutional networks such as the SBA, and their Small Business Development Centers (SBDCs). Capitalizing on their higher English proficiency, many of them were able to access these resources. Others emphasized that they had been fortunate to enter the country with legal documentation, whereas a few utilized some of their connections to obtain merchandise credit and explore other financing alternatives. Peruvians complained, to a lesser extent than Salvadorans, of mistreatment or of discrimination by mainstream institutions.

Last, most informants felt that the local opportunity structure had changed for the better. Both Salvadorans and Peruvians emphasized that the region had progressively evolved into a profitable market for ethnic goods and products. In that sense, those informants who had longer established businesses stressed that the policy environment was by far more favorable today than a couple of decades ago.

Needs

Salvadoran and Peruvian informants identified both similar and different types of needs. Both emphasized an unmet need for information on business regulations in Spanish, and on small business development and microcredit programs available to aspiring entrepreneurs. Likewise, they pointed out a pervasive lack of Spanish-speaking business specialists in SBDCs, and/or municipal programs familiar with Latinos and their markets. Finally, both expressed a need for financial literacy and basic business training, as well as for an effective umbrella organization that could represent their commercial interests in the area. Despite having the Arlington-based American-Peruvian Chamber of Commerce, most Peruvians felt like commercial pariahs.

Interestingly, whereas Peruvian informants strongly emphasized the need for information on various types of financing alternatives to start and expand their businesses, Salvadorans emphasized a need for business training and, most important, technical assistance to guide them through the process. This is consistent with studies that show that immigrant and refugee entrepreneurs sorely need technical assistance and training far more than working capital (Else and Clay-Thomson 1999). Because they usually start their ventures with family and personal savings, many first generation immigrants are reluctant to embark on institutional borrowing. Further, many immigrants distrust banking institutions and, as I will explore later on, remain apprehensive towards debt and/or credit acquisition.

CONCLUSION

In general terms, the US economic and institutional regulatory environment facilitates the development of immigrant entrepreneurship. This is particularly true in the small business sector, which relies on low and semi-skilled immigrant labor in the growing service and sweatshop-type manufacturing sectors. Yet, while business regulations and markets remain relatively open to ethnic entrepreneurs, diminishing federal support for small businesses, and minority business in particular, often translates into ineffective assistance programs. Thus, lack of institutional coordination across states and municipalities, stiff competition for scarce funding among intermediary lender organizations, and poorly funded training and technical assistance programs adversely affect a large segment of the Washington Latino immigrant entrepreneurial population.

Such ineffectiveness is particularly acute in the case of Salvadorans, many of whom remain in legal limbo either with transient visas or, at worst, undocumented. This vulnerable legal status automatically disqualifies them from participating in federal and state-sponsored programs. Thus, despite their bourgeoning numbers, Washington Latinos, including many Salvadoran and Peruvian first generation immigrants, remain economically and politically disenfranchised embedded in a region where the interests of other ethnic minorities and North Americans prevail. This situation, compounded to Washington Latinos' own community dynamics,—including their inability to effectively mobilize themselves under a collective panethnic banner, and their disarticulated political presence—translates into their inability to fully benefit from the scant resources available for minority businesses. The post 9/11 environment has added complexity to this scenario since, despite the nativism and anti-immigrant backlash that ensued after the attacks, it has also created the conditions that allowed larger Latino representation in governance across the region.

Salvadoran and Peruvian men and women's perceptions of the Washington opportunity structure underscores their differential class, ethnic and gender-based endowments. Peruvians perceive less institutional discrimination from mainstream society, including less regulatory roadblocks and personal frictions with institutional representatives. As I will examine in the next two chapters, Peruvians' emphasis on lack of institutional financing alternatives also underlines distinct business practices and needs. In fact, a few of their businesses have managed to break away from ethnic niches and have more demanding working capital needs. Also in line with this, many Peruvian informants seem less apprehensive than Salvadorans to acquire debt and engage in commercial borrowing.

In contrast, many Salvadoran men often felt unfairly treated when it came to complying with municipal business regulations such as zoning laws, licenses, permits, and other such requirements. Their lower levels of English proficiency, coupled to their unfamiliarity with the American system and institutional resources available most likely exacerbated their sense of isolation and marginality. Salvadoran women, instead, despite their lower class resources, did not share such negative perception of governmental business regulations and enforcing mechanisms. As we will see in chapter eight, the answer to Salvadoran women's social resilience might lie in their ties to co-ethnic women and mainstream non-governmental institutions, which mitigate their sense of isolation and blocked mobility.

5 Class Resources, Group Cohesion and Business Strategies

Moving away from a demand side analysis of immigrant entrepreneurship, this chapter focuses instead on its supply side. Thus, we begin an exploration of the ways in which social relations based upon class (albeit ethnicity and gender are naturally interwoven) mediate Salvadoran and Peruvian business ventures. Organized in three sections, the chapter reviews first the factors that have contributed to Salvadorans' stronger group cohesion, including socio-demographic, transnational, and reception dynamics. The second part presents a comparative analysis of participants' class resources, including human, financial, and class-based social and cultural capital. Finally, the last section examines Salvadoran and Peruvian class-based business strategies.

ETHNICITY, CLASS, AND IMMIGRANT SOCIAL COHESION

Individuals' membership in various social groups determines the types of identities they will adopt, reject, combine, and, ultimately, shed. Identity formation not only colors individuals' self-perception in terms of ethnic origin, class extraction, or gender identity, but it affects their internalized views of the community they belong to and of other social groups they relate to. Ultimately, the success of a group at forging a strong ethnic identity may undergird its ability to develop solidarious social relations among country fellow men and women. Almost inevitably, every immigrant group is plagued by class, religious, and/or racial cleavages; therefore a sense of pride in a shared common ancestry, group trust, and a positive view of one's own is paramount to ensure a minimal degree of social cohesion. Social cohesion, thus, underlies the quality of social relations among co-nationals.

The economic sociology of immigration emphasizes that social relations shape and condition economic action. One of the various ways in which immigrants' economic action manifests itself is through its attempts at mobilizing resources to create and develop small businesses. Consequently, the quality of social relations within a community takes on special relevance. To recall from chapter two, focusing on immigrant economic adaptation and on ethnic entrepreneurship in particular, Light distinguishes between class and ethnic resources. In his conceptualization, every immigrant group mobilizes a unique set of ethnic and class-based resources derived from both intrinsic group features and its embeddedness in a particular context of reception. Yet, as the extensive literature on ethnic entrepreneurship has shown thus far, to thrive economically because of its ethnicity, an immigrant group has to command a considerable amount of both types of resources (Light and Gold 2000; Portes and Manning 1986). As I will show, this is not the case of either Washington Salvadorans or Peruvians.

Upon arrival to the Washington area, Salvadorans and Peruvians struggle to adjust to their new environment in multifaceted ways. Endowed with distinct class and ethnic based resources, due to varying degrees of group cohesion and structurally induced factors, Salvadoran and Peruvian resource mobilization strategies will either be class-predominant, ethnic-predominant, or a balanced combination of them both. In tandem with Light's argument, participants' permutation of class and ethnic resources ultimately leads to either collectivist or individualist entrepreneurial styles. Given that, in real life, class and ethnicity intersect, and often times become intertwined in social phenomena, the task of fleshing out the contributions of each becomes quite complex. Occasionally, as it occurs primarily with Salvadoran informants, class and national origin coalesce, posing the risks of conflating them and misinterpreting the data.

My informants' accounts indicate that group cohesion remains the foundation upon which communal interests and collective goals can be pursued, including economic advancement. Yet, it is both social legacies transferred from the homeland and emerging realities in the new environment that converge to endow Washington Peruvians and Salvadorans with varying degrees of social cohesion. The previous chapter has examined in detail the demand side factors in the Greater Washington area that affect Salvadoran and Peruvian entrepreneurs. I discuss next how specific circumstances in their context of exit and in their receiving communities affect group cohesion.

Social Stratification, 'Paisanaje,'[1] Reactive Ethnicity, and Resettlement

As discussed in chapter four, Salvadorans and Peruvians' panethnic categorization under the common label of Hispanic or Latinos/as obscures important differences between the two groups. Beyond their divergent socioeconomic backgrounds, Peruvian and Salvadoran first generation immigrants remain, to a considerable extent, a product of the societies they have left behind. They come with a unique menagerie of human, cultural, social, and financial capital, including internalized prejudices borne out of culturally specific stratified social systems. My qualitative data indicate that when an immigrant community primarily includes single class strata, as is the case with Washington Salvadorans, such class homogeneity reduces class-cleavages and bolsters social cohesion among co-nationals. Conversely, when an immigrant community, such as Washington Peruvians, includes a more heterogeneous population, it tends to reproduce the very racial and class hierarchies it has left behind. Therefore, it weakens its group cohesion. Yanine and Carlos, two of my Peruvian informants explain,

> In my opinion, I think that, in Peru, we have many social and class cleavages. In Peru we don't share a sense of brotherhood, of being part of something together, and this feeling is due to many sociological reasons. I believe that when we all come here . . . if we haven't had unity in Peru, we shouldn't expect to find it here simply because we are immigrants. Despite being in the same boat, we don't feel any solidarity towards Peruvian compatriots. At least, I don't. And, most times, I believe that these things are reciprocal. This is very common in Peru and it happens here as well.
>
> In Northern Virginia, many Peruvians from Lima have huge houses. [They are] . . . 'serranos', 'serranos' (from the mountains). Let me tell you, these people are doing much better here than our middle class. Because in Lima, those belonging to the middle class are only able to boast about their whiteness; that is the only thing they can brag about. I don't believe in this, I don't believe in any of the things I'm telling you. I'm only telling you what I see happening around me. The 'serranos' have indigenous blood; and that is the great difference. They don't mix . . . Like in the United States, the white 'Limeños' (coming from Lima) don't get together with Peruvians who have indigenous blood, neither back home nor here. And here it's even worse. So the problem comes with us, all the way from Peru.

Although, at a national level, Salvadorans are a more heterogeneous immigrant population than predominantly middle class Peruvians, the Washington area demographics virtually reverts this national profile. The Washington Salvadoran community is largely composed of working class and rural peasant migrants, while that of Washington Peruvians bifurcates into a segment with working and lower middle class migrants and another one with upwardly mobile middle class professionals. Unlike its Salvadoran counterpart, then, the Peruvian immigrant community is furthered fragmented by racial cleavages between "serranos" (Peruvian indigenous population predominantly from the sierra) and "Limeños"(Ladino population from the capital city of Lima).

Furthermore, Washington Salvadorans are particularly homogeneous not only in their racial uniformity, but because they come, primarily, from a few rural towns in the Salvadoran Eastern provinces of La Union, San Miguel, and Usulután. As mentioned before, as many as 79 per cent of

Salvadoran male and 92 per cent of Salvadoran female informants originated in these provinces. Meanwhile, over half of female and male Peruvian informants migrated from Peru's capital city of Lima.

This element of 'paisanaje' among Salvadorans plays an important role in laying out the bases for a more cohesive community. Social ties among co-villagers and extended networks of Salvadoran families engaged in circuit migrant routes to the area provide a contrasting model to Peruvians' more scattered, urban, and modernized immigrant population. Ultimately, Salvadorans' ethnic-preponderant business strategies will make up for their class disadvantage. In other words, Salvadoran social relations based around kin and 'paisano' loyalties counterbalance, to some extent, their scarcity of class based resources.

The other key factor that seems to play a critical role in buttressing immigrant social cohesion is the development of a strong reactive ethnicity. To recall from chapter two, the ethnic resilience perspective posits that immigrants' ethnic identity formation follows either a linear or reactive evolution. Whereas linear ethnicity entails a shared identity primarily forged on the basis of cultural memory brought from the homeland, reactive ethnicity is a product of the immigrant experience, an emergent feeling of "we-ness prompted by the experience of being subjected to the same discrimination by the host society" (Portes 1995: 256). More recently Landolt argues that it is both structural factors, such as the level of reception an immigrant group encounters, as well as the extent and quality of its enduring ties with their homeland that converge to galvanize reactive ethnicity (Landolt 2001: 178). My own observations and informants' accounts corroborate this argument, which better explains the more pronounced reactive ethnicity among Salvadorans.

Salvadorans' higher levels of engagement in transnational processes— ranging from periodic remittances, to hometown fundraising activities, to arrangements that make possible for children to be raised by family members in the homeland—further bolster their reactive ethnicity. Although contemporary technological, information, and communication technologies also enable Peruvians to become enmeshed in transnational social fields, their level of transnational social obligations does not match that of Salvadorans. In sum, the Washington Peruvian immigrant community lacks the synergy that transnationalism, a de facto refugee status, a hostile reception level, and a significant numerical presence have granted Washington Salvadorans.

In conclusion, Salvadoran and Peruvian study participants show different degrees of group cohesion. Whereas Salvadorans exhibit a stronger reactive ethnicity with considerable levels of ethnic solidarity among closely tight kin and 'paisano' networks, Peruvians do not. Nevertheless, the latter have access to greater human, financial, and class-derived sources of social and cultural capital. Furthermore, Washington Peruvians seem more assimilated to mainstream circles than their Salvadoran counterparts, often benefiting from higher levels of social and economic incorporation. The next sections will specifically examine the class resources each group commands, addressing how each leverages such resources in articulating business strategies.

SALVADORAN AND PERUVIAN CLASS-BASED RESOURCES

In practice, immigrant groups combine various types of resources in their business undertakings. Yet, this chapter exclusively focuses on Salvadoran and Peruvian class endowments and the way in which these shape their business strategies. Chapter two has already discussed Light's distinction between immigrants' class and ethnic-based resources. To recall briefly, class resources encompass all those assets an immigrant group has access to by virtue of its membership in the bourgeoisie, that is in a worldwide entrepreneurial class that encompasses business owners in the formal, informal and illegal sectors of the economy. Class resources include both material and cultural endowments that range from financial, to human, to cultural, to social capital (Light 1984; Light and Gold 2000). As Bourdieu argues, class-based cultural endowments translate into skills, attitudes, values, and knowledge that allow the bourgeoisies of the world to reproduce themselves and perpetuate their structural position of privilege. Most important, class based group resources allow members to transcend ethnic boundaries, creating loyalties along class lines and linking bourgeoisies worldwide (Bourdieu 1977).

Chapter three described, based on census data, the divergent socioeconomic characteristics of Salvadoran and Peruvian immigrants. My survey and interview data further confirm this gap, showing that Peruvians command group resources that are class-preponderant relative to Salvadorans. Three themes in participants' narratives clearly illustrate this: 1) their immigration motives; 2) their class endowments upon arrival, including human and cultural forms of capital; and 3) their divergent motivations for self-employment.

Immigration Motives

When an individual decides, either as a household or individual strategy, that immigration has become a viable alternative to improve one's life chances, the motivations behind such a decision usually reflect his or her class extraction. My informants expressed a wide range of reasons that led to their migration, pointing out concrete needs and goals that propelled them to seek opportunities here. Clearly, their motivations for migration were directly related both to circumstances that expelled them from their homelands, as well as to factors that attracted them here.

My data show that, whereas many Peruvians came to the Washington area primarily to recapture or maintain a middle class social status, most Salvadorans arrived escaping destitution, war, and political persecution. Further, the majority of Salvadoran informants stressed they came in search of opportunities that would allow them to meet social obligations at home. Informants explained they had debts they had incurred in the process of travelling north since they had received loans from kin and friends to pay their coyotes. Further, they stressed they needed to periodically remit money to their struggling families in their homeland. Finally, despite having substantial family networks in the Washington DC area, Salvadorans remained particularly vulnerable given that their families, themselves undocumented, or at best under Temporary Protected Status (TPS), were unable to sponsor them for legal permanent residency. Blanca, a Salvadoran informant explains,

> When I came to this country, I came like everybody else, to make some money [. . .] I kept on telling myself that I would come to the United States to start a business and that I would do much better here. It wasn't easy. I came like the rest, without a visa. I had a brother in California but he couldn't help me much because he had no papers himself. So, then, when I first arrived here, I had thought I would stay for a couple of years because I had left my four children back home. At the beginning, I couldn't come because we had no money, but my mother helped me out. She stayed with the children and took care of them. My husband also stayed behind working there. It took me a whole month to make it here. My husband . . . he had tried three times before and hadn't been able to cross the border [Blanca laughs]. So, finally, after his third try, I told him I would come myself. So six days after I arrived, I was working. And my husband . . . three times that he had tried and hadn't been able to make it [Blanca laughs again].

Luis also compares Salvadoran migrants' specific circumstances to that of other Latino immigrant groups,

> From El Salvador, we come undocumented, we come anyway we can, but we come. So we arrive without an education, peasants. And South Americans, let's say Peruvians or Colombians, not everybody is able to come here. Only those who have some means are able to make it, those who have studied . . . because, think about it, I think a Peruvian peasant is not even dreaming about coming here. Because he doesn't have the possibility; he doesn't have the money; it is too far. Instead, we, from El Salvador, we come straight from the countryside. I can assure you that very few of us have even visited San Salvador (Capital City). And we come here anyway. That is the truth, that we have little education but [our coming here] benefits the whole country because we send money to our families, and we open businesses here and there. But it is a good

thing for our country that anyone who has a need comes here. Those who come, believe me, it is because we have a real need. The Salvadorans who, let's say . . . are doing relatively well back home, those who are professionals, they don't come here. Only very few of them ever come. Almost nobody I would say. A while ago we had three Peruvian medical doctors working here in the bar, mopping the floors, working very hard. This is not a criticism, but I have never seen a Salvadoran medical doctor coming here to mop floors and wash dishes. Nor have I seen other Salvadoran professionals, lawyers, and the like coming here to do that type of work. That is very hard for them so they stay back home.

Unlike most Salvadorans, many Peruvian informants brought with them at least modest amounts of capital, including severance packages and/or lifelong savings. Some arrived legally sponsored by family members and, rarely, did they talk about remittance obligations. Notably, mostly Peruvian participants reported having arrived originally to pursue an education or leisure travel, which later turned into permanent stays. For example, Carmen describes the circumstances of her migration with the following words,

My brother-in-law was here, he was an American citizen and he sponsored us. We arrived with 'papeles' (legal documentation). My husband was already here when I arrived. He is a computer analyst and my brother-in-law had found him a job at NASA. But my husband missed us so much that he quit everything and went back to Peru. Then, my brother-in-law got mad and didn't want to deal with us anymore. Fortunately, my mother-in-law intervened and asked him to help us again. That's how it all turned out. So the second time around all of us came here but, this time, my husband didn't have that good job anymore. We brought all our savings and that helped us to open our business. Since we had worked many years in the national telephone company back in Peru, when we gave our resignation they gave us a severance package. We saved every single penny and didn't spend anything except the rent deposit.

In sum, while both Salvadorans and Peruvians coincided that economic, political, and social factors had fueled their migration, each group emphasized different reasons. As I will elaborate in chapter seven, men and women significantly differed on their immigration motives.

Human Capital and Class Resources

Occupational Experience

Salvadorans were younger, less educated, and with modest occupational experiences that suited them best for low-wage menial type jobs in the informal ethnic economy or, at best, for jobs in the secondary sector of the service economy. A closer look at Salvadoran and Peruvian occupational histories might provide insight into the different opportunity structures they accessed upon arrival.

Agustina Guzman is the owner of a small "tiendita" (clothing store) in a Washington DC suburb. She arrived to the area many years ago, leaving behind two children and a disgruntled husband. Agustina completed her primary education back in El Salvador, where she worked as a seamstress before migrating to the DC region. With a poor command of the English language, she only managed to obtain dead-end jobs in the personal service sector. Before opening her small business, Agustina worked two jobs, rushing from one to the other. From 6:00 in the morning to 3:30 in the afternoon, she worked as a janitorial assistant at a military base. After her first shift, without time to spare, she would drop by her house, quickly put on her uniform and start her Taco Bell shift at 4 PM. She would then work there until midnight. She was so exhausted from the juggling, low pay, and poor treatment she received from her employers that, when one of her jobs fell through, she decided to venture herself and open her own alterations business.

In contrast, Clara Herrera owns a residential janitorial service and a gourmet coffee catering franchise. Like Agustina, she also arrived to the area many years ago but, instead, her former husband and two daughters were waiting for her here. Clara studied English from an early age and completed postgraduate studies back in Lima. She migrated to the US, primarily, because of the political and economic chaos unleashed by the Shining Path and its guerrilla warfare. Although she barely had time to gather her belongings before the trip, she managed to secure three thousand dollars right before boarding her plane. In Lima, she had worked as a high school teacher and, a few months after arriving in the US, she was able to land a secretarial job at a multilateral organization. While working full-time, she decided to start a janitorial service on the side and try her luck. A few years later, with her side business thriving, she quit her secretarial job and devoted herself entirely to her venture. More recently, she has opened a second business that caters gourmet coffee to hotels and corporations in the area.

As Clara's story illustrates, Peruvians' higher levels of human capital, including more prestigious pre-migration occupational experiences, allow them to diversify their range of possible employment opportunities upon arrival. Thus, their occupations include a wider range of jobs such as sales associates, managers, executives, international civil servants, teachers, government employees, clerks, construction workers, domestic servants, and janitorial workers. Unlike most Salvadorans, some Peruvian participants successfully managed to insert themselves both in the secondary as well as primary sectors of the mainstream local economy.

Paradoxically, however, as Luis' remarks on the differences among Salvadoran and South American migration to the area highlights, Peruvians' higher occupational prestige does not always translate into upwardly mobile outcomes. In fact, only Peruvian participants experienced sharp downward mobility, precisely because of higher human capital endowments they could not successfully transfer from the homeland to the US labor market. Like other non-English speaking immigrant populations coming with substantial levels of human capital, some Peruvian participants underwent "status incongruence" between home and host-country occupations (Light and Gold 2000). The disjuncture between past achievements, expectations, and real opportunities in the new environment led Arturo to eloquently describe his predicament,

> I was in tears. Alone. I used to cry out of powerlessness, of bitterness. You know, the sadness of it all . . . but I wasn't ashamed of what I was doing, of the manual work. It was the investment I had lost in all those years of education, right? My father's shame . . . My father never knew what I did for a living. He died five years ago but he never found out. Because, you know, for him . . . he was in the military. Neither did my brother know. So well, after a couple of months trying to get a job, I decided I had to do something. I began leaving ads under the doors, in cars, everywhere. I connected a phone line, hooked an answering machine to it and used my brother-in-law's small office. So that's how I got started, by myself. I'm not saying that this job has no dignity, but it is not something to boast about either.

English Language Proficiency

Light and Gold argue (2000) that an immigrant group's level of English proficiency upon arrival is a clear class indicator. Hence, Salvadorans and Peruvians' level of English proficiency upon arrival confirms that, on average, the latter command more class resources than the former. Notwithstanding, it is important to underline that in a few notable cases the class background of certain participants intersected with national origin, adding another layer of complexity to the analysis. The cases below serve to illustrate this point.

Karla, a young artist from the capital city of San Salvador, has a small atelier in a trendy area of Adams Morgan. She is a professional artist who paints on commission for a select clientele and for exhibits at local galleries. A middle class Salvadoran with professional parents, she arrived to the area with her family when she was only 12 years old. Since then, she has long become a permanent resident and has completed an undergraduate degree in liberal arts at the University of Maryland. She is fluent in English, Spanish, French, and Italian and, since she received a fellowship to study arts and culture in Paris, she has had the opportunity to travel extensively throughout Europe.

In contrast, Carlos, from a small town in El Salvador, runs his own home improvement business. He has recently arrived to the area, leaving his wife and children back home. After being undocumented for a couple of years, he has only recently initiated immigration paperwork. He speaks little English and spent the first year in this country doing construction work for a small company run by co-nationals. He decided to become self-employed primarily because he realized he needed to maximize profits to be able to send money home, pay debts, as well as finance his immigration lawyer's fees.

As the stories above illustrate, beyond sharing a common nationality, Carlos and Karla have little else in common. Their divergent class endowments steer them into a different opportunity structure that, ultimately, positions them in a more or less advantageous location in the social hierarchy. As will be examined later on, this intersection of class and ethnicity becomes even more evident among Peruvian informants.

Parental Occupation

Salvadoran and Peruvian participants also differed in their parental occupation models. Whereas a vast number of Salvadorans reported parents in the trade professions, a majority of Peruvians had parents in the professional and managerial occupations. A substantial number of Salvadoran participants acquired entrepreneurship skills either through early childhood socialization processes or through informal business training in businesses run by co-nationals or co-ethnics. Instead, Peruvian participants were most likely to have acquired these skills only upon arrival, and while working at businesses run primarily by North Americans. As Esteban, a Peruvian informant explains,

> When I was offered this marketing and sales job at the radio, that was like a gift from heaven. Because at that time I was beginning my research [to start my own business]. So I told them: 'Of course I will take the job.' I started working for them at the end of 1984. And stayed there until perhaps January, February, or March of 1985 and, then, I gave them my resignation. By that time, I had reached a ceiling where I couldn't learn anything else from them. I needed to learn more about the Hispanic market. I did learn a lot with these people because they had good material. In fact, I think the first year of my business I used as much as 70 per cent of what I had learned at the radio. The second and third year that became only like a 10 per cent. But I did learn quite a lot with that job, and I made many contacts there. All of that gave me a big push at the beginning.

Business Experience

Since many Salvadoran participants had already ran businesses back home, they approached their business ventures much as they had done before. In so doing, they held mismatched expectations of what the process entailed in the context of an industrialized economy. Thus, a large number of Salvadorans complained that they "had jumped into business ventures without knowing what they were doing." While their previous business experiences made them confident that they might be able to replicate their successes in their new home, Salvadorans had difficulty adjusting to the unfamiliar American regulatory environment with its certification, licensing, permits, credit, and business plans requirements. Precisely because of their limited exposure to American business practices, Salvadorans encountered more hurdles along the way than their Peruvian counterparts. In some of the worst instances, a few experienced malfeasance and fraud at the hands of other immigrants, including Latinos.

Yet Light and Gold point out that immigrants' class-based resources extend well beyond their human capital endowments. They also encompass cultural capital accrued by virtue of membership in the bourgeoisie, regardless of ethnic or national boundaries. Bourgeois occupational culture, values, beliefs, and aspirations are concrete manifestations of class-based resources. Not surprisingly, a much larger number of Peruvians expressed deeply held bourgeois values, beliefs, and aspirations. Similarly, among Salvadorans, a few middle class informants, considerably acculturated to mainstream American values, also held bourgeois occupational attitudes. For example, Henry several times stressed his desire for self-fulfillment and American-style success. He explains,

> I have always dreamed big . . . in becoming a leader, in succeeding in life! Everything started back in 1982 when my then dentist encouraged me to make some changes in my life. This man, from Irish background, told me: "Henry, you have to open your own business. Given your personality, you'll do really well. You can do it." Then, my former boss at the bank helped me out too. Since he knew I was an honors student and that I did very good work, one day he called me to his office and told me he wanted to help me. He said I could ask him for anything I needed. So I told him I wanted to become the general manager of the division I worked for. Unfortunately, there were many people ahead of me waiting for that job so I couldn't get it. But he insisted I asked him for something else. At that very moment I knew I wanted to start my own company and I told him so. And he did help me. In fact, he provided all my first clients, including his own wife. Now, my dream is to open several offices throughout the country.

In contrast, and critical of some of his co-nationals' lack of aspirations, Samuel, described how some of his employees did not seem to understand the empowering value of education. In doing so, he pointed out that lack of class-related cultural capital in the socialization process of some of his co-nationals adversely affected them. In his own words,

But there are some people . . . maybe because they have very limited education and they just don't think about the future. You know, being able to speak some English . . . but, in my country, there are people with a different frame of mind from yours. They say: "As if reading and writing is going to feed you!" Many people come from the countryside. Actually most of them come from the countryside and a very small number of Salvadorans come from the city or are people who have studied. But the peasant works very hard, full-time during the day and part time in the evenings. They work like donkeys. And what happens? They earn very little. So, I say, why don't they go to school, learn English and some trade, any trade. For example, if somebody comes here without an education, somebody who didn't even know how to read and write comes, he comes only with the idea of working and making some money. The concept of going to school doesn't exist for him. So that's one of the reasons why many people only work, why they don't improve themselves and don't become part of the system.

Self-Employment Motive

Finally, study participants' motivations to engage in self-employment provide another window into the nature and composition of immigrant group resources. My in-depth interview data show that, in both Peruvians and Salvadorans' cases, attitudinal factors remained main determinants of self-employment. Both groups' narratives offered numerous references to motives such as "to work hard and achieve," "because I needed autonomy," "because this is who I am" (identity), "because one has to take risks in life," "because I felt I could do it" (self-esteem), "because I liked challenges," and "because I always had this dream." Yet, whereas Salvadorans stressed themes related to "identity," "dream," and "hard work and achievement," Peruvians highlighted "autonomy" and "risk-taking."

In tandem with ethnic entrepreneurship theoretical paradigms, structural factors emerged as another main determinant of Salvadoran and Peruvian self-employment. Informants vividly referred to instances of discrimination in their new environments, which fueled their determination to become self-employed. Most important, their respective motivations for self-employment highlight Salvadoran and Peruvian differential structural incorporation into the Washington area's labor market.

To recall, the resources theory of ethnic entrepreneurship clearly distinguishes between two types of class disadvantage affecting newcomers upon arrival to the host country (Light and Gold 2000; Light and Rosenstein 1995b). Thus, resource disadvantaged entrepreneurs are those immigrants who arrive with little, if any, human capital and other class-based resources; they are those who had historically been denied access to opportunities other groups have capitalized on. Access to a good education, to a healthy diet, to a reliable healthcare system, to networking opportunities, and to a positive work ethic are group resources that make certain immigrant groups more productive than others. As such, resource disadvantaged entrepreneurs are handicapped from the very beginning, and start their quest for economic incorporation from a lower starting point. Any discrimination they encounter throughout their journey is in addition to that prior discrimination they suffered early on in their lives.

Conversely, labor market disadvantaged entrepreneurs are those who receive below expected returns on their human capital, not because of low productivity, but usually because of discrimination or blocked mobility in the labor market (Bates 1997). Both types of disadvantage are not mutually exclusive, given that immigrants can be subject to both simultaneously, or to none. When immigrants do not have a good command of the English language, have accents, or when their educational credentials are not recognized by American institutions or employers, they suffer labor market discrimination.

My interview data confirm this theoretical argument since Salvadorans disproportionately filled in the ranks of resource disadvantaged entrepreneurs, whereas Peruvians experienced more instances of labor market discrimination. Salvadorans' narratives abounded with references to discrimination, poor treatment, exploitation, and cruel working conditions. This is consistent with their structural insertion in the lower rungs of the secondary labor market and their prior historical exclusion from opportunity structures. Ana Maria explains in her own words,

> I had a very bad experience when we first arrived here. It was very difficult for immigrants then. Now, it is a little easier because many people know their rights and know what to do. In those days, when I got here, they [our employers] would even slap us in the face as they say, and because one was so afraid of 'la migra' (immigration officers), of losing the job, one had to put up with anything. I had very bad experiences with this. And one day I told myself: "Please, God, maybe I cannot do this here and I might have to return back home. But I'm not going to keep on working for anybody else to order me around."[. . .] I once had this Cuban woman . . . she was cruel, mean and cruel. And she was like that with everybody. She abused us, very mean woman.

In contrast, a large number of Peruvians explained that circumstances related to labor market discrimination prompted their determination to become self-employed. Leonor says,

> You know, all the white immigrants who come here, even if they have just arrived, they call themselves American because they are white and because they speak good English. Because that is their fortune. I have always told my husband: "We should sue our governments because they have done a disservice to us. They have forced us to travel around the world with only a sad and single language under our belts. This is not the case of Europeans, who prepare their people with two or three

languages." Our people, however, we have to pay to learn English, but Europeans, they teach languages in their public schools. For example, look at the case of people from the Philippines, they do all their studies in English. Yet, they speak multiple dialects. So they learn English early on. And what happens? Medical doctors and nurses come here and they pass the [revalidation] exams like that. This is my bad luck and I always ask myself: "Why haven't they taught me English in my country?" So to work as an assistant, I decided not to do it. Look, my specialization is care of premature babies. I can get IVs (intravenous catheters) in and out a baby's arm with my eyes closed. And I have to see other people hurting them because they don't know what they are doing, only because they have the certificate, the paper that says they can do it and I don't. I tried to pass the exam twice but the English was too much for me. Then, my children were small and I couldn't take classes at night.

Finally, Salvadorans emphasized that economic reasons had pushed them towards self-employment. They described their efforts at making ends meet as a patchwork of survival strategies that combined full and part-time work. Peruvians, instead, highlighted that a key motivator to become self-employed had been the need to recover or maintain an elusive middle class social status.

To summarize, Peruvian group resources are class preponderant relative to Salvadorans'. In spite of this, the magnitude of such endowments does not compare to that of other Latino immigrant contingents, such as Cubans. Most important, neither the Peruvian nor Salvadoran elite participated in the migration process because they were never hard pressed to leave their countries. Therefore, neither immigrant group includes an entrepreneurial class among its population. Even in the case of El Salvador, where the bloodshed of the civil war produced a mass exodus, Salvadoran elite families were seen as an accomplice of right-wing state terrorism. Hence, they were never interested, or forced, to leave behind their possessions to pursue a new life somewhere else.

PARTICIPANTS CLASS-BASED BUSINESS STRATEGIES

Salvadoran and Peruvians' differential class endowments lead them to articulate common as well as widely distinct business strategies. My qualitative data show some differences in their financing, labor, and marketing practices as well as in their business culture and management styles.

Financing

Not surprisingly, Peruvian study participants had access to a wider spectrum of financing options to start and develop their commercial ventures.

The combination of relatively higher financial and human capital endowments, including their better command of the English language, secured them access to critical information on financing alternatives beyond personal and family sources of capital. Thus, they were able to finance their business ventures through Small Business Administration (SBA) federal government loans, commercial bank loans, personal and family savings, as well as proceeds from the sale of personal property including jewels, stock, and/or real estate. Because of their wider connections to American mainstream institutions and bourgeois social circles, early on they found out about lucrative bankrupt business foreclosures and/or special financing options and took advantage of them. As Maco, one of my Peruvian participants explains,

> Sometimes I had expensive projects, huge entertainment productions where just the investment to provide orchestras or a music band was in the neighborhood of 30,000 or 40,000 dollars. Sometimes I had the money to back these investments up since I have owned my own house for a long time, so I would take out equity loans. Other times, I would use my company's stock as collateral. So you could say that, in a way, the company loaned me the money. But I'd usually prefer to take out loans, even personal loans. But, of course, the only way I could do these things [take loans] was through personal property that I used as collateral.

Yanine also described the favorable circumstances under which she acquired her first clients from her former boss. She explains,

> So that was how I began working for this man, this American. I started as a general administrator in his company and I did pretty much everything for him. In a few months, I lifted the company from scratch. A couple of years later, the man ended up selling the company after having broken it up into sub-companies. He sold me twenty clients because I made sure to remind him that he owed me big time, that he would have never been able to sell his company so high had I not lifted it up the way I did. He ended up financing me the cost of the portfolio of clients he had sold me. I did a good job managing those first clients so I acquired more and more clients. In fact, I even acquired some of the clients that my former boss had sold to other people. I would hear that some of the other poor fellows who had purchased portfolios of clients had no experience whatsoever in managing this type of company and, of course, they started having all sorts of problems, customer service issues, and others. So as these sub-companies started faltering when their clientele became more and more dissatisfied, I bought them one by one. But, whereas the owners had paid a fortune for them, I bought them for a few pennies. But that wasn't my problem . . .

Conversely, Salvadorans had to rely, almost exclusively, on ethnic credit, including personal and family savings. I will address the influence of ethnic resources in the articulation of business strategies in the following chapter. Further, because they had social obligations to remit periodically to their struggling families back home, they found it very difficult to accumulate start-up capital or to further finance their ventures. Frustrated at his inability to obtain commercial credit to finance capital expenditures, Samuel had to creatively resort to alternative financing strategies such as equipment leasing. He explains his predicament with these words,

> Way back in January I wanted to buy some mechanical equipment but, as you know, the first thing any bank requests is your company's tax returns. Think about it! I barely have a year doing this formally. Where was I going to get these tax returns! So . . . some people told me that there were leasing companies and that I could try to apply to one of them. What happens is that the leasing company buys the equipment and rents it to you and you rent it out and start paying it out month by month. But what happens? . . . let me tell you, I am amazed . . . Everybody wants to make money of everybody else! The problem was that I didn't understand how the whole thing worked. The only reason why I wanted to buy the equipment was because, last year, I spent around 20,000 dollars just in four months of rentals! Just for leasing it! Therefore, from a managerial perspective, I could have applied all that money to payments for my own equipment . . . of course, if I had been able to find somebody willing to finance it to me.

Even when they managed to obtain commercial loans, Salvadorans complained they had to wait for long periods of time before becoming eligible to borrow. Ironically, many obtained the loans when they needed them the least. Luis, owner of two popular restaurants in the District, explained that only after having long succeeded with their first business, he and his partner were able to secure a healthy commercial loan.

Further, Salvadorans' vulnerable position, exacerbated by their low levels of English proficiency and their lack of knowledge of business regulations, at times placed them at the center of fraud and malfeasance at the hands of other groups, including other Latinos. For example, when one of her partners decided to withdraw from the business partnership, Blanca almost lost her small restaurant. For a couple of months, she was unable to meet her monthly payments and she felt she ended up paying far more in interest rates than she had to. She explains,

> Yes, we opened it up with 15,000 dollars. So we became partners with a cousin of mine. But the other partner we had, six months down the road, he had to chip in some money, right? And so he came up with the news he didn't have the money and he left the partnership. So they told

us they would take away the restaurant from us in three months if we didn't pay. "So what do we do now? What do we do?", I kept on asking my family. So the owner of the restaurant finally gave us a special financing but we had to pay him with huge interest rates. We ended up paying like 230,000 dollars in the end . . . but we didn't know much about running a business, then. So think about it, what were we going to tell him . . . He did whatever he wanted. . . .

Labor

Labor business strategies are those practices strictly related to the acquisition and utilization of labor in the operation of business ventures. These include aspects such as employer-employee relations, entrepreneurs' hiring and recruitment practices, their utilization of referral networks and access to a cheap co-ethnic and/or co-national pool of labor, and informal business training practices. Not surprisingly, Salvadoran and Peruvian informants' differential class-based endowments directly influenced their labor business strategies.

My in-depth interview data suggest that, in many instances, Peruvians' labor business strategies concealed class interests behind an ideology of panethnic solidarity. This finding is congruent with scholars' contention that the ethnic solidarity thesis severely overlooks class antagonisms among co-ethnics (Anthias 1992; Bonacich 1973). Ironically, most Peruvian informants refused to hire compatriots but extolled the virtues of hiring co-ethnic Central American employees, especially Salvadorans. For the most part, Peruvians preferred Central Americans because they were cheaper, more subservient, better workers, and readily available given their numerical presence in the area. In other words, they hired them not because of social solidarity with fellow Latino immigrants, but because they wanted to maximize their business profits, and Central Americans perfectly met their needs. Carlos M. explains it with these words,

> Sometimes we do five [houses] in a day. We start around 8:00 in the morning and we finish around 5:00 in the evening and the workers leave with 250 dollars in their pocket. But South Americans are not suited for that. I really like them, I enjoy talking to them about almost anything, they are very congenial . . . but the ones who really help me are the Central Americans. I have Guatemalan, Hondurans, Salvadorans. . . . They are excellent workers. "No lloran, pues!"[They don't complain]; they don't expect anything.

Thus, Salvadoran wage earners become typified as menial, cheap, and hard working and enter a hierarchical employee-employer relationship where they are not exposed to ethnic solidarity, but sometimes to panethnic exploitation.[2] Surprisingly, the topic of panethnic exploitation among

Latino immigrants has not received much attention in the ethnic entrepreneurship literature. This problematizes the ethnic solidarity thesis and
raises questions on the exact nature of its social boundaries. Although
scholars have alluded to the limits of ethnic solidarity among Chinese in
New York and Cubans in Miami (Gilbertson 1995; Sanders and Nee 1987;
Portes and Zhou 1992; Zhou and Logan 1989), the matter has not been
explored further and merits more attention.

Further, Salvadoran and Peruvian's attitude vis à vis employee-employer
relations provided another source of contrast. Peruvians showed a wide
range of variation with some informants practicing more or less informal
arrangements than others. Further, on average, Peruvians were more likely
to establish more formal employee-employer relations. This might be indicative of their larger insertion into the mainstream economy, and their higher
degrees of bourgeois occupational culture, including a tendency towards
more bureaucratic and impersonal labor management styles.

In contrast, Salvadorans' hiring practices seemed more motivated by ethnic loyalties. Most participants described informal human resource management styles with practices that had an ethnic character and were less
hierarchical. In spite of this, Salvadoran labor business strategies were not
entirely altruistic or devoid of conflict since, to make ends meet, most businesses largely depended on the owner's self-exploitation, and offered long
working hours, meager wages, few opportunities for advancement and few,
if any, fringe benefits. Since most of Salvadorans' labor business strategies
drew primarily from their ethnic resource base, I will examine these in
more detail in chapter six.

Ironically, while Peruvians' preferential hiring of Central Americans
allowed some of them to effectively maximize their profits with "docile
and hard working employees," it also meant that they had to interact with
these employees on a regular basis. For example, Arturo confided that, at a
personal level, he felt lonely because his employees were good workers but
not appropriate for socialization purposes.

> I think that those that came here first, ten years ago, were people from
> the lower classes. So the people with whom I used to hang out were from
> a much lower social class, and there was a lot of envy, lack of trust, and
> their topic of conversation revolved around women, drugs . . . I didn't
> have anything in common with them except that we worked together.

Marketing

My informants' marketing strategies revolved around two interrelated
factors: the target markets they focused on and the mechanisms through
which they attempted to reach those markets. The market an immigrant
groups targets constitutes a good indicator of its structural position in the

ethnic or mainstream economy of the host country. I will only focus on marketing strategies resulting from Salvadoran and Peruvians' deployment of class-based resources.

Both my survey and in-depth interview data show that most Salvadorans' lack of English language proficiency, their lower levels of education, and modest occupational experiences restricted them to ethnic consumer markets (multicultural and Latino markets). Instead, Peruvians' overall larger class endowments allowed them to break away, even if modestly, to mainstream markets in the general economy. In fact, my survey data show a stark contrast with 77 per cent of Salvadorans and 48 per cent of Peruvians targeting Latino and multicultural markets. Furthermore, my in-depth interview data revealed that only Peruvians had managed to expand their businesses to non-local markets in other metropolitan areas. For example, at the time of our interview, Esteban was about to expand his company and enter a strategic partnership with an organization in the New York metropolitan area.

Ironically, when targeting mainstream markets, both Salvadoran and Peruvian informants with access to class resources sometimes capitalized on the exoticism of their ethnic backgrounds. For example, Karla takes great pride in her Latina identity, and her paintings vividly depict Latino themes and motifs, which her clientele values. She does not target an ethnic market, but a North American one, primarily because of profit considerations. She explains,

> I love it but it's a bit funny because, in one of the exhibits I participated in, a lot of people came by and they kept on bringing this word "exotic" up. Because they [the paintings] had these vivid colors, contrasting colors. When I went to display my work at this one restaurant, the Americans were mesmerized: "Oh . . . these reds . . . I love them!" And I don't really know why but I see that the Americans have a high sensitivity. I'm not saying that the Latinos don't like artwork but . . . the Americans, they truly value craftsmanship and artwork. They become fascinated by it while the Latinos, they do like it but they don't value it as much. They look at a painting and they think it is too expensive. But this is also because of their lower economic status, they can't pay as much and they see it as a luxury.

Concomitant to targeting mainstream markets, a large number of Peruvian study participants utilized mainstream media to publicize their products. More costly and less accessible than ethnic and other types of media, some of my Peruvian informants utilized highly specialized technical publications either when advertising their companies or when recruiting personnel. Notwithstanding, both groups still utilized a variety of ethnic media and relied on informal strategies such as word-of-mouth and referral networks.

Business Culture and General Features

Salvadoran and Peruvian narratives provided multiple examples of the types of business cultures and management styles fostered in their work environments. In general, some Peruvian informants seemed more predisposed than Salvadorans towards incorporating innovative business practices, such as applying information technology and periodic market evaluation tools. This might be related to their larger exposure to bourgeoisie occupational cultural values, including American entrepreneurial practices. Either their prior work experience in American businesses, or early class socialization back home, could be responsible for these attitudes. For example Dori, another Peruvian informant, described how she had been struggling to increase her clientele in the last few months, and how she periodically sought customer feedback to improve her business.

Likewise, as mentioned before, Peruvian and Salvadoran narratives emphasized different factors that led them to the creation of their businesses. In fact, my interview data suggest that while some Peruvian informants prioritized social status concerns over business growth and capital accumulation, Salvadorans did exactly the reverse. In Luis' own words,

> So I say, many of those who come here, well . . . maybe not many but some of those who already have their own small businesses, they think they know it all. This is one of the main reasons why a business fails. They have their small businesses starting to do well so they go and get their BMWs, their SAAB, a Mercedes . . . to show off. I don't know . . . most people are like that. Or, maybe it is that these are people who are used to these things because they have had them in the past. We, at least, I have never had anything so having a car like those is not something that makes me crazy. Or sending your child to a private university because that's where you have to send him. Let me tell you, no, I have always prioritized my business, invested everything in my business so that it will grow, more and more. I have been left behind, and I'm not sure whether that is good or bad, but that is what my partner and I have always done. Seven years ago I still rented a 300 dollar room and my partner, he rented a small 600 dollar apartment. Many people open a little restaurant and they already want to live beyond their means, they spend more than they can. So then, their businesses cannot grow. For us, no, our dream first.

Finally, because of their larger class and human capital resources, Peruvians were far more likely than Salvadorans to operate franchises or to have larger size businesses that could enter into strategic organizational partnerships. Conversely, Salvadoran businesses included a disproportionate amount of self-employed subcontractors, many times working for other Latino-owned companies, including Peruvians'.

CONCLUSION

Washington Salvadoran and Peruvian study participants belong to Latino immigrant communities that substantially differ in their degrees of group cohesion. Closely tight social ties among Salvadoran co-villagers from a few sending communities in Eastern El Salvador, their widespread participation in transnational practices, and their early exposure to a colder and more hostile reception in this country converged to bolster Salvadorans' reactive ethnicity. Reactive ethnicity seems to be at the center of group mechanisms conducive to solidarious social relations among co-ethnics.

In contrast, the Washington Peruvian immigrant community is more acculturated to the American mainstream but it remains internally fragmented due to pronounced class and racial cleavages among co-nationals. Notwithstanding, Peruvian newcomers arrive to the US with group resources that are class-preponderant relative to Salvadorans'. Three themes in participants' narratives clearly illustrate this: 1) their immigration motives; 2) their class resources upon arrival, including human capital and class-based cultural capital; and 3) their motivations for self-employment. Paradoxically, despite their higher human capital resources, only Peruvian informants experienced incidences of downward mobility. Perhaps for this reason, many Peruvians gave primacy to social status concerns over business growth and capital accumulation.

Further, my data confirm that Salvadorans disproportionately fill in the ranks of resource disadvantaged entrepreneurs, whereas Peruvians experience more instances of labor market discrimination. This is consistent with the structural insertion of the former in the lower rungs of the secondary labor market and their prior historical exclusion from opportunity structures. In contrast, a large number of Peruvians explained that circumstances related to labor market discrimination and status incongruence prompted their decision to become self-employed.

Salvadoran and Peruvians' differential levels of class resources allowed them to articulate divergent business strategies in the areas of financing, labor, marketing and management. First, Peruvian study participants had access to a wider spectrum of financing options to start and develop their commercial ventures. The combination of relatively higher financial and human capital endowments, including their better command of the English language, secured them access to critical information on financing alternatives beyond personal and family sources of capital. In contrast, Salvadorans had to rely, almost exclusively, on ethnic credit. Further, because they had social obligations to remit periodically to their families back home, Salvadorans found it difficult to accumulate start-up or working capital.

Second, Peruvians were more likely to establish formal employee-employer relations. This might be indicative of their larger insertion into the mainstream economy and their higher degrees of bourgeois occupational culture, including a tendency towards more bureaucratic and impersonal labor management styles. As important, Peruvians' labor business strategies often times concealed class interests behind a romanticized ideology of panethnic solidarity. In contrast, Salvadorans' hiring practices seemed more motivated by ethnic loyalties. Most participants described informal human resource management styles with practices that had an ethnic character and were less hierarchical. In spite of this, Salvadoran labor business strategies were not entirely altruistic or devoid of conflict.

Third, most Salvadorans' lack of English language proficiency, lower levels of education, and modest occupational experiences restricted them, for the most part, to ethnic consumer markets (multicultural and Latino markets). Instead, Peruvians' overall larger class endowments allowed them to break away, even if modestly, to mainstream markets in the general economy. Interestingly, when targeting mainstream markets, both Salvadoran and Peruvian informants with access to class resources often capitalized on the allure of their exoticism. Although many Peruvians marketed their products through mainstream outlets, both groups still relied on a variety of ethnic media, including informal referral networks and word-of-mouth.

Last, related to their larger exposure to bourgeoisie occupational cultural values, including American entrepreneurial practices, Peruvian informants seemed more eager to incorporate innovative business practices than Salvadorans. Conversely, Salvadorans had difficulty in adjusting to their unfamiliar regulatory environment and its host of certification, licensing, permits, credit, and business plan requirements. Precisely because of their limited exposure to American ways of doing business, that is their lack of information and knowledge on business basics in the context of the US economy, Salvadorans' accounts emphasized hurdles they faced along the way to a larger extent than Peruvians' narratives. We will explore next the economic power of ethnicity, and the ways in which social relations, bounded by ethnic loyalties, often compensated for and/or complemented immigrant class-related mobilization strategies.

6 Ethnicity and Business Strategies

Continuing with a supply side analysis, this chapter examines the economic power of ethnicity,[1] and the mechanisms through which it mediates Salvadoran and Peruvian entrepreneurship. The chapter is organized in two sections. First, it compares Salvadoran and Peruvian ethnic-based resources, including cultural and social group endowments. Equally important, it highlights the strategic value of family and extended kin in the management of immigrant businesses. Last, it reviews Salvadorans and Peruvians' business strategies, demonstrating that ethnicity significantly patterns their financing, labor, marketing, and daily management practices.

SALVADORAN AND PERVUVIAN ETHNIC RESOURCES

As noted before, in practice, immigrants blend various types of resources to develop business ventures. For the purposes of this chapter, however, I will focus on Salvadoran and Peruvian's ethnic resources and how these manifest themselves in their formulation of business strategies. I first examine some of their ethnic-based cultural capital features, and then turn to a comparative analysis of some of their sources of social capital, including ethnic and panethnic forms of solidarity, family-based resources, and family businesses.

Cultural Capital

Beyond the class-based endowments explored in chapter five, immigrants also accrue cultural and social capital by virtue of their membership in a group of co-ethnics. Such endowments have a definite cultural flavor and are group-specific features that compatriots capitalize on to derive economic benefit. As is the case with class-based resources, ethnic endowments include knowledge, skills, attitudes, and values; but instead of being shared by all persons of a common class position, these characteristics are tied to ethnic group traditions. Religious beliefs, attitudes about the importance of family and social life, and cooking or language skills based on ethnic origin are some examples.

My qualitative data indicate that Salvadorans' group resources are more ethnic-preponderant than Peruvians'. My informants showed different degrees of social cohesion, reactive ethnicity, sojourner mentality, and divergent attitudes about prosperity and progress. Further, they also differed along internalized notions of group superiority and degree of relative satisfaction.

Reactive Ethnicity and Immigrant Work Ethic

Salvadoran and Peruvian small business owners seemed to differ in their levels of reactive ethnicity. In the previous chapter, I described how the confluence of tight social ties among Washington Salvadoran co-villagers from a few sending communities in East El Salvador, their widespread participation in transnational practices, and their exposure to a cold and hostile reception in this country all bolster Salvadoran's reactive ethnicity. Instead, the Peruvian immigrant community, albeit more acculturated to the American mainstream, remains socially fragmented due to pronounced class and racial cleavages among co-nationals.

Further, both Salvadorans' and Peruvians' narratives exuded a strong immigrant work ethic that extolled the importance of persistence, determination, and hard work in achieving goals and overcoming challenges. Although nationals from both groups unequivocally valued the concept of prosperity and progress, Salvadoran informants showed a tendency to link such notions to deeply held religious beliefs. Peruvians' narratives, for the most part, lacked such connection between religious motivation and notions of individual prosperity. In fact, religious beliefs seemed to galvanize Salvadorans' mutual assistance efforts, as informants felt empowered by their religious convictions.

Although most of the fieldwork conducted for this study has not systematically explored intra-group differences in religious participation and its effect on immigrant entrepreneurship, evidence from ethnographic work conducted among Washington Salvadorans suggests that their high levels of participation in congregational life might enhance mutual assistance among co-nationals (Verdaguer 2001). In fact, some Salvadoran informants vividly described how their participation in religious congregations had facilitated their access to informal co-national and/or co-ethnic networks where they had obtained loans, information on jobs, or had recruited employees or clients.[2]

Sojourning Orientation and Relative Satisfaction

Both my survey and interview data suggest that Salvadorans have a stronger sojourning orientation than Peruvians. In fact, 24 per cent of Salvadorans indicated they wanted to eventually settle back home, whereas only 10 per cent of Peruvians wished to return. To recall, ethnic entrepreneurship scholars argue that immigrant groups with sojourning orientations tend, among other strategies, to work harder and accumulate investment capital faster than other groups who lack such transitory outlook (Bonacich 1973; Bonacich and Modell 1980). The rationale behind this theory is that sojourners' ultimate goal is to maximize profits so they can return to their places of origin sooner. Although neither Salvadorans nor Peruvians are "sojourner groups" in the classical sense of the term, Salvadorans resemble sojourner-migrants more closely, primarily because of their refugee mentality, including their initial hope to return back home in a near future. Yet, in spite of this quasi-sojourning mindset, Salvadoran informants found it hard to benefit from its theoretical benefits, primarily because their transnational social obligations detracted from their ability to accumulate start-up capital and expand their businesses.

Many of my informants explained they had initially planned to stay in the United States only for a short time but that, as time went on, it became increasingly difficult to go back. Rocibel, one Salvadoran informant comments,

> [. . .] many of us left, not because we wanted to but because of the war. We had to leave. The war was long and, once here, we started our families and then they didn't want to leave. Because our children, they want to be here so we cannot leave them until they get married. So, in the long run, one ends up staying here.

Highlighting the sojourning character of their American lives, many Salvadorans bitterly complained about the meager conditions in which they lived, attributing their sorrows to the heavy weight imposed by transnational social obligations. For example, Antonieta explains,

> I arrived here without a long-term goal. Because, you know, my plan was to look around, work a little and then go back home. Here we live like . . . excuse my language . . . like dogs. We have a double life here. We don't even have money to buy curtains or a good bed . . . all the money goes back home. Right here, a person dies tomorrow . . . so who did he work for? Oh, no. I don't think that way. I'm not going to keep on living poorly here to say: "I have my country, I have things in my country . . ." In the meantime, one suffers here. Here there are people who have eaten an egg and have died . . . they never made it back home. But I think that not all people think alike. Some always think: "Oh . . . no, but I don't have papers [legal documentation]. . . .

Related to their modest human capital endowments and mild sojourning orientation, Salvadoran participants exhibited higher degrees of relative satisfaction than their Peruvian counterparts. Scholars explain that immigrants are willing (and content) to take on jobs that natives reject because of the wage differentials between home and host country, and their lack of acculturation to prevailing labor and living standards (Light and Gold 2000). Immigrants' relative satisfaction becomes a group ethnic resource when it generates an available cheap co-ethnic labor pool that toils hard for little pay. Thus, Salvadorans' sojourning mindset further fostered their relative satisfaction given the many needs and social obligations they arrived with. Yet, as Samuel points out, workers' relative satisfaction sometimes became a liability rather than an asset,

> Look, part of my problem is that the people working for me sort of reject the American system, they resist it. For instance, they don't want to learn English. They only work to live . . . to barely subsist. How can I put it . . . they don't work with the idea of settling down here, of growing here, of buying a house, of doing all the things that people who want to become somebody do. You think about getting a house, then about another thing and so on and so forth. You always have to go up one more ladder. These people, no, they are comfortable in their room, with their rent, with the little money they have to go out on Friday or Saturday and, maybe, a few bucks to send back to El Salvador or wherever.

And Roberto, another Salvadoran informant confirms,

> The problem we have is that we are "comformistas" (conformists). We are too conformists, do you understand? And. . . . I don't know if this is because of our customs, our traditions. But, if we, Latinos, if we worked smarter and with more enthusiasm, I think we would get ahead. Many people are very laid back. So, if they earn ten dollars an hour, they are happy. But what happens? The day you don't work, that day you don't eat. [. . .] The problem is that we come from cultures that tell us we have to be poor.

Yet, as Antonieta pointed out previously, some Salvadorans graduate from an initial relative satisfaction to develop an entrepreneurial drive that reveals a sense of autonomy, ambition, and enhanced self-esteem.

In contrast, as indicated by their motivations for self-employment, Peruvians' levels of relative satisfaction proved much lower. Their desire for autonomous employment was based, primarily, in their lower levels of tolerance for wage work under what they perceived to be exploitative conditions. Interestingly, their narratives frequently highlighted Salvadorans' relative satisfaction with menial type jobs. As Gladys eloquently describes below, relative satisfaction becomes exacerbated by differential access to class resources, such as English language proficiency,

You know, Central Americans are very useful workers. They can build you a house; they can do anything else. The problem is that they have to work for somebody else and they don't speak any English. So they can't negotiate to offer their services. For instance, the other day I read an add in the paper: "I clean houses." So I work for a janitorial company, I take a friend of mine to that job, and my friend takes another friend . . . and everybody ends up cleaning houses. Why? Because nobody is capable of introducing himself, of filling out an application and of sitting for an interview. They are afraid, afraid to open their mouths, of not understanding. So what is the end result? All of us, Latinos, we are conditioning ourselves to do a certain type of job by default, because nobody gets a job as a cashier and draws friends to that other job. Because, cleaning houses . . . that is the lowest type of job that we can do.

Finally, related to their lower levels of relative satisfaction and higher human and cultural capital, a considerable number of Peruvian participants espoused an ideology of ethnic superiority, particularly vis à vis Central Americans. Often times, they refused to perform tasks they considered inappropriate for their level of education. Interestingly, they preferred to hire Central Americans to perform manual work, rather than co-nationals, arguing that their compatriots were not suited for those types of jobs. Ironically, many of them avoided working for co-ethnic Latinos because they did not want to be exploited.

Sources of Social Capital

Social Boundaries and Mutual Assistance

Scholars offer two models for the interpretation of the economic value of ethnicity. On the one hand, immigrants possess a culturally specific toolkit with values, skills, and attitudes derived from their ethnic tradition or historical experience (Light 2000; Aldrich et al. 1990). Some of the characteristics discussed in the previous section are part of Salvadorans' and/ or Peruvians' unique cultural repertoires. On the other hand, other interpretations highlight the value of ethnically derived sources of social capital marked, primarily, by boundaries in immigrants' social relations (Barth 1969; Cornell 1996). When a group establishes social boundaries, cooperation and assistance among members ensue. Ethnic boundaries are, for the most part, effective at promoting solidarity and cooperation among individuals given that ethnicity is a primary source of personal and collective identity. Yet, this type of ethnicity is not linear, but reactive (Light and Rosenstein 1995a; Portes 1990). As my qualitative data confirm, reactive ethnicity seems to be at the center of group mechanisms conducive to solidarious social relations among co-nationals. Group trust, reciprocity expectations, and bounded solidarity are some such mechanisms.

For the most part, Peruvians' narratives underscored an underlying sense of distrust, especially of co-nationals. Salvadorans' accounts, instead, revealed a more trusting and less cynical attitude toward co-nationals and co-ethnics in general. For example, Carmen, a Peruvian informant, explains,

> I don't mess around with anybody and nobody messes around with me. One has to be distrustful of people, "m'hijita" (my little daughter, meaning my dear). Peruvians don't help you; they destroy you. If they can stab you in the back, they'll do it. There is much envy. We are not like the Chinese who help each other out.

Yet, Agustina, a Salvadoran small business owner, tells quite a different story. In her own words,

> I like hiring our own because those of us, from the same place, we understand each other. And people from outside, they only try to slow you down. Because those from outside . . . they don't really want to work. And we, Salvadorans, we know how hard we have to work to get anything.

It is precisely group trust that undergirds both reciprocity and solidarity because, as Carlos points out, "solidarity comes only after being able to establish trust among ourselves."

Yet, Salvadoran accounts often times included personal anecdotes which underlined existing tensions among compatriots. This, thus, partly corroborates Menjívar's (2000) and Mahler's (1995) argument that Salvadoran immigrant social relations become commodified in the United States, destabilizing home-based networks and normative codes of behavior among kin and friends. To illustrate, Agustina explained how a Salvadoran co-national to whom she rented a commercial space inside her own store had betrayed her trust. She says,

> There is much selfishness, however. We sublet this room to this guy right there, right? When his lease expired, what did he do? He went to the rental office to see if he himself could rent the whole space. And the manager told him: "No, Mr. and Mrs. Perez came here first." Think about it! He wanted to push us out of the main area and send us to the little room he is in now. And he came here only because I helped him. Because if I had said no, he wouldn't be here. He came on a Mother's Day. And believe me, he makes very good money. Now I'm only waiting for the end of the lease to see if it is true that he'll stay there. He only pays rent and doesn't want to help with any of the utilities. And believe me, he sees bills coming into his business . . . big time.

Given the varying degrees of group trust within their communities, Salvadoran and Peruvian informants interpreted reciprocity expectations in different terms. Whereas Salvadorans expected co-nationals to meet some of their expectations and reciprocate, at least, some of their favors, Peruvians had much lower expectations. For example, Javier says,

> Well, I'll be very honest. The Peruvian is very selfish. The Peruvian is the type of person that, if he sees you are doing well, he can bring you down. He is not like the Salvadoran or the Chinese. Salvadorans see that a brother needs help and they are there to support him. I don't know if you know but, when a Chinese arrives from his country, a group of compatriots get together and give him money to start a business. If he wants to do it fine but if he doesn't . . . too bad for him. But the Peruvian, no, he is very selfish.

Furthermore, many Peruvians restricted their reciprocity expectations to familial and friendship circles. In fact, when coming from co-national strangers, Peruvians resented such expectations and criticized them as cold and calculating behaviors. For example, Silvia says,

> We help those who have helped us and, of course, our family. I don't know but I have seen that Peruvians are a bit too "calculadores" (calculating, conniving). "I help you only if you help me." Do you see what I mean? As though they are always expecting something in return. I think that to help people out, they have to be family or very close to you. But, just for the mere fact of being Peruvians . . . no way. But if they are family or friends, yes, we help them.

Salvadorans' narratives, instead, placed an emphasis on reciprocity expectations, whether when compatriots met such obligations, or when they reneged them. For example, Marlon described how he had worked out an agreement with fellow Salvadoran business owners whereby they would help each other out when in need of extra personnel during times of crisis. Moreover, other Salvadoran informants expressed disappointment when co-nationals failed to return favors, dispense information, or showed ungrateful behavior. For example, Agustina complains,

> When we wanted to open our shop, he [my husband] went for advice to Sandra. He had worked for her before, building a porch in her store. And the man there told him: "Look, I can't give you that information because all of us have to pay our dues . . ."

Bounded Solidarity: Ethnic, Panethnic, and Transnational Solidarity

As previously noted, ethnic sources of social capital are primarily organized according to group boundaries in immigrants' social relations (Barth 1969; Cornell 1996). Bounded solidarity ensures both that assistance and cooperation among group members take place and that non-members are effectively excluded from membership privileges. Salvadoran and Peruvian narratives highlighted various dimensions of bounded solidarity among and between co-ethnics. In fact, informants identified commercial, social, panethnic, ethnic, and transnational levels of solidarity. Nevertheless, they often alluded to a breakdown in solidarious relations, which manifested itself through cannibalistic competition, panethnic fragmentation, and exploitation among co-ethnics.

In general terms, both Salvadorans and Peruvians highlighted the existence of a divide between their commercial and social lives, suggesting detachment in business matters within the American context. Whereas a large number of Salvadorans' perceived themselves to be solidarious with co-nationals in their daily lives, both groups stressed such solidarity did not extend to commercial practices. Chapter seven will later examine how this pattern differs along gender lines. In Arturo's own words: "In Perú, or in Latin America, commercial relationships become social friendships, but here this is not the case." Or, as Roberto explains: "I am willing to help insofar as whatever they ask of me doesn't adversely affect my business."

Some Salvadorans complained about the lack of "organized solidarity" within the immigrant community, blaming it on co-nationals' individualist tendencies, their lack of education, and their precarious living existences. As Luis describes,

> There isn't a solidarity that we could say . . . is organized. We are not like the Jews. I don't think that we are in the same conditions here that other Latino immigrants. This is because ours is a new group of immigrants. We haven't gotten organized yet. We have arrived with many needs and we do whatever we can. We don't even have our own Salvadoran Chamber of Commerce.

Yet, in listening to study participants' stories, it became clear that Salvadorans did engage in mutual assistance exchanges, commercial and non-commercial. Further, they did it far more than Peruvians. Salvadorans' ethnic solidarity manifested itself in informants' sharing of business-related information and resources, their hiring and informal training of co-nationals, and their pooling of capital with family and friends. For instance, Vidal, a Salvadoran restaurant owner, sadly remarked that some community members were envious of his success, and that he had learned not to let that bother him. Yet, a few minutes later, he vividly narrated how he had found invaluable help in a former Salvadoran boss who had not only trained and mentored him, but also loaned him commercial appliances for his kitchen. In his words: "The community, you know, there are some envious people, so one has to learn to choose the right friends." Yet, he adds, "but then, they [his compatriots] drive miles to come to my restaurant, just to support me."

With less ambiguity, Roberto, another Salvadoran informant, concludes,

> Yes, Maria, we, Salvadorans, we help each other. Not only do we help ourselves. That's the way my country is . . . if your country has a need, my country gets together to help you out. Because whenever there have been natural disasters somewhere else . . . I feel bad to say this, but when . . . I don't remember what exactly happened in Bolivia, it was only we, Salvadorans, who helped them out. That's the way we are used to doing things in my country. There's much unity, brotherhood. A Salvadoran feels proud when another Salvadoran gets ahead. Do you know what I mean?

In contrast, most Peruvians' narratives contained, almost invariably, negative comments about co-nationals, whether in commercial or social settings. So distrustful were some Peruvians of their own compatriots, that a few informants had totally distanced themselves from their community, primarily relating to out-group members. Such distancing from compatriots might be due to a weaker reactive ethnicity and a higher degree of social and economic incorporation into American society. In fact, scholars contend immigrants seeking to distance themselves from their own community is a clear indication of the progressive dissolution of their ethnic sources of social capital and, concomitantly, of their faster acculturation to American society (Portes and Zhou 1992).

Notably, informants' exchange of assistance with co-ethnics proved a bag with mixed blessings. Whereas Peruvians often times extolled the virtues of Central American immigrants, endowed with convenient docility, industriousness, and consumer loyalty, Salvadorans denounced abuses and malfeasance, primarily at the hands of other Latino immigrants and ethnic minorities. In fact, many Salvadoran informants bitterly complained about South Americans' arrogance and poor demeanor. Antonieta explains that she usually had "problems" with South Americans who only came to her store to bargain and look down upon her merchandise. She states,

> But they come here, ask around, bother me and leave without buying anything. So I feel bad. I feel uncomfortable because I sense they don't like my merchandise. I even feel tricked upon. Because the reason why they come the most . . . I don't think it's because of the clothing I carry. I am Salvadoran and I know the taste of my people, but for the South Americans, I don't know their taste. And they come anyway and ask: "Is this 18K gold?" And I say, "No, it is 14K." And they go "Ah, no, in my country, we have 18K."

Likewise, Blanca and Carlos describe how their accountants, of Bolivian and Peruvian origin respectively, had "miscalculated" their tax burden and, as a result, they had had to pay expensive penalties. In fact, as it turned out, their accountants were later convicted and sent to jail because they had pocketed their clients' money. Blanca explains,

> When we first opened the business, we had quite a bad streak . . . and the accountant misinformed us. We didn't know it but we weren't paying the taxes we had to pay. So, one day, here came a man with lots of papers. "I want to speak to the owner," he asked. I swear I didn't know anything. And he tells me: "You have to close your business." "Why!", I asked him. And he told us . . . we owed like 10,000 dollars, which had become 38,000. He [the accountant] was Bolivian. At the beginning he would tell us that he had made a mistake . . . then, they sent him to jail.

Ironically, even when underscoring the good qualities of Salvadorans, Peruvians' accounts denounced lower levels of solidarity within their community. For example, Grace attributes the initial success of her catering business to the unrelenting support she had received from her Salvadoran-exclusive clientele. In her words,

> For a long time, I only worked only for Salvadorans. Of course, each Salvadoran I worked for brought me more and more Salvadorans. The first two years were exclusively Salvadoran. Very decent people, wonderful people. I gave them all my materials [for cake decorations] and they would bring them all back without a deposit or anything. I think they treated me as a Latina and, after getting to know me better, they realized they would benefit from my services. With them, I didn't have to overcome the prejudices of those who see Latinos as people who will be late, who are impulsive, who will trick you. When you deal with a Peruvian, he treats you like that because he remembers where he comes from. With the Salvadoran . . . no, they are wonderful.

Yet, as mentioned before, Peruvians' positive opinion of Salvadorans was primarily related to their qualities as cheap co-ethnic labor pool and loyal customer base. Again, this suggests that these expressions of panethnic solidarity conceal, underneath, an ideology of class exploitation. As Portes and Espiritu point out, panethnic labels can sometimes give place to fictive ethnic solidarity, which conceals other interest and affects collective behavior. Thus, class cleavages prevented Salvadorans and Peruvians from socializing together and, often times, from joining forces under Latino panethnic umbrella organizations. For example, Carlos illustrates why collective efforts at putting together a Latino community organization tend to fail.

> We, Latinos, we have many social problems. We put too much emphasis on our egos and everybody wants to stand out. [. . .] When we expanded the group to people from other nationalities, some of whom

believed they were more entitled to be here, the whole issue of the fund allocations came up. Everything started right there. We broke up the group for nothing. As I am telling you, for what I have seen in meetings with Latino businessmen, each one wants to "lucir como el mejor pavo real" (put up the best show in town).

Another theme related to panethnic social relations revolved around informants' cannibalistic competition either among themselves or with other Latino immigrant groups. Although some level of competition permeated most informants' commercial activities, it seemed particularly pronounced among Peruvians, and between Salvadorans and other Latino groups. Several informants complained about existing tensions with neighboring Latino-owned businesses which were "stealing" their clientele. In one extreme case, a Salvadoran informant confided that he had received telephone threats from a nearby Mexican competitor who had pledged to ruin his business if he stayed in the neighborhood.

Last, Salvadorans' bounded solidarity transcended national borders to reach sending communities in El Salvador. Although Peruvians are also immersed in transnational social fields where sending and receiving communities become intertwined, Washington Peruvian study participants' level of transnational social obligations remained below that of Salvadorans. As a consequence, while the latter were constrained in their ability to accumulate investment capital, the former were not. Yet, as demanding as these transnational social obligations might prove, they also reinforced Salvadorans' co-national ties. As I will examine in the next chapter, this will have important repercussions for Salvadoran women entrepreneurs.

Family Resources and Family Businesses

Family values emerged as a key theme that permeated most Salvadorans' and Peruvians' narratives. Most informants highlighted the significant role their families played in their lives, including unrelenting assistance in the conceptualization, start-up, and operation of commercial ventures. Families provided financial, labor, and moral support to study participants who, at times, overemphasized the familial boundaries of social solidarity among co-nationals. Even when informants were not in marital or consensual unions, extended family proved instrumental in the creation and development of businesses. Thus, my data corroborate scholars' contentions that familial resources remain the cornerstones of ethnic economies (Espiritu 1997; Phizacklea 1983; Sanders and Nee 1996; Ward 1991; Ward and Jenkins 1984).

Despite the fact that study participants utilized family resources in distinct ways, numerous Salvadorans and Peruvians made use of relatives in their daily business operations. To illustrate, my survey data show that 54 per cent of Salvadorans and 35 per cent of Peruvians used their spouses' assistance, 42 per cent of Salvadorans and 30 per cent of Peruvians used their children's assistance, and 59 per cent of Salvadorans and 49 per cent of Peruvians used other relatives' aid. In sum, Salvadorans deployed more familial resources than their Peruvian counterparts. I will examine interesting gender differences in the utilization of familial resources in the following chapter.

Moreover, 32 per cent of Salvadorans and 4 per cent of Peruvians ran their businesses in partnership with spouses. Thus, Salvadorans show higher incidences of familial business partnerships than Peruvians. This scenario is congruent with the fact that there are more married participants among them, that they primarily run mom and pop shops, and that the Washington metro area is home to a large number of Salvadoran families from the same sending communities in eastern El Salvador. Instead, Peruvians run a wider spectrum of businesses in both the ethnic and mainstream economy, and have more diversified business partnerships with extended family, friends, and acquaintances. In most instances, Peruvian informants drew moral support from their families but relied, to a much lesser extent, on their contribution as unpaid or paid labor.

Finally, unlike Salvadorans, a few Peruvian informants expressed profound disillusionment with their families. Whether by refusing to pool together financial resources or by putting personal interests first, some of these families let informants down. Javier, for example, bitterly complains about his family hindering rather than facilitating his success.

> I have a serious problem. I can't ask them [my family] for help. Because if you do well, they believe that it is only because of them. "He had that because of me; I made him do it." You know what I'm saying? They are never satisfied with what you are doing. And this is not new, I have always wanted to do things on my own, but they never like it if others get ahead. They always want to be the only ones. When I first arrived here, I was very submissive, very shy; I would put up with many things. Now not anymore. Whenever I find out something I don't like, I tell everybody, my mother, father, whoever . . . I gather them all and I tell everybody what I feel. Then, I turn around and I leave. If they get blue in the face out of anger, so be it but I have learned to let it all out. Sometimes, for instance, my uncle, for whom I work part of the day, tells me: "Hey, there is a small house there, you go and do it." But I know better. He's trying to win me over . . . but I know the wolves.

ETHNIC-BASED BUSINESS STRATEGIES

As was the case with their unequal access to class resources, Salvadorans and Peruvians differential ethnic-based endowments largely shaped their business strategies. I will examine these next, looking at their financing, labor, and marketing practices as well as their business culture and management styles.

Financing

This time, it was Salvadoran participants, not Peruvians, who had access to a wider spectrum of financing options for their commercial ventures. They tapped into various sources of ethnic credit, including family and friends' loans, merchandise credit, personal savings, and pooling of resources. In fact, my survey data show that 45 per cent of Salvadorans and 12 per cent of Peruvians received financial assistance from family and friends. Further, they frequently relied on the direct support of family members who, by maintaining a second job on the side, provided the bare necessities that allowed informants, and their businesses, to survive those first difficult years. In Rocibel's own words,

> My husband's support, that was important. Since we got married, that's how we live together. Everything goes to a common fund and we take out for whatever is needed. We don't divide things; this is for you and this for me. No, because the way I was brought up in my country, a marriage is not a business partnership; it is a unity where two become one.

Ana Maria also stressed that her parents had proved critical to her success. She explains,

> I think I was very lucky, very lucky. Because my father, he already worked for Gigante Express. Actually, where Gigante Express stands now, there was a small office. Where I have my shop now, that used to be a dentist office. So I started going to my father's on Saturdays and Sundays. One day, thieves got in and they stole everything I had, everything. By then, my mother had loaned me 3,000 dollars. So she told me: "M'hija (my little daughter), don't worry." I remember being sitting down in the stairs, devastated after my mother said: "I told you not to do anything yet because you had to wait until you saved more money to do something better." Disappointed, I replied: "Alright, then, I'll close tomorrow." And she told me: "No, m'hijita, this is going to be a lesson for you. Here you have 1,000 dollars and your father will give you another 1000. And let's go to New York to buy everything you need to replace what has been stolen."

Despite the meager conditions under which some of their businesses operated, partly because of remittance obligations, many study participants displayed an astounding capacity for capital accumulation. Antonieta, for example, proudly describes how, for years, she had accumulated money from previous tax returns so she could open her own store.

Of course, I have always had savings. Whatever refund check I would ever get from income taxes, I never blew it off going shopping; I saved every single penny. I started with 1000 dollars and here I am. I saved every refund from my taxes, year after year. I also invested it. I would take out 2,000 dollars and I would say to myself: "From this, I will make 2,500". Now, I'm thinking that I would like to save any help my son gives me so I can open another business.

Moreover, only among Salvadoran participants did ethnic credit become available through the intervention of religious institutions, primarily in the form of congregations. Often times, religious leaders acted as brokers between potential investors and aspiring entrepreneurs in a congregation. For example, Roberto describes how his Pastor played an instrumental role in securing that first loan that enabled him to get started.

So, what happened? We started to pray and pray because we didn't have any money. We were barely covering the cost of producing the newspaper. And we were working from the house. One day as we prayed, the Lord told me that I had to open the press and motivate myself. I didn't even have 2,000 dollars then . . . and they were asking me for 10,000 to get the machinery! So I asked the Lord: "If you have been able to change my life, Lord, we are asking you now for 10,000 dollars. Where am I going to find this money?" So I spoke to my Pastor and he found somebody who lent me the money. That's why I'm telling you, God is always with us.

Salvadorans' heavy reliance on ethnic sources of credit underlines two related factors: 1) their lack of access to commercial loans, and 2) their general distrust of financial institutions. In fact, their inability to obtain commercial credit both exacerbates their reliance on ethnic credit and fosters their participation in microloan schemes. Interestingly, it was primarily Salvadoran participants who used the services of such microcredit programs, frequently affiliated to immigrant social service agencies and/or other nongovernmental organizations. Further, their distrust of financial institutions might be rooted in the collective memory of many who lost substantial deposits from the collapse of an informal bank founded, during the 1980s, by a Salvadoran from Intipucá. Undisputedly, the collapse of the Salvadoran-owned "Banquito" [Little Bank], as it was called, left an imprint on some of my informants' minds. As an officer from a social service agency summed it up, the Banquito incident adversely affected Latino immigrant consumer confidence in financial institutions for years to come.

In contrast, Peruvian participants relied less on family loans and more on institutional forms of credit, whether from commercial or governmental sources. Like Salvadorans, many of their businesses were subsidized by other family members' incomes. Mothers, fathers, and spouses worked in secondary jobs to ensure the survival of their businesses. Further, as I examined earlier, their class resources facilitated their access to federally sponsored programs, such as the SBA procurement program, by allowing them to weather higher entry barriers in industries such as information and communication technology. Yet, Peruvians' ethnic endowments also contributed to their participation in such programs. Among other requirements, to qualify for the SBA 8(a) Business Development program, participants have to be members of an ethnic minority group. Thus, Peruvian informants' Latino identity proved a valuable asset in this regard.

Labor

Once again, in contrast to Peruvians, Salvadoran participants' labor strategies drew primarily from their ethnic-based resources. Let's examine participants' hiring practices, referral networks, informal labor recruitment, informal business training, and self-exploitation practices next.

Hiring Practices

Almost all participants agreed they preferred to hire co-nationals or co-ethnics from referral networks. In fact, many informants explained they did not even need to advertise in ethnic or mainstream media; just word of mouth or placing an ad in their stores generated a pool of potentially qualified candidates. Further, despite their efforts to reassure me of their willingness to hire Latino co-ethnics from any national group, most Salvadorans actually employed larger numbers of co-nationals. In fact, many of them liked to use co-national referral networks because they could better trust these individuals, feeling more comfortable with their own. As Carlos describes,

> We have people from El Salvador, which is the majority. When we first arrive here we tend to only trust our own people. There's a group of people who say: "Don't mess around with those people." You probably might have heard comments like that. And so as time goes by and you start getting to know other people, well, you realize that you just can't talk like that.

And Samuel confirms,

> There is a comfort zone among people of the same group, right? And you know how we, Salvadorans, are. This is natural because we sometimes don't feel like going out there to explore what is unfamiliar.

Yet, as much as they preferred to hire co-nationals, or even co-ethnics, some Salvadorans also expressed reservation about hiring from external groups beyond familial circles to fill in supervisory level jobs. As many explained, those positions had to remain within the confines of highly trusted individuals such as family members. In Sandra's own words,

> All my managers are family members. For instance, the girl that manages the Alexandria store, she is my husband's cousin. We almost always keep family [in the stores] because I have had bad experiences with non-related employees. One has to trust these people, you know. . . .

Interestingly, a couple of Salvadoran informants preferred to hire North Americans of middle class extraction since this strategy reduced labor market discrimination and furthered the expansion of their businesses into mainstream markets. Marlon comments,

> But, at the same time, I look at this from a different perspective, from the point of view of the company's image. Although a lot of people don't want to see it, there is a lot of discrimination going on here. And sometimes, let me tell you, it is very evident, very obvious. There are times when . . . I tell you, they [those who discriminate against us] are such good actors . . . they should win an Oscar . . . So it has happened to me, several times, that people look down upon us but, when I have an American in charge, things tend to run smoothly. So these are tactics that I sometimes have to use.

In contrast, my interview data show that Peruvians preferred not to employ co-nationals but Latinos from other national groups. Corroborating this, my survey data indicate that whereas 42 per cent of Salvadorans and 13 per cent of Peruvians would hire co-nationals, 32 per cent of Salvadorans and 43 per cent of Peruvians would hire other co-ethnics. Peruvians' reservation to hire co-nationals might be explained by various factors. First, as already examined, Peruvians' lower levels of group trust seem to be rooted in internal racial and class cleavages brought from the homeland. Second, Washington Peruvians seem to have typified Central Americans as better, cheaper, and more docile workers. Third, their predominantly middle class origin, status incongruence between home and host occupations, and their sense of superiority vis à vis other Latino immigrants occasionally gets in their way of effectively performing mundane tasks, such as those involved in running personal service, retail, and construction businesses. Following this logic, many Peruvians often prefer not to hire co-nationals given the abundance of cheap Central American workers in the Washington area. In Edi's own words,

> I rather hire Latinos, with the exception of Peruvians. Peruvians only think about themselves. I was born in Peru but I think differently because I grew up here. Besides, my clientele is, for the most part, Central

American, especially Honduran. So, you see, I need somebody who will treat people well, who will not feel above my clients; otherwise, I'll lose them and that doesn't work for me.

Informality and Labor

Another important theme that emerged from informants' narratives was the intersection of the formal and informal economies in their daily business operations. Participants shared stories of informality that ranged from the hiring of undocumented employees, to the modest beginnings of start-ups in the unregulated informal sector. Often times, to fill in vacancies, many informants resorted either to unregulated day laborer sites or to referral services provided by social service agencies. As they explained it, their objective was to find possible recruits and not to find out about candidates' legal status. One Peruvian informant even provided reliable and safe transportation for his undocumented employees, mostly Central Americans, so they would get to the workplace on time.

Yet, it was primarily Salvadorans who emphasized the importance of hiring recently arrived undocumented co-nationals both to help them out as well as to benefit from their pleasant disposition. As Vidal points out,

> I like hiring whoever needs the job. I have had many many people right here, newcomers, their first job . . . and they have stayed with me for a long time. I know that some people say that I do this [hire them] out of necessity, and that really hurts me. Right now, for instance, I have two girls in the kitchen, the very first job they have had in this country. And I like these people because they care about their jobs. They are happy with their first jobs, they take care of them because they say: "This is my first job." And they always remember it, like their first boyfriends.

Moreover, during production peak times or delivery deadlines, some Salvadorans engaged in informal labor exchange practices with co-nationals. Carlos, for example, described how he frequently exchanged these types of favors with co-national friends. Yet, he strongly emphasized that reciprocal expectations stood behind these practices. He explains,

> Look, right now, we are trying to work out some issues with the foreman of the construction company. They are in charge of doing all the work before we can go in and do what we do [drywall and painting]. They are behind schedule so we'll have to give them a hand. But, see, the type of work they want us to do . . . it requires a lot more people than what I can provide. It is precisely during these situations that one makes money. They tell you: "We need this by such and such date, get all the people you need to get it done. It doesn't matter how much it costs." At that very moment, one has to move fast. I only need to make a phone

call and I know I can count on my friends and "compadres" (close country fellow men). They come with an army of workers . . . but I do the
same for them. We are there for each other, that's how we get by.

Informal Business Training

In employing a much larger number of co-nationals than Peruvians, Salvadorans provided their compatriots with more opportunities for informal
business training. Peruvians, instead, ended up primarily training other
Latino immigrants, including Salvadorans. A major consequence of such
an arrangement is that Peruvians' labor practices frequently fail to arouse
employees' loyalty based on reciprocity expectations enforceable within co-
national boundaries. Because they employed fewer compatriots, Peruvians
had much lower expectations in terms of employee loyalty. Precisely because
of this, they expressed less disappointment than Salvadorans who, often
times, complained about lack of loyalty, loss of human resource investment,
and being taken advantage of. This finding resonates with Menjívar's and
Mahler's argument that social relations among Salvadorans become commodified upon their arrival to the US. It also questions the overly harmonious ethnic solidarity thesis where business owners employing co-nationals
are repaid in kind. For example, Samuel described how difficult it proved to
retain co-national employees, even after having trained and counseled them
on various personal and business related issues. He says,

> Life is not fair, as they say. You hire a worker who doesn't know
> anything and you train him. Once he knows how to do this and
> that, all of a sudden, they contact him from a different company and
> he leaves you. He goes there not as an apprentice but as an expert.
> For instance, there is this guy we even brought from New York. He
> wanted to come here so we even got him a place to stay. We kept his
> belongings in our own house . . . I think he worked with us for . . .
> maybe four months? From one day to the next, he got another job
> offer. And he kept it all to himself, until the very last day. Everything
> was "chévere" (cool) till he got his suitcases out and pum! He was
> gone; he didn't work for us anymore. And those are the things that I
> resent. Because it turns out that people end up kind of using you . . .
> do you know what I mean?

Finally, because many Peruvians had occupational histories that included
prior work experiences in North American companies, their informal training afforded them some advantages over Salvadorans. Thus, their informal
training in mainstream businesses allowed them to acquire American style
management skills that further facilitated their breaking away from the
ethnic economy.

Self-Exploitation

Both Salvadorans and Peruvians resorted to self-exploitation to see that their businesses survived and succeeded. They worked exceedingly long hours, sometimes averaging fifteen hours per day, and juggled between their businesses and part-time wage work on the side. For example, Blanca vividly described the challenges she came up against in running her small restaurant. She says,

> And when we first opened, I didn't only work here. I sold "pupusas" (Salvadoran delicacy filled with meat or cheese) at home. I sold at the festivals. I would go to soccer games . . . I worked everywhere, here and there. Whenever I would go to the festivals, people would form a circle around me, to protect me, you know. So that the police wouldn't see me [she had no permit to sell food]. So, as I'm telling you, here you don't do anything but work, and work some more. I don't think I'll resist much longer. Either I retire or I die.

Yet, whereas Salvadorans met some of their labor needs with family members, some Peruvians found it hard to find trustworthy individuals in whom to delegate; which, at times, exacerbated their self-exploitation. While they often did have the financial resources needed to hire staff, it was the lack of confidence in others' abilities that led them to self-exploitative practices. Arturo explains,

> The real issue is how far can I stretch myself. . . . Here, I can find people to help me clean, to help me manage but to manage on their own . . . that is different. Every time I go on vacation, I spend five hundred, six hundred dollars in long distance phone calls. "How are you doing? What's going on? Please call me back." I don't know if this is an overreaction but this is the only way of keeping my clients. Delegating to others . . . that is the jump I have to do because I can't do everything. And I know that, at some point, I'll have to hire somebody to help with this.

Directly related to their self-exploitation, both groups of informants expressed a pervasive sense of isolation. Perhaps more acute for Salvadorans, they generally attributed their sense of isolation to long working hours and confinement to their stores. In fact, many participants stressed that their necessary self-exploitation prevented them from meeting friends, acquaintances and, even, kin. Carlos' words eloquently capture the daily struggle Salvadorans face to fulfill long term objectives,

> I feel that we arrive to the land of opportunity and we get stuck here. This is because of the way in which we live, fragmented, isolated. It

happens to many of us, mainly because of ignorance, of lack of education and of time. We arrive here having to work two jobs to support our families, to pay our debt from the trip and so forth. And that's how we spend our days, and time goes by, we get old and, then, we just don't want to get started any more.

Thus, Salvadorans' sense of isolation might constitute an expression of their more pronounced marginality. Echoing Menjívar's argument, lack of time, self-exploitation, heavy social obligations, and a hostile receiving context can converge to weaken immigrants' social networks. As I will discuss in chapter eight, when such is the case, co-national networks become less effective as conduits of information and favors, including commercial assistance.

Marketing

Not surprisingly, Salvadorans' ethnic preponderant resources translated into an almost exclusive targeting of ethnic consumer markets through ethnic media. As noted earlier, a larger number of Peruvian informants targeted mainstream markets, utilizing mainstream media and more formal advertising channels. As the effects of class and ethnic resources are, in practice, difficult to tease out, Peruvians' larger class-based resources allowed them entry into sectors of the economy that remained off limits for most Salvadorans. This is not to say that Peruvians did not target ethnic markets or that they did not utilize ethnic channels to advertise their businesses. In fact, they did, but to a much lesser extent.

In contrast, Salvadoran business owners used a wide variety of ethnic venues to market their companies. They utilized Latino newspapers, magazines, television and radio, informal congregational newsletters, bulletin boards, and flyers. They also capitalized on their participation in charitable activities, such as hometown association and parish-sponsored events to promote their businesses. Most important, Salvadorans' referral networks proved powerful mechanisms to recruit potential employees and advertise their companies.

Business Culture, Structure, and Management Style

The most salient difference between Salvadorans and Peruvians' business culture was that the former relied, to a larger extent than the latter, on familial resources to run and develop their businesses. As mentioned before, Salvadoran participants had more businesses in partnership with spouses than many Peruvians who, instead, had partnerships with individuals beyond their familial circle. Even when Salvadorans' partnerships did not include spouses, they involved brothers, sisters, cousins, or other extended family. Such tightly closed circles, where families and businesses became intertwined, inevitably influenced Salvadorans' business development plans.

In fact, most Salvadorans revealed business expansion plans that involved family members in the operation of chain stores across the metro area or in nearby states. Haydee, for example, vividly explained she was soon to open a second restaurant in the Columbia Heights neighborhood of Washington DC. Since she would not be able to run both places simultaneously, she had decided to delegate some of the managerial responsibilities to one of her brothers. Then, she added, she hoped to develop a franchise scheme that would also involve the participation of some of her other siblings.

Related to such family orientation, Salvadoran narratives often alluded to cooperative practices among co-nationals. In fact, many Salvadorans who were recent newcomers partnered with old-time relatives and/or friends to start new business ventures. More an expression of familial or ethnic-based paisano loyalties, this practice connected Salvadoran businesses across the Washington metro area in myriad of ways. As Rocibel explains,

> The family always brings in more family. Friends bring you over, guide you, teach you, help you with this or tell you: "Do this, do that". And, in seeing that people do well here, newcomers think to themselves: "If he's doing well, I might be able to do well too." And that's how they decide to open their business. Nowadays, it is not as it was before, when you had to wait four, five, six years to open your business. Now, people come here and in three years they have their own business. They come and, perhaps, they partner with other Salvadorans here who want to expand their businesses. And that's how it works. It's like a chain reaction; everything is much easier now, everything!

Further, a few Salvadoran participants often integrated co-nationally owned subcontracting companies to their business operations. For example, Merci described how her commercial janitorial business relied on teams of co-national subcontractors who worked on assigned locations and independently managed staff. She says,

> This is what has worked for us in the last few months. And we're going to do exactly the same with stores that are close to each other. We hire a small group of employees and a team leader, and we give her the contract. And she has to worry about managing and paying everybody else. What we do, however, is provide her with the equipment and necessary training so they can operate the machinery appropriately.

Likewise, Salvadorans' business culture, largely based upon familial ties, prioritized business succession among kin and extended kin. For example, Blanca and Victorina both had been at different ends of the family succession process. Blanca had undersold her second restaurant to one of her daughters who ran it, benefiting from her mother's well-established reputation.

Victorina, instead, bought her apparel store below market price from her own daughter. She says,

> So, then, my daughter told me: "Alright, 'mami' (endearing term for mother), I will sell you this store. So don't worry anymore, you'll have your own place. I'll keep the other two and, with that, we'll have more than enough. This way, you'll be close to my father and in a place you like [heavily Latino-populated neighborhood]. "Because we had been in this neighborhood for a very long time, since the time my father opened his store upstairs, on the second floor.

Finally, my interview data show that neither group buys merchandise predominantly from co-national or co-ethnic wholesalers simply because there are few Latino-owned wholesalers. Perhaps the most notable exception are exotic produce wholesalers, exclusively catering to ethnic bodegas and, more recently, to mainstream chain stores offering ethnic products. Business owners in ethnic niches did, by mere necessity, occasionally buy from co-nationally-owned companies. Thus, in this sense, because Salvadorans were overrepresented in the food retail industry, they purchased more goods from other co-ethnics than Peruvians. Further, Salvadorans were also more likely to buy products from other ethnic minority groups, such as Middle Easterners and Asians.

CONCLUSION

Washington Salvadorans seem to be able to mobilize more ethnic-based resources than their Peruvian counterparts. This might be indicative of two interrelated processes: 1) the weakening of Peruvians' ethnic identity and ethnic sources of social capital; and 2) their overall faster social and economic incorporation to mainstream American society. Salvadorans showed higher degrees of reactive ethnicity, sojourner mentality, and relative satisfaction. Further, informants differed along internalized notions of group superiority and attitudes about prosperity and progress, either religiously or secularly based.

The use of fictive panethnic labels blurred informants' social boundaries. Yet, such panethnicity often proved counterproductive as it created more group cleavages than commonalties. Because of class and national rivalries among Washington Latinos, panethnicity often turned into a liability rather than a group asset. Further, both Salvadorans and Peruvians highlighted the existence of a divide between their commercial and social lives. Whereas a large number of Salvadorans' perceived themselves to be relatively solidarious with co-nationals in their daily lives, both groups stressed this solidarity did not extend to their commercial practices. Notwithstanding, Salvadorans' accounts suggest that they did engage in various types of mutual assistance exchanges at commercial, non-commercial, local, and transnational levels. More important, informants' stories indicate that Salvadorans tended to engage in assistance exchanges to a larger extent than Peruvians.

Furthermore, findings from the study corroborate scholars' contentions that familial resources remain the cornerstone of ethnic economies. Salvadorans relied more heavily on familial resources to run and develop their businesses and had more businesses in partnership with spouses and kin. Peruvians, instead, although they certainly leaned on family for moral and financial support, utilized less frequently relatives as paid or unpaid labor, and had partnerships with individuals beyond their familial circle.

Salvadorans' heavy reliance on ethnic sources of credit underlines two related factors: 1) their lack of access to commercial loans, and 2) their general distrust of financial institutions. In fact, most Salvadorans' inability to obtain commercial credit both exacerbates their reliance on ethnic credit and fosters their wider participation in local microloan schemes. In contrast, Peruvian participants relied on ethnic as well as institutional forms of credit, whether from commercial banks or government-sponsored programs.

In employing a much larger number of co-nationals than Peruvians, Salvadorans provided their compatriots with more opportunities for informal business training. Peruvians, instead, ended up primarily training other Latino immigrants, including Salvadorans. A major consequence of such an arrangement is that Peruvians' labor practices often times failed to arouse employees' loyalty based on reciprocity expectations enforceable within co-national boundaries. A related theme to co-national hiring was the intersection of the formal and informal economies in their daily business operations. Nevertheless, because more Peruvians had occupational histories that included prior experience in North American companies, the informal training they provided to co-ethnics afforded important advantages over Salvadorans. Thus, some Peruvians' informal training allowed co-ethnics employees to acquire American style management skills that further facilitated their incorporation in mainstream markets, occasionally breaking away from the ethnic economy. Next, let's explore the ways in which gender also patterned participants' practices and access to entrepreneurial opportunities.

7 Gender and Resource Mobilization Strategies

This chapter examines how gender, as main organizing category, interacts with class and ethnicity to mediate Salvadoran and Peruvian entrepreneurs' access to resources and their articulation of business strategies. The chapter is divided in four parts. First, it focuses on gender stratification in the immigrant economy. Second, it discusses how gender socialization processes differentially shape men's and women's motivations for migration and self-employment. Next, it engenders Salvadorans' and Peruvians' cultural, ethnic and social capital, tracing participants' gender role ideology back to Latin American ideological constructs such as 'Marianismo' and 'Machismo.' Equally important, it reviews gender patterns in informants' deployment of familial resources and in their levels of social solidarity. Finally, it discusses gendered business strategies, exploring the ways in which class, ethnicity, and gender remain interwoven in informants' commercial and personal lives.

GENDER STRATIFICATION IN THE IMMIGRANT ECONOMY

As illustrated in chapters five and six, the ethnic entrepreneurship literature has made important contributions to current theorizing on the role of class and ethnicity in immigrants' entrepreneurial activities. Socially-oriented economic action, scholars conclude, is primarily shaped by the interaction of changing opportunity structures and unique immigrant group characteristics (Light and Bhachu 1993; Light 1984; Aldrich et al. 1990; Waldinger 1993). Yet, while these factors are critical to immigrant business development, the literature suffers from a myopic tendency to overlook the role of gender as an analytical organizing principle. In fact, Morokvasic (1993) has criticized Waldinger's interactionist model for underestimating the role that gender plays in conditioning entrepreneurs' access to opportunity structures. In all, except for a few notable studies (Espiritu 1997; Gilbertson 1995; Sanders and Nee 1989; Zhou and Logan 1989), immigrant entrepreneurship theories remain gender blind.

A key source of personal identity, gender significantly patterns the human experience. It organizes social interaction, including access to resources, decision-making processes, and opportunity structures. It is contested, negotiated, and re-constructed, and other stratifying forces such as race, age, class, and ethnicity interact with it to produce, reproduce, and/or alter hierarchies of power across multiple social settings. Because gender is a relational construct, men's and women's experiences remain two sides of the same coin, and to understand one, we need to grasp the other.

Salvadoran and Peruvian patriarchal ideology, including normatively prescribed behavior for men and women, circumscribes immigrants' social relations. Therefore, gender unevenly patterns entrepreneurs' spatial mobility, business styles, and commercial strategies. It significantly shapes immigrant entrepreneurs' resource mobilization strategies, including access to information, personal networks, and various types of assistance.

Feminist scholars have extensively discussed how both the general and immigrant economy rely on a gendered[1] division of labor where women provide a cheap pool of labor (Boyd 1989; Espiritu 1997; Pedraza 1991; Phizacklea 1983). Gender-segmented labor markets, occupational segregation, and the feminization of a growing contingent workforce are common features of the global economy. Gender role ideology informs the types of jobs men and women are eager to perform, and the types of businesses they choose to run. Within the immigrant economy, this gendered division of labor translates into men and women operating businesses in industries with differential profit margins. Therefore, while women's start-ups are in lower profit margin industries, such as personal service and retail, that of men's concentrate in the more profitable construction, manufacturing, or business service sectors.

Participants' survey data in Appendix B show that Salvadoran and Peruvian women's businesses were concentrated in apparel, retail, and personal services. Instead, men's businesses showed large representation in business services, retail, and construction trades. Usually, women's businesses provided services that were an extension of their nurturing roles as mothers and wives. They ran daycares, catering services, restaurants or carryouts, beauty parlors, janitorial services, and apparel retail stores. Men, instead, ran businesses in lines of work perceived as masculine because these required either physical strength or technological know-how entailing higher human capital investments.

Yet gender does not operate in a vacuum. As scholars have pointed out the complex overlap of gender, class, ethnicity, race, legal status, and other group identities situate individuals at different locations of the power hierarchy (Pessar and Mahler 2003; Young and Dickerson 1994; Chow et al. 1996; Fernandez-Kelly and Garcia 1991). The experiences of Salvadoran and Peruvian study participants eloquently illustrate how differential group endowments predispose men and women to respond to structural forces in divergent, and often gendered ways. I turn to this topic next.

GENDER, CLASS, AND ETHNICITY IN LATINO ENTREPRENEURSHIP

As discussed in previous chapters, immigrant groups intertwine class and ethnic resources to pursue commercial ventures. Washington Salvadoran and Peruvian resource mobilization strategies differed to the extent that each group predominantly utilized one type of resource over the other. In addition, gender significantly mediated informants' entrepreneurial pursuits, making resources available by virtue of their membership in female or male groups. A closer look at the interaction of gender, class, and ethnicity provides nuanced insights into Salvadoran and Peruvian entrepreneurial experiences.

While women concentrated in retail and personal services in general, the Salvadoran cohort had a larger proportion of mom and pop stores exclusively in ethnic niches. Instead, Peruvian women tended to break away into the mainstream economy, running export/import, wholesale retail, and entertainment promotion businesses. Further, while most women seemed strongly influenced by their maternal occupational models, it was Salvadorans' experiences, in particular, which suggested their entrepreneurship was a continuation of a culturally specific tradition. On the other hand, whereas men concentrated on retail, services, and construction, Salvadorans, in particular, ran restaurants, construction businesses, and general retail stores. Peruvian men, instead, ran business services such as communications, marketing, and information technology as well as home remodeling and painting firms. Notably, Peruvian men were the only study participants who owned manufacturing type businesses.

Gendered Beginnings: Motivations for Immigration and Self-Employment

Patriarchal gender relations within the family and community circumscribe individuals' aspirations, motivations, options, and decisions. From an early age, socialization processes engender individuals' dreams and roles, from preferences for toys and professional careers, to attitudes about parental obligations and sexual behavior. Because the aspirations of Salvadoran and Peruvian men and women are shaped by dynamic gender relations and ideology, their motivations, aspirations, and actions are gendered. Their motivations for immigration and self-employment throw some light on the distinct types of expectations, needs, and obligations that propelled them to migrate and, ultimately, start their own businesses.

Motivations for Immigration

My survey data show that whereas women stressed economic factors, men emphasized political circumstances as main determinants of their immigration to the United States. As important, only women highlighted factors related to social control and gender oppression, including the need to escape from domestic violence and 'machista' societies. For example, Agustina explains,

> I came here escaping from my husband. I got married back in El Salvador [to her first husband]. Only after being here for a while did I marry him [her second husband whom she points to]. I had never wanted to come here; you know . . . I had to come. I was forced to come. You know, I couldn't take it anymore, so much suffering down there. You know how it is, he would go with other women, would get drunk, would hit me . . . so much suffering. Until one day, I felt I 'd had enough, I grabbed my two children and I came here to some relatives' home nearby.

On the other hand, men highlighted reasons such as the need to escape recruitment by guerrilla or military forces, to indulge their curiosity, or to embark on trips that served as symbolic rites of passage. Javier, for example, describes how he had decided to come to the US

> I came here because I wanted to get out of my country. Things were pretty bad down there and everybody would tell me: "Go to the US, you'll be able to study there." And everybody would tell me how things were great here. But, of course, as soon as you are here, you realize that things are not that easy or that perfect. But I came here to become an electrical engineer one day. You know, I don't want to stay in this country. I would like to work, get my degree and then go back home to practice my profession there. So I would go back with a piece of paper, a diploma from here, which is the most prestigious thing back home. Don't you think it's the most prestigious thing? When you go back there with a degree from the US, you know, that opens doors for you everywhere. That's my goal. Maybe I won't be able to study right now, but soon, one day I'll have my degree and my children will be able to build on what I will give them because of that. That's my goal and why I came here.

In looking at the intersection of gender, class and ethnicity, Salvadoran women highlighted reasons related to domestic violence, poverty, and destitution, as well as to social networks of family and female friends luring them to the area. Instead, many Peruvian women listed reasons congruent with their primarily middle-class lifestyles. They talked about frustration in professional jobs where gender discrimination precluded them from moving up the ladder, and about lifelong dreams of pursuing studies in this country. For example, Elizabeth says,

> Well, I came here because I wanted to do an MBA here. To tell the truth, I also wanted to go to a place where I could be on a level playing field with men. I wanted to have the same opportunities men had and be able to advance in my professional goals.

In sum, whereas both men and women expressed a few commonalties in their reasons for migration, more frequently, their commonalties cut along nationality or class, and not along gender lines exclusively.

Motivations for Self-Employment

My in-depth interview data show that Salvadoran and Peruvian men's and women's motivation to engage in self-employment differed significantly. Their motivations highlighted family-related, attitudinal, contextual, economic, status, and human capital-related factors. Invariably, women stressed that family-related factors pushed them to seek self-employment; many of them indicated that their businesses were part of a family strategy that conveniently allowed them to combine private and public responsibilities and roles. As Gladys points out,

> See, when I first arrived, I had a two-year old. So from what I earned, I had to pay a lot of money in baby-sitting expenses. So I thought: "If I have my own business, then I can bring her with me to work." And that's how it happened. I brought her with me until she was about four years old. And, let me tell you, sometimes it was quite difficult, because I had to come back and forth several times, back and forth. Sometimes, people would come to the store and it would be closed . . . and that was my loss. But I had to go back and forth because I also had the older kids coming in the school bus everyday.

Although both men and women coincided that a main reason why they had opened their businesses was to attain work autonomy, only women highlighted the need to do work that was consistent with an inner sense of identity. This is congruent with the types of businesses they ran in feminized services and professions, capitalizing on their nurturing and caring abilities. Men, instead, stressed that opening their own businesses responded to a desire for personal fulfillment and prosperity.

Further, women's narratives emphasized, to a larger extent than men's, that contextual factors had led them to self-employment. In fact, it was mostly women who explained that self-employment was often times a response to harsh discrimination and exploitative working conditions.

Moreover, whereas many highlighted factors related to their resource disadvantaged position, men tended to stress labor market disadvantage. Equally important, while many women engaged in self-employment as a survival strategy to mere destitution, a substantial number of men indicated the main reason they had started their businesses was to maximize profits margins. As Carlos comments,

> I think that the construction industry is very profitable. Look, if there were no winter season, it would be incredible . . . think that, if I'm telling you that I already have work commitments for the next 13 months, the demand way exceeds the supply. So, you look at the work you put into something, and how much a company pays you for it, and you start adding things up. If I make ten dollars an hour and I work eight hours, then I earn eighty dollars, right? But, if what I do is worth at least a hundred and fifty dollars, then, my boss is keeping seventy dollars out of what I make. Then, I prefer to work independently and to keep those hundred and fifty dollars myself. I think that, in my case, the higher profit margin motivates me to work on my own.

It should be underscored that most women drew a good deal of their self-employment motivation from gender-specific cultural and human capital endowments such as culinary, sewing, and other traditionally domestic abilities. Many described their parental occupational models and previous work experience, including informal business training in family-owned businesses at home, as critical in their decision to become self-employed. This is in contrast to men, who primarily stressed prior work experience as influential in their decision. Blanca, for example, reminisces,

> Well, I have been cooking since I was a little girl. My grandmother, my aunts, and my mother . . . my mother in particular, they taught me. Since I can remember I have been working . . . I might have been about eight years old. Just like my mother, I was one of the first children, actually, her second daughter. So . . . poverty is very tough in my country, very tough. So I'd help my mother in everything. Actually, all my sisters helped her out too so we all worked early on. We would cook in the house and then go outside, to the streets and sell our food door to door.

Last, more men than women indicated that social status concerns had motivated them to open their own operations. For some Peruvians, the emphasis was placed on the need to either recover or attain a better lifestyle for their families. But a few Salvadorans also pointed out this need. For example, Carlos explained that he had decided to open a grocery store so that his wife could attain some level of social prestige and mobility in her work life. He says,

Our idea was that, since she [his wife] cleaned houses, well . . . we wanted something different for her, something better. So we thought that, maybe, a small business would let us live in a different way. So, basically, the idea was to try to improve my wife's situation and, of course, both of us would benefit. Then, I talked to her and told her: "Look, I'm planning to do this, do you think we can do it?" And, since she has always trusted my opinion, she told me: "If you think we should do it, just tell me." You see, she is an excellent worker, when she works, she doesn't even raise her head from the working table.

More Peruvian than Salvadoran women emphasized family related factors in their decision to become self-employed. Many Peruvians highlighted the need to find flexible employment opportunities that would allow them to better combine their private and public spheres. They preferred self-employment over wage work because it allowed them to bring children to the workplace, to work from home, or to retain autonomy and flexibility to combine maternal and work related chores. For example, Grace vividly explained how she valued the possibility of setting her own working hours so she could drive her children to and from school. She proudly asserts,

Above everything else, I'm a mom. When I got pregnant both my husband and I knew that I'd have to stay home, because that was what we had discussed. I was phobic to the idea of leaving my children [in a childcare facility]. Actually, it was very sad because I had a very good salary and I had built a good reputation at work. They had given me plenty of training and I had many benefits. But I had to quit anyway because I needed a job that would allow me to take care of my children, a job that would give me the time to pick them up and drop them at school and at sports practices . . . all those things you have to do in this country.

Such prioritizing might be indicative of Peruvians' predominant middle class origin. It might also suggest that these women perceived their own labor in family businesses as an extension of domestic responsibilities. Paradoxically, Salvadorans' narratives did not reveal such a strong preoccupation with combining economic and social reproduction responsibilities. Although these women certainly juggled family and work duties, their access to wider networks of extended family and friends—which provided critical assistance with caregiving duties—might have eased this anxiety.

In fact, Salvadorans' economic vulnerabilities placed them in a different situation from Peruvians. Either as rural migrants escaping destitution or transnational mothers leaving children behind, Salvadoran women were forced, sometimes at great personal cost, to distance themselves from the daily aspects of mothering.[2] "Transnational motherhood," as

Hondagneu-Sotelo (1998) calls it, does not affect all women, but only those of lower socioeconomic status.

In terms of attitudinal factors, whereas the need for autonomy was an important theme for Salvadoran women, identity-related factors stood out for a considerable number of Peruvians. These findings might suggest that Salvadorans' strong desire to escape harsh discrimination and exploitative working conditions is an important determinant of their self-employment. Instead, a number of Peruvian women started commercial ventures that they believed would meet underserved market demands. As Clara explains,

> When I first started my janitorial company twenty years ago, this was a very good business because there was much demand and very few companies offering these services. Now, it isn't anymore, but then it was. The same thing with my brand-new gourmet coffee catering service. I think that, during the next five to seven years, this will be a good business. After that, I will probably sell it off because the market will be saturated by then.

Finally, Salvadoran women emphasized the strong influence of mothers, grandmothers, and other female relatives in their personal and working lives. Almost half of all Salvadoran survey respondents reported having mothers in the trade and petty-trade professions. Thus, their self-employment became a continuation of what they had always known, replicating skills learnt from previous generations of women in their families (cultural capital). Peruvian women, instead, although also influenced by their mothers, lacked this intergenerational informal business training.

On the other hand, men embraced risk-taking as a necessary evil to succeed in business. Conversely to women, Peruvian men emphasized that the need for autonomy had been paramount in their decision to become self-employed. This is suggestive of their higher aspirations as well as of their lower tolerance for work they perceived to be below their abilities, or for working conditions they felt were exploitative. In fact, Peruvians highlighted, to a larger extent than Salvadorans, that contextual factors, such as labor market discrimination, had fueled their decision to open their own businesses. Again, this confirms the higher incidence of status incongruence between home and host occupations among Peruvians. Cato, for example, comments,

> When I started working for other people I started thinking that it wasn't going to be for long. I was very aware of the treatment immigrants received in those days. You could feel the discrimination everywhere. You could feel it as they say in English, "right away." I lost many, many jobs, especially construction jobs, because I was treated poorly. Whenever they mistreated me, I'd throw the tools on the ground and just leave. And I'd think to myself: "I won't starve."

In those days, I was already doing painting jobs, home remodeling projects, and I knew that other companies would hire me. That's how I got started. And so, one day, I started working on my own. Now, it's been many years I work on my own. I don't like having bosses, perhaps because of my personality, and because of the poor treatment Latinos receive.

In contrast, Salvadorans' narratives emphasized that values such as hard work and achievement had propelled them to "try it on their own," which might be indicative of their more modest aspirations and class background. Finally, whereas some Peruvian men underscored that a need to enhance their social status had motivated them to become self-employed, a few Salvadorans emphasized religious beliefs. Some talked about religion as a strong motivational force that inspired their ventures and recast their notion of individual prosperity in religious terms.[3] Interestingly, neither Salvadoran nor Peruvian women emphasized that personal religious beliefs, premised upon the achievement of individual prosperity, had fueled their self-employment. As I will address in the next section, this is consistent with Latin American gender role ideology and its traditional emphasis on women's private roles as mothers and wives and men's public roles as family heads and providers.

ENGENDERING CULTURAL, ETHNIC, AND SOCIAL CAPITAL

Chapter two reviews in detail the various forms of capital that facilitate immigrant entrepreneurship. To recall, in Light and Gold's (2000) formulation, immigrants possess distinct permutations of class and/or ethnic-based resources, which, in turn, inform their class and ethnic-based cultural and social capital. To rectify their omission of gender, I argue that gender significantly patterns immigrants' cultural and social capital since men and women become exposed to, and informally trained in, feminine and masculine occupations largely informed by gender ideology. Just as important, class often mediates the engendering of cultural and social capital because women and men from distinct class backgrounds acquire divergent occupationally relevant cultures, values, and skills. I turn to this topic next.

Cultural Capital: Gender Role Ideology, Role Models, and Religious Influences

As examined in the previous chapters, immigrants arrive to their new environment endowed with group-specific cultural and social capital based on class and/or ethnic loyalties. Gender role ideology—including normatively prescribed roles, aspirations, values, and behaviors for men and women—is an integral part of an ethnic group cultural tool-kit. Immigrants' class and ethnic-based capital is, thus, gendered since their traditions differentially endow men and women with skills and knowledge based upon a culturally-specific gendered division of labor. Whereas some women's occupationally-relevant cultural capital includes feminized culinary, home economics, and petty-trade skills, men's often encompasses skills perceived as masculine, such as construction trades, technical, and/or vocational work.

But class mediates immigrants' gendered cultural capital, endowing some men and women, and not others, with certain skill sets. For example, the economic vulnerabilities of Salvadoran women engaged them, at an early age, in female-dominated petty-trade, seamstress, and culinary related activities. Arguably, their female role models effectively predisposed many of them towards developing certain types of entrepreneurial skills. Their grandmothers, mothers, aunts, and sisters effectively passed on to many of these women occupationally relevant gender-based cultural capital. This might partly explain their significantly higher self-employment rates relative to Salvadoran men (see Table 3).

Instead, many middle-class Peruvian informants were not engaged, early in life, in the same types of activities as Salvadoran women and men. Further, few informants received informal training working in a relative's business. Actually, very few Peruvians reported parental occupations in the trade professions. Similarly, few Peruvian women reported having been engaged in home chores at an early age given that their families were financially better off. Their larger class resources, thus, allowed many Peruvian informants' mothers either to be full-time housewives, or to delegate many social reproduction duties to domestics. Therefore, many Peruvian women of middle and upper-class background lacked the gendered cultural capital that working class and peasant Salvadoran women possessed. Instead, they were transmitted other, sometimes more lucrative, types of gendered cultural capital, such as knowledge and information on how to femininely dress for success, or values and attitudes about the importance of advancing one's education.

Most notably, both Salvadorans' and Peruvians' cultural repertoire shared a gender role ideology informed by Latin American ethnorcligious constructs such as "Marianismo" and, its antonym, "Machismo." Derived from "Maria," the Virgin's name, Marianismo dictates that women emulate Virgin Mary's virtuous qualities. Thus, they are subject to strict standards of social control, such as requirements for chastity, subservience, and self-sacrifice. Marianismo gives primacy to women's nurturing roles as mothers and wives, but restricts their professional aspirations and limits their independent latitude of action in public spheres. Men's masculinity is expressed, instead, through an exacerbated virility, and an emphasis on men's roles as breadwinners and defenders of family honor. As I have already illustrated in the previous section, participants' motivations reflected, to varying degrees, the influence of Marianismo and Machismo ideology on various aspects of their private and public lives.

Thus, both Salvadoran and Peruvian narratives largely reflected traditional gender role ideology, albeit partially modified along class lines. For example, even Peruvian women, coming from more modernized backgrounds, succumbed to traditional gender role ideology as they struggled to reconcile Marianismo values with their own business aspirations. In fact, many Peruvians were fully cognizant of and resented the gender discrimination they experienced in their professional and commercial lives. As we will see later on, gender ideology particularly informed participants' labor business strategies.

As important, immigrants' gender relations underwent substantial transformation in their new environment, as men and women adapted to different social expectations and codes of behavior. Further, Salvadoran and Peruvian men and women substantially differed insofar as sojourning orientation. Whereas most women seemed comfortable with the idea of permanently resettling in the US, a substantial number of men wanted to return back home. This pattern is consistent with Grasmuck and Pessar's (1996) finding for Dominican women in New York, who also preferred to stay in the US rather than return to their homelands. As gender relations evolved and some women became empowered through newfound freedoms, they seemed more predisposed towards resettling in their new communities. Men, instead, particularly Salvadorans, retained a pronounced sojourning mindset, perhaps as an expression of resistance to weakening patriarchal authority and altered gender relations within the family.

Gender and Family Resources

As examined in chapter six, family members constituted a critical resource for Salvadoran and Peruvian business owners. Their assistance took various forms, including relatives' unpaid labor, tax, or bookkeeping consultations, translation and cultural broker assistance, subsidies through relatives' part-time work, and provision of valuable business information, childcare assistance, and emotional support.

Yet, my data indicate that women were more likely than men to integrate family members in their daily operations. In fact, as many as 52 per cent of women and 37 per cent of men acknowledged receiving spousal assistance in running their businesses. Fifty-two per cent of women and 21 per cent of men indicated that they used their children's assistance, and 66 per cent of women and 41 per cent of men used other relatives' help. In sum, women deployed family resources in their business operations to a larger extent than men; a finding which reflects most women's working routines, where private and public responsibilities become continuously intermingled.

Men, instead, although they acknowledged their family's moral and emotional support, did not rely as much on relatives' active involvement in business operations. Most notably, men rarely involved children in their business practices. Again, this might be partly indicative of men's bifurcated lives where, for the most part, working and private spheres remain separate.

Thus, women made use of substantial familial resources in their daily business routines. They involved husbands, brothers, sons, parents, daughters, and in-laws in various capacities, ranging from supervising to production to consulting services. Strikingly, women involved children and teenagers in their businesses as cultural brokers, translators, administratives, receptionists, and in other such capacities; a finding which echoes earlier research on immigrant children and their role as facilitators in settlement processes (Valenzuela 1998).

Survey data confirm such gendered pattern in participants' utilization of family resources, highlighting differences across nationalities. In fact, 66 per cent of Salvadoran and 54 per cent of Peruvian women utilized their spouses' assistance in running their businesses; 54 per cent of Salvadoran and 50 per cent of Peruvian women used their children's help; and 73 per cent of Salvadoran and 39 per cent of Peruvian women utilized other relatives' assistance. In other words, Salvadoran women deployed, to a larger extent than Peruvians, familial resources in their business operations. Many Salvadoran women not only benefited from their children and other relatives' unpaid labor, but from subsidies from sons, brothers, spouses, and fathers who helped to facilitate their initial start-up phase. Further, their extensive networks of co-national family-owned businesses in the area supplied an additional layer of support, which proved instrumental in the acquisition of information and advice. For example, Antonieta explains,

> Well, you know, the wife of Florencio Ramos, the owner of Mi Rancho Restaurant, she is my cousin so we are family. And I had had this idea of opening my own store for a very long time. Many times I talked to them about it, and they would tell me: "Antonieta, do this or do that. Go there and find out about such and such." In fact, they were helpful in giving me advice and some information but since they had a restaurant, and I wanted to start a clothing retail store, there were many things that didn't apply to what I wanted to do. But, yes, Florencio and Margarita [her cousin-in-law] know a lot of people in the area and told me many things that were useful.

In contrast, both groups of men expressed reservations at the idea of involving children and other relatives in their business operations. In fact, my survey data show that: 1) 50 per cent of Salvadoran and 29 per cent of Peruvian men used their spouses' assistance in running their businesses; 2) 26 per cent of Salvadoran and 15 per cent of Peruvian used their children's help; and 3) 28 per cent of Salvadoran and 25 per cent of Peruvian men integrated other relatives in their operations. Thus, Salvadoran men deployed family resources to a larger extent than their Peruvian counterparts, with types of assistance that ranged from family loans, to business partnerships, to family paid and unpaid labor, and to moral support.

Further, due to the gendered division of labor in the economy, many Salvadoran and Peruvian men operated businesses in male-dominated industries such as specialized construction and home improvement trades. Moreover, a vast majority of male informants justified the exclusion of spouses and children from the workplace with arguments informed by traditional gender role ideology. They considered certain types of work inappropriate for female family members and, thus, preferred to keep home and business affairs strictly separate. For example, Vidal explained how he preferred his wife and children not be involved in the running of his restaurant since family life was too important to be neglected by the demands of one's business. He says,

> My wife, she seldom works here. If anything, she comes here in her spare time, to help a little. But I don't allow her to come here too often because she needs to be home with our children. You know, for our family, for the children, because one can't neglect one's family because of the business. One has to take care of both things, because both are important. What's the purpose of having a business and making money if my family disintegrates?

Gender, Ethnicity and Social Solidarity

In general, the data does not reveal striking differences in patterns of social solidarity between male and female informants. It does suggest, as explored in previous chapters, significant ethnic solidarity contrasts along nationality lines. Salvadoran and Peruvian men and women equally indicated they would not necessarily limit themselves to hiring co-nationals, but would also employ Latino co-ethnics of various nationalities. In fact, 30 per cent of all women and 35 per cent of all men indicated they would hire co-nationals, whereas 70 per cent of women and 73 per cent of men reported they would hire co-ethnics. In spite of this, notable differences emerged among participants' responses. These included dissimilar levels of group trust, uneven participation in informal business training, and distinct degrees of transnational solidarity. Most notably, social status and deeply rooted masculine values interfered with some participants' ability to seek assistance.

Group Trust and Transnational Solidarity

Women's narratives abounded with stories of female camaraderie and mutual assistance. As I will examine in chapter eight, women primarily relied on same sex networks of friends and acquaintances to acquire the initial know-how that enabled them to launch their commercial ventures. Salvadorans, in particular, seemed to share a stronger group trust than Peruvians, probably stimulated by their active engagement in various community development projects and philanthropic activities. They leaned on fellow women entrepreneurs for advice and information, purchased merchandise from each other, and even belonged to international feminist collectives. For example, Karla, a young Salvadoran woman, belonged to a group of women artists who pooled resources to market their artwork on a collective website. She explains,

> Recently, they have contacted me so I became part of a website of a group of women artists. And I wasn't even looking for this, this group contacted me directly. They saw me in an exhibit last year and they told me: "We like your artwork very much and we would like you to be part of our group." So, being in this group is a real privilege because it makes things easier for us. This is a feminist group, with women from all over the world. They are trying not to have multiple members from the same country, and the leader is a woman from India. She does sculpture. This all started with a feminist women's conference in New York, and this woman I'm telling you about drafted a proposal. In fact, she is very good at that because she has worked in economics stuff, writing proposals, and other things. It's incredible how different people, with so many different skills, get together and create something. We all are artists and, at the same time, we have other abilities. We are currently in the process of applying for grants and other sources of funds. In the meantime, each of us has contributed from our own pocket to organize exhibits and the website but, in the future, the idea is that we'll be able to obtain funds to subsidize our exhibits.

Although Peruvian women also expressed a sense of solidarity and trust towards fellow women, such connections did not seem as institutionalized as with Salvadorans who, through engagement in social activities of various sorts, solidified such ties. For example, Juana, a Peruvian informant, describes her social circle with these words,

> In Peru, we have the celebration of the Lord of the Miracles (El Señor de los Milagros) in October and that's when we meet. Actually, I am friends with the woman who keeps the picture of the Lord of the Miracles. I'm very close to her. The other people that go . . . well, I see some of them from year to year but I'm not that familiar with them. There are around fifty women from different parts of Peru who show up every year. Sometimes, they even bring their husbands and children. But other than that, no, we don't meet regularly. The people I see more frequently, though, are friends from different parts of Latin America whom I occasionally take with me to work.

On the other hand, Salvadoran men's group trust did seem relatively stronger than that of their Peruvian counterparts. While Salvadoran men sought advice and various other types of assistance from each other, they did not seem to partake, to the extent their women did, in community type activities that fostered ties and cemented group trust. Instead, Peruvian men seemed cautious about others, especially co-nationals or Latinos. As detailed in previous chapters, informants' narratives suggested that ethnic solidarity was more prevalent among Salvadoran men and women than among Peruvians.

Salvadoran women's active engagement in transnational philanthropic activities constituted an exclusive feature of this group. As I will examine in the next chapter, many Salvadorans belonged to formal and informal networks of fellow women who gathered for collective projects. In coming together for these activities, including hometown association fundraisers, community development projects, and social events, they not only built on their associational and organizational potential, but further galvanized their resource mobilization capacity. Although some Salvadoran men indicated having participated in such philanthropic networks, it was Salvadoran women's sheer labor which primarily staffed these efforts. This is consistent with Levitt's (2001) findings that immigrant women disproportionately bear the brunt of transnational community work, either in religious or secular settings.

Informal Business Training

My survey data show that as many as 46 per cent of Salvadoran women had mothers in the trade professions, including petty-trade in the informal economy and other self-employment activities. In fact, many Salvadoran women proudly pointed out they followed a long line of mothers, grandmothers, and other female ancestors in the profession. Thus, they frequently received more informal business training at the hands of fellow women. To illustrate, Agustina describes how she entered the seamstress profession.

> Back in El Salvador, my sisters had a 'sastreria' (tailor shop) and I started working for them when I was a teenager. They taught me plenty there and, a few years later, I opened my own sewing academy. I did that for a few years before coming to this country. That's why I decided to start sewing here, too.

Instead, at least half of all Peruvian women had mothers who had been either professionals or exclusively homemakers, and thus received less informal business training from fellow women.

Conversely, men exhibited the opposite pattern. Salvadorans reported less informal business experience than their Peruvian counterparts since most had come from rural areas, with parental occupations in agricultural production or factory type work. Therefore, Salvadoran men lacked role models and informal business training in the trade professions. Peruvians, on the other hand, coming from more modernized backgrounds, reported a larger amount of parental occupations in professional self-employment capacities and various types of trades.

Social Status

Peruvian men's social status concerns and traditional gender values concerning a masculine identity constructed around the role of "the good provider" (Bernard 1995; Noon 2001) occasionally affected some participants' ability to benefit from social solidarity with co-nationals and co ethnics. For example, men's extreme frustration at their inability to fulfill traditional masculine roles at times interfered with participants' ability to seek assistance from friends and acquaintances. For example, Arturo described how he had become depressed at his inability to fulfill his family provider role. He says,

> I studied at the "Universidad Agraria" in Perú. I'm an industrial engineer and worked many years for the government. When I graduated from the university, I did a masters in policy planning and started working with the government. In the 1990s, I went to Barcelona (Spain) to do an MBA and, during that time, there was a change of government in Perú. Think about it, when I first started working in the government in 1972, I was earning an average of 500 dollars per month. It was a good salary. But, after nine years, I ended up earning around 320 dollars a month! So, imagine, my salary went down and so did my self-esteem because I couldn't even fulfill my breadwinning responsibilities. I could no longer support my family and I started feeling depressed. Eventually, since my wife had family here, I decided to give it a try [migrate to the US]

Further, caught in a vicious circle, with his masculine pride and self-esteem hurt, Arturo refused to seek assistance from old-time co-national friends and acquaintances in strategic institutional circles. He needed to save face vis à vis these friends from home because he felt he had been stripped of his masculine identity as the good provider. In other words, internalized masculine values constructed around notions of conditional self-worth—based on men's competition against others and on their upholding masculine roles as good providers, exemplary athletes, or successful businessmen— occasionally acted against men's best interest (Bernard 1995; Kimmel and Messner 2001; Messner 1990; Noon 2001). As Arturo explains,

> I had some Peruvian friends at the IDB and the World Bank but they were leading a lifestyle that was well beyond my means. I had tried,

at the very beginning to make some connections there, but after a month or two, I realized I had to get going somehow. I don't like going around asking people for help and making them feel sorry for me. One asks for help when there is a very serious problem. Sometimes, to share a problem, I'd even tell my wife, so that she'd feel more involved in the business, but I don't share these things with anybody else. I don't believe this would help me much, actually. I would even look funny in front of some of my friends. Besides, many people could use that information the wrong way. Here, we, Latinos, we have a great flaw, which is that we are very envious. We resent others and friendship is not as genuine. Here, I only have two friends, my brother-in-law and my cousin.

As mentioned before, status concerns were very prominent in Peruvian men's and women's narratives, although they seemed to interfere, most poignantly, with men's assistance seeking behavior. In contrast, Salvadorans did not share the anxiety of maintaining an elusive middle class standing. As a consequence, status concerns did not interfere as much with Salvadorans' ability to reach out and seek assistance. In all, looking at participants' quest for social status, two patterns emerged. Either they focused on: 1) attaining social status back home through periodic remittances, which sometimes came at the cost of leading marginal existences in the US; 2) maintaining or recreating the social privilege they had previously enjoyed in their homelands; or 3) gaining status in both places through participation in projects benefiting the homeland as well as through professional and commercial activities in the US. Whereas many Salvadorans followed the first strategy, and many Peruvians the second, a considerable amount of Salvadoran women fell in the third category.

GENDERED BUSINESS STRATEGIES

Salvadoran and Peruvian participants' uneven access to class and ethnic resources often led them to articulate qualitatively distinct business strategies. Moreover, men's and women's resource mobilization practices differed, more or less, in areas such as financing, labor, management, and marketing.

Financing

Confirming previous research, family loans remained the cornerstone of Salvadoran and Peruvian men's and women's financing strategies (Light and Gold 2000; Ward and Jenkins 1984). Unlike Korean or Haitian entrepreneurs, who make use of 'kyes' or 'scans,' participants did not resort to organized forms of ethnic credit, such as rotating savings and credit associations

(ROSCAS). They did, however, resort to personal and family savings, loans from family and friends, commercial and merchandise credit, microcredit programs, credit cards and, to a minimal extent, SBA loans.

For the most part, women had access to ethnic capital from family members and female friends. In fact, my survey and qualitative data revealed that women received financial assistance mostly in the form of ethnic loans and indirect subsidies. Over 30 per cent of all women surveyed indicated having received direct monetary assistance or indirect subsidies through free housing or rent. Further, because many women felt disconnected from mainstream banking institutions, they relied, primarily, on personal savings. Interestingly, most women expressed apprehension at commercial credit. As Carmen explains,

> A loan? That is like walking into the lion's den! It's like the credit cards, 'm'hijita.' A business goes down when it has debt. My husband has that habit . . . that all debts have to be paid in full by the end of the year. We can't roll them over into the following year. When you have debts you are enslaved.

Men, instead, had access to more diversified sources of start-up capital. In addition to the availability of ethnic credit, some also had access to commercial and institutional loans. Further, unlike most women, they also received financial assistance from friends and acquaintances of the opposite sex. Some even financed their start ups through credit cards and home equity loans. Others benefitted from favorable terms of payment in, for example, the male-dominated construction industry, which allowed many to defray the initial cost of working materials. For example, Carlos described how he usually requested that his clients pay in advance a third of the total fees so that he could use that money to buy materials.

Beyond these gendered patterns, male and female financing strategies differed according to class and national origin. Thus, Salvadoran women relied, to a larger extent than Peruvians, on loans from family, female friends, and acquaintances. In fact, 35 per cent of Salvadoran and 8 per cent of Peruvian women surveyed reported having received loans from such sources. Some Salvadorans pooled personal savings with other women to launch collective marketing initiatives, while others participated in microcredit programs. Karla, for example, earlier described her joint venture with a group of international feminist artists who launched a collective website. Another Salvadoran informant, Mercedes, described how she had received a small loan of 500 dollars from a microcredit institution which helped her cover childproofing expenses in her family daycare business.

Beyond family loans, Salvadoran women were only able to obtain ethnic credit through connections with friends and acquaintances of the same sex. As already mentioned, they received microloans, while men rarely participated in such programs. Again, this might be indicative of normatively prescribed mores for male and female behavior, including restrictive social interaction and spatial mobility. Salvadoran women could only accept money from family or, at most, female acquaintances. Otherwise, it could be misinterpreted and they taken advantage of by men. To illustrate, Haydee explains,

> As I told you before, I was fortunate because my father helped me a lot at the beginning. Since he paid for all of my expenses when I started working, that's how I saved money to buy the restaurant. With the saving I had . . . around 30,000 dollars, plus a loan I got from my cousin Juana, that's how I started. Even though I had all these men mentors I told you about, the Jewish and the Iranian men, I couldn't accept money from them. That could have given them the wrong idea and, you know, people like to gossip a lot. They would have said worse things about me than what they even say now.

Therefore, restrictive gender ideology interfered with some Salvadoran women's ability to diversify their ethnic credit portfolio. Perhaps to counterbalance this shortcoming, many women acknowledged the benefits of microcredit programs, taking full advantage of them. In contrast, men obtained loans from female lenders without concerns about social stigmatization, even when these were distant acquaintances. For example, Carlos says,

> So, one day, this woman I had met when I was a real estate agent realized I was in real trouble. I had been asking all of my friends for money, but they didn't have any, except for this one who did offer me five thousand dollars. But that amount, it really wasn't of much help to me. She really loaned me a lot more money. And she gave it to me like that . . . no questions asked.

As important, culturally specific factors influenced women's higher participation in microcredit programs since debt and credit acquisition is not perceived as being status building in Latin America as it is in the United States. Actually, for some men the idea of carrying public debt (as opposed to family and personal loans) threatened their sense of masculinity, stigmatizing them. In this sense, women seemed to operate more freely than men. To illustrate, Salvador explains his predicament when starting his janitorial franchise.

> Personally, I don't like the idea of going out there asking money of those I don't really know. And organizations, and community programs . . . even less. Everybody then finds out . . . Here, people live indebted and they don't mind. But, in my country, it is not like that.

Back home, carrying debt is something to be ashamed of. Here, it isn't and everybody works just to pay his or her debts.

Like their Salvadoran counterparts, Peruvian women also relied on family and female credit. Yet, because of their higher-class endowments and the more favorable structural embeddedness of their networks, many Peruvians were able to take advantage of lucrative financing opportunities such as special financing, SBA loans, or business foreclosures. For example, Elsa explains,

> I have never felt discriminated against. In fact, many years ago I received a huge loan from the SBA. Think about it, they gave me 200,000 dollars to expand my restaurant and open a new branch. So, no, I never felt blocked because of my sex or nationality.

Finally, because many Peruvian men were more affluent and highly educated, a few managed to access a much wider portfolio of financing options than Salvadorans. They used home equity and stock collateral along with family loans and personal savings. Like their Salvadoran counterparts, Peruvian men occasionally financed their ventures through the use of credit cards.

Labor

Salvadoran and Peruvian participants' labor strategies drew from class, ethnic, and gender-based resources, including internalized gender role ideology and gender segregated co-ethnic pools of labor in the informal economy. Next, I will examine participants' hiring practices, and their use of referral networks and informal arrangements through which they capitalized on paid and unpaid labor.

Hiring Practices

As examined in chapters five and six, Salvadoran's and Peruvian's hiring practices largely benefited from accessibility to cheap co-ethnic pools of labor. For business owners, this availability generally entailed bigger profits; for employees, it often meant working in a culturally familiar environment, albeit with low wages, minimal (if any) fringe benefits, and long working hours. To recall from chapter five, a prominent theme that cut across informants' narratives was the exploitative conditions under which most Salvadorans often worked—an exploitation that came, primarily, at the hands of other Latino immigrant groups, including Peruvians.

In line with this, Salvadoran's and Peruvian's hiring practices showed a similar pattern of exploitation between members of the same and opposite sex. Neither did participants hire co-nationals and co-ethnics following notions of ethnic solidarity, nor did women or men hire employees because they belonged to their same sex. In sum, participants' accounts do not reveal altruistic gender solidarity in men's and women's hiring practices but, on the contrary, reveal discrimination and, at times, even exploitation. In fact, many participants often complained about exploitation at the hands of fellow women and men. For example, Yanine comments,

> I knew English and I spoke it very well but Micky [her husband] didn't, so I decided to look for something, some type of work. Then, I found out about a Colombian woman who needed somebody to give her a hand, actually somebody who could be "her right hand" in the janitorial company. So I applied for the job. She hired me but then, she got me doing everything, from cleaning houses, to supervising, to administering . . . everything. She really was exploiting me, because I would only return back home around 8:00 p.m. every day. Yet, I was determined to learn the business so I could start my own later on. And I did tell this to the Colombian, that whenever I found something better, I would leave because I was being exploited and I knew it.

Furthermore, traditional gender role ideology informed participants' preferences in hiring practices, with most informants using it to justify discriminatory and exploitative working practices. For example, many men and women rationalized exclusionary practices, arguing that certain types of work required women's feminine or men's masculine skills. Many men, acknowledging the 'machista' (patriarchal) market they serviced, ended up playing on the attraction employees of the opposite sex provided. As Edi, a grocery store owner explains,

> Generally, the way we do it is that we interview three or four people. Mostly younger girls, though, because we like to work with women. You know, this is what gets the attention of our clients the most. So what is important is that they be women, that they like to work, and that they be friendly with our customers.

Therefore, most men preferred to hire women to market, and even exploit, their sexual attributes. Invariably, both Salvadoran and Peruvian men appreciated women's feminine docility, attention to detail, nurturing abilities, hardworking nature, and social disposition. As important, they valued women's physical presence and sexual allure to attract a male clientele. An important exception was in manual occupations or male-dominated industries, such as construction or security, where men explicitly avoided hiring women because "that wasn't the type of work women should do." To illustrate, Marlon explains why he preferred not to hire women in his painting business,

I try not to mix people of the opposite sex. Perhaps this is because that's how I got trained in this line of business. I have never seen a woman involved in this work [painting and home remodeling]. So, to avoid the conflict . . . I think that what we do is not inappropriate but, in fact, there are no women applying for these jobs. It is not that they are not qualified but that the working environment is not appropriate for them. And so to avoid problems. . . .

My data show that whenever businesses served a predominantly ethnic clientele, men emphasized the value of hiring female co-nationals or co-ethnics because of their sexual endowments. Vidal, for example, emphasized how important it was for his Salvadoran restaurant to have female cooks and waitresses. His remarks accentuate the underlying sense of sexual predation in some of these businesses. He explains,

Kitchen work, well, you know, that is more a woman-type of work. Because the cooking that women do . . . I had a man, actually two men, that were a total failure. So, in the kitchen, I have all women. Salvadoran food, in particular, 'tortillitas,' 'pupusas,' 'tamales' . . . women are better at that. They cook them instinctively, that's their job. You see, we are in a neighborhood that has a lot, a lot of men and they come looking for women. They like a feminine presence and that's how it is around here. If I change the environment and I give them male waiters, I would loose many many clients. So I have to adapt to what people want. At the same time, though, I tell everybody that they have to respect the women working for me. From the door outside, that's not my problem, but here, inside the restaurant, I want respect. I don't like obscenities or anything like that. This is a place to work. If they [his waitresses] want to give out their phone numbers to clients and they make arrangements outside the restaurant, I don't care. I don't want to know. So, yes, I prefer to hire women; they are necessary and it's out of convenience.

Instead, when their clientele included mainstream customers, men's hiring preferences did not overemphasize women's sexual attributes, but their docility and supporting type qualities. For example, Luis described how most women in his restaurant worked in the kitchen, not as cooks, but in the preparation area where vegetables and fruits were chopped ahead of time. With the exception of one middle manager, women did not occupy leadership roles in his business. He says,

In the kitchen, there are more men but in the preparation area, more women. For instance, they chop tomatoes, slice onions . . . If the chef needs shredded carrots, then they peel them, cut them, and throw them in a food processor. That's the type of work women do in our kitchen. Not that we discriminate, but we are not going to staff the grill with a woman, that is so hot and greasy. They wouldn't put up with it. There are certain jobs that we think are too heavy for women. But we do have one woman in our management team.

Further, one informant went to the extreme of suggesting that women who challenged traditional gender role ideology were probably homosexuals. For example, Carlos proudly explained how there were almost no women in his line of business. And if there were, he concluded, they certainly had to be lesbians.

We don't hire women because they disturb the whole work environment. There's much tension when women are around. My workers would get too excited . . . how could I say it . . . it just wouldn't work. But there are a few moving companies staffed exclusively by women. Because there are some very strong women out there . . ."Amazon," they are called. I think they are lesbians, you know?

Similarly, women also showed pronounced gender preferences in hiring practices. Whereas some resisted their sexual objectification and avoided hiring other women because that created sexual tensions in the workplace, others played on women's sexuality to retain their male customers. For example, Blanca and Haydee say,

I prefer men waiters. They are faster. But, there are many places where they prefer women. But I don't like it. I don't know . . . but you are selling food, not image, not sex, neither for men nor for women. In the kitchen, on the contrary, I prefer women.

I don't really care although I have all waitresses. Men don't like being waiters here. In the kitchen, I have all men, even my husband!

Most women hired other women because of similar reasons than men, including their being an attractively docile and inexpensive pool of labor. Yet, often times, women also preferred to hire men for specific roles and functions. Actually, both Peruvian and Salvadoran women occasionally hired men as a strategy to counterbalance gender discrimination in the workplace. Dori, for example, only hired men to staff her ticket office, avoiding potential free riders and arguments with male clients. Karla, on the other hand, also preferred men agents because she felt they had innate negotiating skills that women lacked. They both explain,

I would have liked to hire all women, you know, but you need men in certain jobs. I need a man on the door, for example. Even if it just as image, but I need a male presence there. I also prefer men in the ticket office. Before, I used to have a woman there but, you know, the Latino community is somewhat difficult. When they see a woman, part of our culture says that women have to be treated differently. For this reason, it's good to mix both men and women staff.

I'd really want to hire a male agent because I feel that, as a woman, I have come across many obstacles because, you know, they don't take us seriously.[. . .] Because I've been in situations where it would have been advantageous to have had a man do certain things. For example, I have an exhibit and I need to do a press release. In most of these places, there are always men doing these things. I have managed to do these things on my own so far but, sometimes, it has been an uphill battle. I feel that, if a man represents me . . . I have already experienced instances where a male friend has made a phone call for me, or has acted as my agent. Men go: "We would like to know what you'll give us in exchange so we can sign the contract and we need to have everything guaranteed." I see that men put the cards on the table. Instead, we, women, we can't do that, we go around the bushes. Because we don't want to look as too aggressive. But men, it is much easier for them.

Informality, Labor, and the Informal Economy

As examined earlier, women and men entrepreneurs differed in the extent to which they utilized kin in the operation of their businesses. Women not only staffed their businesses with paid and unpaid relatives, but they frequently brought infants and small children to the workplace. In fact, as mentioned earlier, that was one of the key reasons why some opened their businesses to begin with. In that sense, informality was much more prominent in women's commercial ventures.

Likewise, the co-ethnic pools of labor that men and women resorted to in the informal economy were often gender segregated.[1] Thus, men had access to convenient male-exclusive day labor sites scattered throughout various neighborhoods in the metropolitan area. This contingent, accessible, and cheap workforce provided many benefits to men entrepreneurs. For example, Carlos extolled the virtues of day laborers to assist him in providing moving services. He says,

Here there's a lot of manual labor available . . . ugh! There are places like some Seven Elevens where people gather early in the mornings to wait for folks to drive by and offer them a day job [day laborer sites]. There are a lot of Central Americans around here who don't like to work for somebody else. So you have a huge pool of workers available . . . like in University Boulevard and Riggs [Langley Park area in MD], or in Culmore [in Falls Church, Virginia] they gather by the hundreds. So, occasionally, I go there when I need somebody on the spot. But I have to be careful because these people enter my clients' homes and that is very risky. I'd rather hire people and try them out with other jobs first. What ends up happening is that you hire some day laborers and, if everything goes the right way, you end up training them and working with them for a while.

Women, instead, with businesses in retail and personal service industries, resorted either to personal referral networks or to informal recruiting practices during social events such as church-sponsored functions and community activities. For example, Merci describes how she sometimes advertised vacancies in her janitorial company,

> Occasionally, when we go to Sunday services, I ask the Pastor or one of the deacons if they could announce that I have vacancies in my company. We ask them to come to talk to us after the service, and that's how sometimes we find workers who can either work out or not. But this has always been a good system for us, really.

Marketing

As examined earlier, women's businesses concentrated in retail and personal services, whereas men in services, retail, and construction. Yet, while Salvadoran women had a larger proportion of mom and pop stores, exclusively in ethnic niches, Peruvian women tended to break away into the mainstream economy with export/import, wholesale retail, and marketing businesses. Within group differences between Salvadoran and Peruvian men were not as pronounced as among women. While Salvadorans reported 43 per cent of Latino, 30 per cent of non-Hispanic white, and 27 per cent of multicultural markets, Peruvians reported 35 per cent of non-Hispanic white, 32 per cent of Latino and 12 per cent of multicultural markets. In sum, men's and women's businesses in the immigrant and mainstream markets did not differentiate along gender, but along nationality lines.

To market their services and products, Salvadoran and Peruvian men and women utilized various advertising strategies. While many women made use of referral networks, word of mouth, varied forms of ethnic media, direct mailing, and flyers, men focused on referral networks and ethnic media. As important, many women emphasized the value of on-site event marketing strategies that allowed them to display products and/or services to a captive audience of potential clients. For example, Grace described how each time she catered an event, she would gain many additional customers since they tasted, first-hand, the quality of her food. Likewise, Gladys also explained how she had come to an agreement with her parish whereby she was allowed to display her hand-made baptism and first communion cards in their bookstore. As parishioners would attend services, they would later shop there, spotting her cards and ordering some for their family events.

Salvadoran women, in particular, talked about their participation in philanthropic causes that served as effective marketing strategies for themselves and their businesses. Rocibel explained how her participation in various community-oriented associations had helped her develop a strong network of co-national men and women business owners. Participating in these meetings not only helped her attain social status within the immigrant community, but also made her known to potential job seekers who might be suitable stylists for any of her beauty parlors. Finally, Karla explained that donating a few of her paintings to charitable causes had been instrumental in helping her build strategic relations with prestigious individuals and institutions. She says,

> More recently, I have been focusing on developing contacts or, as you say here, on public relations. I have been actively participating in several exhibits, in auctions . . . I've donated some of my paintings to special auctions and this has given me very good results. Not only because I'm helping a good cause . . . In this case it was to benefit Latino HIV patients at the Whitman Walker Clinic. You feel good about doing a good deed and you end up receiving back because of it. So I have met many people because of these charitable activities. For example, Carol Schwartz purchased one of my paintings and, you know, she competed against Mayor Anthony Williams in DC's elections. So I became somewhat involved in governmental circles and I even visited her house . . . Oh, her house . . . forget it, it's like a mansion, like a gallery. And the fact that my painting is there! Because she frequently organizes charitable events, dinners and the like. She does a lot to benefit the poor. So, because of this connection, many people have been exposed to my artwork. They have seen my painting there.[. . .] And I have also participated in other events like last year, when I did a portrait for the people at the Chamber of Commerce, and other works for the Ibero-American Chamber of Commerce . . .

Interestingly, men's marketing strategies differed from women in that they tended to draw a distinct line between social and commercial activities, at times even refusing to utilize social events for personal marketing purposes. To recall from an earlier narrative, Vidal, for example, described how he did not like to mix family and commercial life, rarely allowing his wife to work in his restaurant. Further, Javier explained how he belonged to several soccer leagues in which he played weekly. Yet, he refused to informally advertise the services of his painting company during such events. He explains,

> Well . . . when I play soccer, if people come around asking me if I do residential or commercial painting, I respond: "Yes, I paint. But don't talk to me now about painting-related issues, talk to me about soccer."

I never mix these things. On the other hand, if somebody tells me, when we are at work: "Hey, Peru is playing now", I tell him or her right there that we are working, and that we first need to finish our job. Only then can we go watch the game. One has to know when to do what, otherwise people start saying this guy is such and such. If one is not serious and doesn't put things in their right place, things don't work out.

In all, the lack of divide in women's social and commercial lives might be a function of the constant overlap of their private and public spheres, compounded by their early gender socialization in relationship building and nurturing type roles as family and community caregivers.

Business Culture and Management Style

The most salient difference between participants' business cultures revolved around women's informal work environment. Further, my data show that women-owned businesses displayed higher levels of ethnic succession than men, and that women tended to establish more linkages with ethnic vendors and providers. In fact, 12 per cent of Salvadoran and 4 per cent of Peruvian women purchased their businesses from other immigrant women entrepreneurs, from countries as diverse as China, Iran, Korea, and El Salvador. Interestingly, only Salvadoran women reported having purchased their businesses from co-national or co-ethnic men and women owners. Peruvians, instead, purchased their businesses primarily from other ethnic minorities and from North Americans. Incidentally, most informants started new businesses rather than purchased previously owned firms.

Looking at differences among nationalities, many Salvadoran women showed occasional resistance to innovative practices. For example, Antonieta explained that a friend had suggested she purchase merchandise online so she would minimize time and energy. Yet, she felt that that was not the right way to conduct commercial transactions. She explains,

> Well, you see, a while ago this woman from Mexico, Mrs. Lourdes, came here and told me that I could buy and sell merchandise over the internet and that I should think about doing that. But I told her that I wasn't interested. Because, you know, I don't understand anything about Internet. Why am I going to mess around with something I don't understand? I know how to buy and sell merchandise but I need to see it, to touch it first. It's very different buying something after having seen it firsthand than buying it without having seen it at all. Like buying from a catalog . . . sometimes you get some real bad products when you buy like that. Therefore, I prefer not to use Internet for that.

Instead, some of the more affluent and educated Peruvians tended to be more innovative, implementing regular evaluation techniques to assess market demand and customer satisfaction. For example, Grace, upon completing her catering assignments, distributed evaluation forms for her clients to complete. Similarly, Dori utilized an online survey to obtain feedback from her multicultural clientele. Finally, some men used particularly adventurous benchmarking techniques to explore the competition. For example, Luis vividly described how he occasionally conducted participant-observation in far-away restaurants across the country. He explains,

> My partner and I, we are self-taught people in this business [restaurants]. One thing we are fully aware of is that we don't know anything, and we are always eager to learn new techniques, new things. We've never thought that we know it all. We are always researching the market, on our own. For instance, if they tell us: "In New York there's this fantastic restaurant and they serve this and this . . ." We find out where it is located and I go there. And if I see that, indeed, they are doing something really different, I try to get into the kitchen. I've already done this in the past, that is going to restaurants from which we feel we can learn something, and ask for work as a dishwasher or waiter as if I have just arrived from El Salvador. With my humble appearance, I go there and I tell them: "Sir, I'm looking for a job." And this has generally worked for me, and if they don't give me the job, I insist and insist and insist.

Most probably, this type of strategy would have remained off limits to most women, either because of competing family obligations or because of tighter social control and concomitant stigmatization.

CONCLUSION

While Salvadoran and Peruvian women's businesses concentrated in retail and personal services, men concentrated in retail, services, and construction. Salvadoran women had a larger proportion of mom and pop stores in ethnic niches whereas Peruvian women tended to break away into the mainstream economy, running export/import, wholesale retail, and marketing businesses. Salvadoran men ran restaurants, retail stores, and construction businesses while Peruvians concentrated in business services and home remodeling trades.

Patriarchal gender relations within the family and community circumscribed participants' aspirations, motivations, options, and decisions. Men's and women's narratives highlighted gendered motivations for migration and self-employment, with women stressing economic factors whereas men emphasized political circumstances leading to their migration to the US. As important, only women highlighted emigration factors related to social control and gender oppression, including their need to escape from domestic violence and patriarchal societies. Further, women underscored that family-related considerations had pushed them towards self-employment as part of a family strategy that conveniently allowed them to combine private and public responsibilities.

To this end, women deployed family resources in their business operations to a larger extent than men. Not only did they staff their businesses with paid and unpaid relatives, but they frequently brought infants and small children to the workplace. This finding resonates with women's Marianista (traditional) gender ideology, which assigns primacy to maternal duties and family responsibilities. Thus, women's working routines entailed a constant juggling of private and public roles. In contrast, men justified the exclusion of spouses and children from the workplace with arguments similarly informed by traditional gender role ideology, which considers certain types of work inappropriate for female family members.

Resonating with earlier findings, the data reveal significant contrasts in co-ethnic solidarity along nationality lines. Salvadoran women seemed to share a stronger group trust than their Peruvian counterparts, possibly stimulated by their active participation in community and philanthropic activities. Notwithstanding, many Peruvians established valuable relationships with members of external communities, partly as an indication of their higher levels of economic and social incorporation into American society. Paradoxically, Peruvian men's social status concerns and occasional sense of inadequacy, when failing to live up to masculine constructs as "good" family providers, undermined their ability to benefit from social solidarity with friends, co-nationals, and co-ethnics.

Family loans remained the cornerstone of Salvadoran and Peruvian men and women's financing strategies. For the most part, women had access to ethnic capital from family members and female friends. Further, because many felt disconnected from mainstream financial institutions, they relied on personal savings. In contrast, men had access to more diversified sources of start-up capital, including ethnic and commercial credit from members of the opposite sex. Therefore, traditional gender ideology interfered with women's ability to diversify their ethnic credit portfolio. Perhaps to counterbalance this shortcoming, many women from lower socio-economic backgrounds resorted to microcredit programs. Notably, cultural and gender specific factors influenced women's more active engagement in microcredit since acquiring debt is not as status building in Latin America as it is in the United States. In fact, for some men the idea of carrying public debt, as opposed to family and personal loans, threatened their sense of masculinity, stigmatizing them.

Similarly, traditional gender role ideology informed gender preferences in participants' hiring practices. Informants' used ideological constructs to justify discriminatory and exploitative working practices, and neither Salvadorans nor Peruvians hired co-nationals and co-ethnics following notions of ethnic solidarity. Further, neither women nor men hired employees because they belonged to their same sex. Yet, in the informal economy, men and women did resort to gender segregated co-ethnic pools of labor. Thus, whereas men had access to convenient male-exclusive day labor sites, women, instead, resorted to referral networks or to informal recruiting practices during social events.

Finally, participants' management and marketing strategies differed in that only men tended to draw a distinct line between social and commercial activities. Women's overlap of private and public spheres, compounded by their early socialization in relationship building and caregiving roles helps explain the lack of such divide in their social and commercial lives.

8 Social Networks, Social Capital and Embeddedness

This chapter describes the ways in which Salvadoran and Peruvian participants' class, ethnic, and gender-based networks act as conduits of financial, training, assistance, and/or emotional support for members. It discusses the distinct types of social capital such networks accrue, and how their resulting social embeddedness grants members uneven access to entrepreneurial opportunities. Although the exploration of gendered networks remains an analytic cornerstone, other structures of difference are equally examined through an intersectional lens given the interwoven nature of class, ethnic, and gender-based boundaries in participants' lives.

SOCIAL NETWORKS

Social network analysis assigns primacy to interpersonal ties and the social capital they accrue by virtue of individuals' membership in networks. Thus, social networks constitute a middle ground between individual and structural forces impinging on people's daily lives. They are means for the acquisition of scarce resources, channel information, confer a sense of mutual trust and collective identity, and can either constrain or exacerbate the purely instrumental behavior of group members. Immigrant networks remain pivotal because newcomers' degree of economic and social incorporation into the host society largely depends on their connections to others who control valuable assets. Therefore, it is important to examine Salvadoran and Peruvian formal and informal networks, whether class, ethnic, and/or gender-based, because it is the networks of relations to which individuals belong that determines their group embeddedness—or structural positioning—in the receiving society. Through accruing and deploying social capital, social embeddedness plays a strategic role as it determines group members' access to varying opportunity structures.

Overall, Washington Salvadoran and Peruvian participants showed wide quantitative and qualitative variation in their access to formal and informal networks of co-nationals, co-ethnics, and outgroup members. Confirming previous research on immigrant gendered networks (Grasmuck and

Grosfogel 1997; Hagan 1998; Hondagneu-Sotelo 1994; Menjivar 2000; Repak 1995; Curran and Saguy 2001; Curran and Rivero-Fuentes 2003), informants also participated in men and women-exclusive networks that differentially mediated their access to business opportunities and resources. In fact, women tended to participate, to a similar extent as men, in referral networks to obtain information, learn the ropes, and recruit employees. Women networks provided participants start-up capital, childcare services, strategic business information, paid and unpaid labor, informal business training and, equally important, moral support. Nevertheless, a closer look at such networks revealed qualitative differences in the types of social circles Salvadoran and Peruvian women and men were able to access.

To illustrate, many Salvadoran women developed a wider range of connections to co-national and co-ethnic, as well as to North American, women and men working in social service agencies. Furthermore, they effectively circulated information about available programs within their own networks. For example, Mercedes described how she learned, through a Salvadoran friend, about the family daycare-training program offered in Spanish by Fairfax County. There, she made important connections to North American organizational representatives who, in turn, have been referring interested families to her for the last few years. She says,

> The Fairfax County course I told you about was terrific. I met other Hispanic family daycare providers there as well as Mrs. Joystick and Stout from the Office for Children and Families. They have been referring me children since then. And that's many years ago . . . It's really sad that they did away with that pilot training program for Spanish-speaking women!

On the other hand, most Peruvian women belonged to women networks in mainstream associations that rarely connected them to fellow Latinas. For example, Grace explained how she participated in the International Society of Cake Decorators, the Association for Female Executives, and the Association of Women Business Owners. These organizations primarily included North American and, perhaps, a few ethnic minority women. When I asked Grace if she had met any other Latinas through these networks, she commented: "Oh, no! There are very few of us in these organizations. The only other Latinas I have met at these conferences are Latin American women who live overseas, but that's it."

As was the case in Menjivar's study (2000), Salvadoran women's networks seemed more adept than men's at bridging beyond their immediate social circle. This was particularly true insofar as access to community resources, perhaps as an extension of women's responsibilities in traditional caregiving roles. As immigrant families re-settle in an unfamiliar environment, it is primarily women who resort to social service agencies and community organizations to seek information and assistance. Thus, many Salvadoran women learned, early on, about church-sponsored emergency food distribution and/or children insurance programs. These initial connections made it simpler for some to later on find out about microcredit and/or entrepreneurial training programs available in their communities.

Similarly, men also participated in men-exclusive networks that assisted them with business-related information, start-up capital, business referrals, informal business training, and other types of assistance. However, for some Peruvian men, their networks ceased to be effective at providing them access to resources. In fact, a salient theme across many male participants' narratives (of both nationalities) revolved around their refusal to seek assistance from others, whether within co-national, co-ethnic, or external communities. To illustrate, neither Carlos nor Arturo sought assistance from male friends and acquaintances, nor did Salvador or Roberto resort to available community development corporations and microcredit assistance programs. None of these men sought assistance from others because they strongly felt their masculine pride would be hurt. Thus, patriarchal notions of masculinity, virility, and honor interfered with men's assistance seeking behavior, making their networks ineffective in extreme cases.

Formal Networks

Three-fourths of all Salvadoran informants belonged to formal networks composed of co-villagers, co-nationals, or other Latino co-ethnics. They were members of hometown associations, Latino church-based foundations, immigrant congregations,[1] neighborhood business associations, cultural and women's organizations, and county-based Latino chambers of commerce. Most notably, Salvadoran informants participated in formal networks of an ethnic character, focusing either on mobilizing resources to benefit their homeland, or on organizing community activities to advance their social and economic incorporation into American society.

In contrast, only one-fifth of all Peruvians belonged to formal networks, including professional, trade associations, and philanthropic institutions. Remarkably, almost all of these formal memberships connected Peruvians to mainstream institutional circles. They belonged, for example, to the American Janitorial Association, the National Association of Business Executives, the International Society of Cake Decorators, the National Publishers' Association, and other similar organizations. Ironically, although Peruvians could have resorted to the Washington-based American-Peruvian Chamber of Commerce, none of them did because they perceived it, at best, ineffective.

In addition, Salvadoran and Peruvian women informants participated, to a larger extent than men, in formal networks of various sorts. Salvadoran women networks primarily revolved around the co-national or Latino immigrant community; they participated in immigrant hometown associations, Latino religious congregations, and various philanthropic and cultural organizations. Notably, their networks simultaneously connected them to their home and host communities. This pattern resonates with Levitt's (2001) finding that immigrant women disproportionately bear the brunt of transnational community work.

In that sense, Salvadorans' active engagement in transnational community work furthered network members' associational capabilities and enhanced women's social prestige within co-national and/or co-ethnic circles. For example, a few Salvadoran informants belonged to a group called 'Club de Damas Latinoamericanas' (Latin American Ladys' Club) which, since the early 1990s, has gathered prominent Salvadoran entrepreneurs in the Washington metro area. As participants explained, a large proportion of women in this group were 'Intipuqueñas' (from the small town of Intipucá), some having arrived to the area as far back as in the mid-70s. Reflective of most of the Salvadoran population in the area, group members were not college educated. Further, they often participated in other co-ethnic associations such as the Salvadoran Cultural Association, the Salvadoran-American Association of Northern Virginia, the United for Intipucá Foundation, the Chirilagua Association, and the Friends of Usulután Foundation. In her research, Landolt (2000) also identifies the 'Club de Damas,' which she describes as an organizational embodiment of Marianismo values.

Many Peruvian women, instead, participated in formal professional networks that connected them to mainstream social circles. Unlike their Salvadoran counterparts, they did not participate in transnational community activities, such as hometown fundraising events, nor in Latino cultural associations aimed at integrating Peruvian newcomers into the fabric of American society. Like their male compatriots, most women refused to participate in the only co-national organization available to them, the American-Peruvian Chamber of Commerce. As Yanine explains,

A while ago I visited the Chamber [Peruvian-American Chamber of Commerce] and, actually, I thought they had much to learn before being able to provide valuable services to those of us who are running businesses. These people are more into social organizing but they are not very informed about business resources. They are somewhat funny in their approach.

Therefore, Peruvian women networks remained fragmented in terms of connections to fellow co-national and/or co-ethnic women. Instead, their ties effectively linked them to professional women and men from external communities. As will be examined later, this will have repercussions for the types of social capital their networks might be able to accrue.

Men's networks differed along similar patterns, except for the fact that Salvadoran men were not as actively involved as their female compatriots in community projects. Many Salvadoran informants were fully aware of the existence of 'paisano' hometown associations, which they had even supported through monetary contributions. Nevertheless, they did not seem as actively engaged in the day-to-day operation of such organizations. Yet, a few Salvadoran men did belong to Latino cultural associations with a stronger focus on immigrant resettlement assistance. In contrast, many Peruvian men belonged to formal professional networks that linked them to mainstream social circles.

Informal Networks

Both Salvadorans and Peruvians had access to informal networks through participation in religious, social, and sports activities such as soccer leagues and ethnic festivals. Yet, Salvadorans' informal networks, primarily based upon familial and paisano loyalties, were denser and tighter than Peruvians. To recall, Salvadoran businesses catered, primarily, to a co-national and Latino clientele with a few of their providers being co-ethnics. Such a web of connections sometimes allowed their networks to faster diffuse information among members. For example, in chapter six, Grace, a Peruvian informant, alluded to the effectiveness of Salvadoran referral networks to expand her customer base.

In contrast, Peruvians' informal ties reached beyond familial circles to encompass friends and acquaintances not necessarily of co-national or Latino origin. Their business providers were, almost exclusively, American companies, and they targeted both ethnic as well as mainstream consumer markets. As noted in previous chapters, Peruvians' weaker reactive ethnicity adversely affected their ability to develop solidarious relations with co-nationals, both commercially and socially. Nevertheless, precisely because their informal networks included a diverse set of connections beyond compatriots, they allowed members access to valuable information from a wider range of sources. Illustrating this, Marco described earlier how his connection to an American friend had proved instrumental in his decision to start his tortilla factory. In explaining his rationale, he concluded: "Help among Peruvians, no. Here who helps you out is not the Peruvian, María, who helps you is the American."

Most notably, Salvadorans and Peruvians had access to gendered informal networks of extended family, friends, associates, and acquaintances. Through their participation in these, they found assistance in a wide range of personal and business related activities, from technical guidance, to recruitment, to public relations, to moral support. Informants participated in sport leagues, church-sponsored functions, cultural events, and business related activities, diversifying their social ties and expanding their web of connections.

Maternal role models proved particularly influential for women participants as 90 per cent of women emphasized that their mothers had played a defining role in their decision to become business owners. Moreover, many pointed out other family members had also been significant role models in their lives. For example, Silvia described how her aunt had taught her the beginning business ropes, providing her with an initial customer base. Maria also shared that her mother had significantly influenced her decision to open her rotisserie. She explains,

> When my mother sent me the chicken recipe, that gave me the push to get going. She bought the recipe back at home for $10,000 and that kind of forced me to start my own restaurant. I'm quite grateful to her for that.

Along with maternal influences, most women informants consulted with male family members, friends, or acquaintances on business related issues. They resorted to men from a wide range of ethnic backgrounds, including co-ethnics, Middle Easterners, Africans, and North Americans. Many women emphasized the critical roles these men had played in their lives as commercial mentors and advisers. Haydee, for example, already described how her male mentors had often advised her on critical business decisions. Similarly, Silvia explained how her friend John had always been supportive of her and her husband. She says,

> Sometimes, when I can't find my husband and I have an urgent question, or let's say that his cell battery died, I call my friend George. Look, sometimes I have a client right in front of me, and they have a question that I can't answer, so well, I call George. This is the man who was once my husband's boss. He has exactly the same type of business we have, identical. He is from Africa, another immigrant. He has always been such a strong support for us! So, anything, anything I need, he tells me: "Call here, call there, do this, do that." And he gives me the numbers.

Men often acknowledged they had received critical support from mothers, wives, and other female relatives. Yet, most of them did not consider the women in their lives as business mentors, or individuals they would resort to if in need of business advice. In fact, most men strictly relied on other men's guidance when consulting on business related issues. Moreover, as previously noted, social status concerns occasionally interfered with men's ability to obtain assistance from co-national male networks. As examined in chapter seven, an important exception to this gendered pattern entailed men's borrowing practices from men and women lenders alike. In contrast, due to stigmatizing social mores, many women felt restricted to borrowing exclusively from fellow women, which placed them at a considerable disadvantage given that it was primarily men who commanded larger financial resources.

Looking across nationalities, Salvadoran women's informal networks seemed particularly effective at information diffusion, assistance, and mentoring. For example, several women described ritualistic women-exclusive trips to wholesale retail stores at the company of co-national or co-ethnic acquaintances who graciously initiated them into the nuts and bolts of business ownership. As Antonieta says,

> One day, one of my friends told me she knew a woman who frequently traveled to New York to buy [merchandise] from wholesalers. So I told my friend: " Can you take me or tell your friend to let me go with her to New York?" Because her friend, you know, she really didn't know me and here I was, asking to have her take me with her! She did agree and that's how I started working in this industry. Those were the first trips I did with several other women who were doing the same.

Likewise, a few informants established partnerships with fellow women business owners to capitalize on shared resources and maximize visibility. Still, others developed flexible arrangements, which allowed them to purchase products and acquire information from one another. For example, Ana Maria explains,

> She buys from me occasionally. She comes to the store and buys stuff. Sometimes, she comes, specifically, because people have come to her store looking for a baptism dress, a 'quinceañera' (fifteen years celebration) dress, or something like that. Then, she calls me and tells me: "Look, they have asked me for such and such a dress." So, if the price is 60 dollars, then I sell it to her for 50 so she can increase a bit and get some profit. Sometimes [before she opened her own store], she would come and tell me: "Look, Ana, I'd like to open my own store. What should I do, where do I have to go?" So I told her to go to New York and gave her some addresses. Of course, I wasn't going to give her absolutely all my contacts, because I have to protect my own business, too. But I did give her basic information so that she could get started. Then, it's up to her to develop it. I also sold her several of my used videos . . . I think that around 300 videos . . . yes, around 300 I sold her. And I told her that she could get started with that. I also connected her with my father so that she could act as representative for Gigante Express (money wire and mail services to and from Central America), right there in the neighborhood where she has the store.

Despite the general camaraderie among many Salvadoran women, a couple of participants expressed strong feelings of isolation because of their non-traditional views and lifestyles. Haydee, for example, explained that, at times, she felt she had no other women to relate to. In fact, she felt other women were critical of her for choosing a busy entrepreneurial career over a traditional Latin American domestic lifestyle. Clearly, she felt stigmatized by co-national men and women who gossiped about her. She says,

Actually, most of the women I know don't understand me. I think I only have one who sort of understands me, but the rest—they don't care about what I do. If they see me, they greet me. They even congratulate me if they have to but. . . . maybe it is hard for them. So sometimes, I feel as though what I'm doing is not right, almost like there's something wrong with me. I realize that some of the things I believe in are not things they agree with . . . like, for example, I always say that it's not that important how many hours you spend with your children, but the quality of the time you spend with them. What really bothers me, though, is that people invent stories about my business and me. Like those stories that somebody gave it to me, or that I inherited it from an old man whom I married for interest, and things like that. These things all bother me.

Peruvian women networks, instead, focused on either recruiting women for contingent work, or on occasional collaboration for multi-branding purposes. Yanine and Clara, for example, had women-exclusive workforces in their janitorial companies, and were constantly recruiting new female candidates. Dori, instead, described how she occasionally promoted other women's businesses in her events. She explains,

She had a travel agency where people also get training on how to become a travel agent. And she gave me tickets back and forth to Miami so I could offer them as raffle prizes during my promotional events. I also have another woman friend, you know her, and she is the owner of the cappuccino catering service. Well, she also has given me several bags of coffee to add to the raffle.

Yet, Peruvian women's co-national networks did not always seem particularly supportive of women. Dori, for example, bitterly described how some of her Peruvian women acquaintances and friends had never supported her business. Many, she explained, had never attended any of her events and, to add insult to injury, had no qualms in supporting men competitors, including those from a different nationality. Disappointed, she attributed this lack of solidarity to Latina women's internalized gender prejudices.

Network Features

As examined in chapter two, there are various network features that can shape the degree to which a network of individuals accesses opportunity structures. Among these, internal class differentiation or multiplexity can be of strategic importance (Boissevian 1974; Fernandez-Kelly and Schauffler 1996; Granovetter 1973, 1985; Portes 1995; Portes and Sensenbrenner 1993). Relatively large and dense networks, with high levels of internal class differentiation, are the most effective at generating normative regulations, reciprocity expectations, and attitudes within a group. In other words, social networks exhibiting a heterogeneous class base further facilitate ties among persons of dissimilar status, or what Granovetter (1973) calls "weak and strong ties."

Thus, in Granovetter's formulation, networks characterized by such mixed ties remain the most efficient since they maximize the array of opportunities available to group members. As individuals successfully interact with others who belong to different institutional circles, they increase the flow of information and resources available to the network and the community as a whole. Further, Lin (2001) has called attention to the specific type of action members of a network seek to advance, concluding that actors motivated to maintain embedded resources are better served by stronger ties with persons of similar status. In contrast, actors motivated to gain new resources for their network are better served by cultivating weaker ties to external institutional circles, thus obtaining access to better social capital for instrumental action.

Washington Salvadoran and Peruvian study participants belonged to networks that substantially differed in their degree of internal class differentiation and density. Whereas Salvadoran networks encompassed a relatively homogeneous group of working class individuals, primarily from similar sending communities in Eastern El Salvador, Peruvians' networks included a more heterogeneous group of working and middle class newcomers, more loosely connected along national lines. Thus, Peruvians' networks showed a higher degree of internal class differentiation than Salvadorans', with group members generally bridging to mainstream social and institutional circles. This was, in great part, due to their class-based bourgeois cultural capital and plentiful human capital endowments, including English language proficiency and wider familiarity with American lifestyles and values. Notably, Peruvians' networks revolved around central members who monopolized strategic resources in the communications, marketing, and IT industries. Through their centrality in such networks, a few select Peruvians mobilized resources to advance their own interests, including those of kin and close associates. A closer look at one such Peruvian key actor might help illustrate this centrality.

Maco is a partner and sales manager at a well-known publishing company at the center of all Latino businesses in the Washington metropolitan area. Simultaneously, he has a side business as an entertainment promoter, organizing events such as concerts and parties for a loyal and exclusive multicultural clientele. His position in sales has allowed him to develop an extensive network of contacts, which he expeditiously taps when promoting events at restaurants and discotheques. Thus, he capitalizes on the business connections he has cultivated through his publishing business. His centrality and reputation in the Latino business community has allowed him to commercially assist his siblings, who also help him run his side business. More recently, he has helped his brothers start a home improvement business by advertising the company for free in one of his various business publications.

Instead, Salvadoran networks often remained inwardly-oriented or, at best, secluded within the Latino community, with occasional linkages to outside social circles. Two notable exceptions included women's connection to social service agencies and microcredit programs and, for more affluent participants, linkages to mainstream social circles of higher-class extraction. Therefore, Washington Salvadorans' networks, while denser and tighter, lacked internal class differentiation, or what Lin calls resource heterogeneity (Lin 2001: 67). Despite their higher levels of co-national ethnic solidarity (strong ties), Salvadorans' networks failed to grant members access to higher quality opportunity structures because most of them remained constrained within a resource poorer community.

In contrast, although Peruvians' networks showed a higher degree of internal class differentiation, their networks did not always provide co-nationals access to better opportunities because their ties were neither dense nor closely knit. Moreover, as Peruvians' social cohesion was weaker relative to Salvadorans', members' access to valuable opportunities remained an individualist rather than a collectivist pursuit. Paradoxically, Peruvian's weaker ethnic group cohesion might well be a manifestation of their more advanced levels of economic and social incorporation into US society.

As empirical studies have eloquently demonstrated, immigrant networks are dynamic and therefore they either strengthen or weaken over time, differentially affecting distinct segments of an immigrant community (Hagan 1998; Menjívar 2000). In line with this, the effectiveness of study participants' networks at allocating resources fluctuated over time. For example, Salvadoran women's networks successfully facilitated members' initiation into business ownership. As described earlier, when seasoned business owners escorted aspiring and novice entrepreneurs on "purchasing trips" to New York City, they taught newcomers the ropes, sharing vital information on business wholesalers and providers. These women-exclusive initiation trips were particularly useful to network members not only because close friends took others on these hand-on activities but, also, because friends of friends were involved in this chain of assistance. Therefore, Salvadoran women's membership in these social circles carried extensive privileges.

Notwithstanding, as time went by and many of these novice entrepreneurs settled in their commercial routines, they failed to keep in touch with initial mentors and peer business owners. In fact, many Salvadoran women talked about the social cost of self-exploitation, namely their lack of time to pursue personal interests and their seclusion in enclosed working environments. Therefore, while their networks eased their transition into business ownership, often times the fast-paced and intensive nature of their routines weakened the effectiveness of their networks in the long run. Without time to replenish their bonding connections, some women's networks weakened or even eroded. Antonieta explains,

> Of course, I'm interested in being informed, informed about the opportunities out there. But, look, being inside this store all day long . . . it's pretty rough because sometimes it feels as though I'm back in my country. I don't even find out about things that happen around me sometimes . . . I spend all day long inside this business, from morning to evening. When I get back home, dinner, my granddaughter . . . you know. Sometimes I spend weeks without seeing any of my friends . . . it's because here there is no time, no time at all.

Conversely, men's networks remained more stable over time. Given that, for the most part, men's workload did not add social reproduction duties to business responsibilities, and that their commercial roles frequently involved public relations and sales—with far less seclusion within the workplace—men's networks tended to stabilize or, at times, even expand. Thus, this pattern is congruent with Hagan's study (1998) on Guatemalan Mayan immigrants in Houston, Texas, in which she found that gendered networks differentially mediated men and women's access to the 1996 IRCA legalization program.

SOCIAL CAPITAL

Social capital allows individuals to use their membership in particular groups to gain access to valuable resources. Thus, it can be a manifestation of class, ethnic, and/or gender- based resources and can exert positive as well as negative effects on members of a network (Fernandez-Kelly 1995; Portes and Landolt 1996; Waldinger 1995). To recall from chapter two, scholars have categorized social capital into two distinct types (Foley, McCarthy and Chavez 2001; Edwards, Foley and Diani 2001). While 'bonding' social capital allows immigrants to develop feelings of social belonging, trust, and reciprocity within a closed circle of family and friends, 'bridging' social capital facilitates their connection to groups and institutions beyond their closest circles. In so doing, bridging social capital facilitates access to valuable resources outside an immigrant's community, including information about jobs and services. Similar to Granovetter's concept of "weak and strong ties," 'bonding' and 'bridging' capital represent distinct but complementary network assets. They are also directly related to the level of internal class differentiation of a network and the type of action it intends to advance (Lin 2001).

Most scholars concur that networks that seek to improve their socioeconomic standing are best served by both their ability to maintain group cohesion, solidarity, and internal trust, as well as by their ability to capitalize on bridging connections to others who control valuable assets (Edwards, Foley, and Diani 2001; Granovetter 1975; Light and Gold 2000; Portes 1998). In other words, co-national networks endowed with complementary types of social capital are more effective at advancing collective interests.

Salvadoran and Peruvian participants' divergent class and ethnic endowments, coupled with their participation in networks of distinct character, largely determined the type of social capital participants were able to accrue. Whereas Salvadoran networks primarily provided members with bonding social capital based upon ethnic loyalties, that of Peruvians' granted them moderate access to bridging social capital organized around class boundaries. Yet, poorer in reactive ethnicity, Peruvian informants lacked the bonding social capital necessary for the strengthening of collective identity. Saddened and amused by the story he was about to share, Esteban illustrated this point with the following story.

> I have never benefited from any Peruvian solidarity . . . or Latino [solidarity], for that matter. My lawyer once told me this story about Latinos, which I think is accurate. It kind of bothered me but, at the same time, I felt it was true. Once upon a time there was a man catching crabs on the beach. I don't know if you know how people catch crabs. Well, they use a type of fishing rope they throw in the sea and, once they have caught the crab, they place it in a cooler. It's very simple. So the story goes that this man, as he was catching crabs, was placing some of them in one cooler and others in a different one. But, while one of the coolers had a cover, the other didn't. A person who was nearby was curious enough to ask the man: "Look, I've noticed that you are placing some crabs here and others there, and that you cover one cooler and not the other. Why are you doing this?" And the man replied: "Well, these ones here, the ones I am covering, you see, I have to cover them because otherwise they would escape. The others, I don't because they are Latinos, and when one of them tries to escape, the rest grab onto it and pull it down."

On the other hand, Peruvians' class-based bridging social capital often facilitated commercial expansion into mainstream markets. Ricardo, for example, belonged to a family of upper-middle class extraction with multiple connections to the United States. Since he could remember, his father had been involved in Florida's commercial real estate business. Thus, everybody in his family had frequently traveled back and forth to the United States to visit friends and business associates. Upon completion of his BA in Lima, Ricardo completed an MBA at an American university, making valuable connections and acquiring professional and status credentials. Not long after that, he landed a lucrative executive level job with a US-owned communications corporation. A few years in that capacity enabled him to make strategic contacts which allowed him to launch his own advertising company later in his career.

Most scholars conclude that only ethnic entrepreneurs who deploy both ethnic and class resources are able to graduate their ethnic economies to higher levels of maturity (Light 1984, Light and Gold, 2000; Portes and Manning 1986). In line with such theories, the experience of Salvadoran and Peruvian study participants suggests that networks that accrue both ethnic and class-based bonding and bridging social capital might better promote the collective advancement of immigrant economies. In fact, participants' experiences suggest that unless both complementary resources are present in immigrant networks, entrepreneurs suffer either one of two fates: 1) they remain survivalist type entrepreneurs in struggling businesses in ethnic niches or; 2) their commercial individualist ventures permeate the ethnic and mainstream economies with little, if any, galvanizing power to advance the immigrant economy to which they belong.

Furthermore, confirming empirical findings on the negative effect of social capital[2] (Fernandez-Kelly 1996; Portes and Landolt 1996; Waldinger 1995), Salvadorans and Peruvians agreed that many aspects of co-national and/or co-ethnic relations were conflict ridden. A number of Peruvian informants pointed out that, by recruiting and circulating information within closed social boundaries, co-ethnic referral networks sometimes excluded them from valuable opportunities. Others emphasized the difficulties of hiring family members who, coming to the job with "airs" because of their connection to the business owner, refused to engage in certain type of work. For example, Maria explains,

> I've already had a big problem with my brother-in-law. We hired him and he made the other workers feel bad. He started talking to them as though he was superior, as though South Americans were any better than anybody else. So, you see, he was creating all sorts of conflicts. I was forced to fire him because he was creating a lot of resentment among my employees, right? He thought that, because he was family and from South America, he had to work less! He thought he could order people around, sit down and read the newspaper . . . and that the others had to cover for him . . .

Salvadorans' demanding transnational obligations, in particular, often proved a social capital liability. Frequently, their potential for capital accumulation and social collaboration was severely weakened by extensive remittance demands. Last, as examined in chapter six, the blurring of informants' national boundaries with the use of fictive panethnic labels often proved counterproductive since it created more cleavages than a sense of shared identity. Ultimately, concealing class interests and national rivalries, fictive panethnicity often turned into an ethnic liability.

Gendered networks also differed in the qualitative nature of their social capital. As already noted, Salvadoran women's networks effectively accrued bonding social capital among co-nationals and, even, co-ethnics. Their paisano-based loyalties, active transnational engagement, and widespread kinship ties were instrumental in strengthening ethnic connections. Among Salvadorans, women's networks differed from men's in that the former were able to accrue at least modicum levels of bridging social capital. Through their membership in multiple formal and informal networks of co-nationals and co-ethnics, including their participation in mainstream microcredit and business training programs, Salvadoran women proved more resourceful. In this sense, gender and ethnicity significantly mediated the types of social capital participants' networks were able to accrue, which might partly explain why Salvadoran women's self-employment rates remain higher than those of their male counterparts.

In contrast, confirming recent scholarship on ethnic identity formation among Peruvian immigrants in New Jersey (Paerregaard 2005), Peruvian men and women's networks often lacked bonding connections among compatriots due to class and racial antagonisms brought from the homeland. Notwithstanding, Peruvian networks showed wider linkages to mainstream social circles, accruing bridging social capital, which Salvadorans often lacked.

In all, women's narratives emphasized the empowering nature of business ownership and women mentors. In fact, this was a theme that emerged from women's accounts exclusively. Yet, there were a few qualitative differences across national origin. Whereas Peruvians emphasized the empowerment they had granted others, for example, by assisting employees start their own businesses, Salvadorans underscored the empowerment they, themselves, had obtained from their status as business owners. As they galvanized their associational and organizational capabilities through participation in women-dominated community activities, many Salvadoran women experienced substantial empowerment. Many participants talked about attaining a newfound leverage vis à vis men in their lives, whether through business ownership or pioneering the chain migration of offspring, spouses, and extended family. A few participants even expressed a profound sense of liberation and exhilarating empowerment after setting themselves free from domestic violence and other forms of patriarchal oppression in their lives. To illustrate, Agustina comments,

> I think that, from the time I arrived here, I have been reaching all of the goals I set for myself. We [her husband and she] not only have this business, but we also belong to a very active community. We frequently meet with members of the Committee [Committee Pro-Chirilagua] to organize events for the community. I am a member of this committee, the one for fundraising. It's very beautiful to be able to help the community, you know? And I feel good being part of that. Besides, being

my own boss also gives me some say in what goes on around here. You know, when he [her husband] has been fooling around, I have threatened to leave him and now he knows what's good for him.

SOCIAL EMBEDDEDNESS

Drawing from economic sociology, Granovetter (1995) argues that social expectations play a key role in determining market (as well as non-contractual) transactions. Assigning priority to the overarching structures in which social relations are situated, he distinguishes between "relational" and "structural" embeddedness. Whereas relational embeddedness refers to behavior induced by reciprocity expectations arising from economic actors' personal relations with one another, structural embeddedness refers to the broader network of social relations to which economic actors belong.

Following Granovetter's logic, despite Washington Peruvians' weaker co-national group cohesion and relational embeddedness, their networks retained a more advantageous structural position than Salvadorans'. Their class-preponderant resources, coupled with their higher levels of bridging social capital and less hostile reception levels, translated into a more favorable structural embeddedness. Further, Peruvians' higher incidence of weaker ties facilitated their instrumental actions. Paradoxically, however, precisely because of their weak relational embeddedness, Washington Peruvians typify what Light (1984) calls "individualist" entrepreneurs, unable to advance the collective interests of the entire Peruvian immigrant economy.

In contrast, Salvadorans seemed to better fit Light's collectivist entrepreneurial typology since their ethnic-preponderant networks, rich in bonding social capital, granted them a stronger relational embeddedness. Naturally, their weaker bridging connections translated into a less favorable structural embeddedness, exacerbated by a more hostile reception level. As a result, their strong ties enhanced the maintenance of network resources, but also impeded members' accrual of new assets.

On the other hand, women's networks showed both commonalities and contrasts. Despite the sense of empowerment conferred by the entrepreneurial experience, patriarchal ideology continued to circumscribe women's mobility, social interactions, attitudes and practices. For Salvadorans, in particular, traditional gender mores and lower socioeconomic status often restricted their access to financing sources, lest they be stigmatized as a form of social control. Nevertheless, contesting such limitations, their networks mobilized around active participation in transnational and local community projects, hence making it possible for women's agency to redefine the terms of their opportunity structure. In striking contrast, Peruvian women's co-national and co-ethnic networks showed higher levels of multiplexity, but lower density and reactive ethnicity. In spite of this, most participants had access to valuable opportunities, information, and connections by virtue of a more privileged socioeconomic standing.

Salvadoran men's networks were as dense and closely knit as their women compatriots. Yet, in contrast, they presented lower levels of multiplexity since they rarely participated in social circles beyond their immigrant community. Neither were they as actively engaged as their female counterparts in community, cultural, or collective commercial projects. Chapter four has already addressed some of the reasons behind Salvadorans' lack of a collectively organized presence in the Washington metropolitan area.

Among Peruvian men, their co-national and co-ethnic networks showed higher levels of internal class differentiation than Salvadorans, but less density and weak cohesion. Like Peruvian women's ties, their networks worked best at accruing bridging social capital, which allowed them to capitalize on financing, technical, and networking opportunities from diverse social circles. Remarkably, a sizable number of their businesses were positioned in higher profit margin industries, such as information technology or communications. In fact, out of all participants, Peruvian men were the group that best managed to break away from the ethnic niche. Like their Salvadoran counterparts, Peruvians also remained free from the unrelenting juggling of private and public responsibilities.

In sum, a nuanced understanding of immigrant social stratification (segmented assimilation) is predicated upon an intersectional analysis that weaves multidimensional structures of difference in individuals' lives. Thus, social embeddedness analysis needs to account for the fact that neither all Latinos nor all men and women are created equally. Gendered and racialized immigrants occupy unique positions in the social hierarchy, despite attempts at homogenization. The intersectionality of gender, ethnicity, and class in Salvadoran and Peruvian experiences brings to bear that Latino men and women do not share similar barriers by virtue of a common ethnic or gender identity. Whereas, for example, Peruvian women obtained better access to financial markets and mainstream circles, Salvadoran men lagged behind these women, despite male privileges and patriarchal gender relations.

CONCLUSION

Washington Salvadoran and Peruvian participants belonged to formal and informal networks of co-nationals, co-ethnics, and/or outgroup members. Salvadorans participated in formal networks of an ethnic character, focusing on mobilizing resources to benefit their homeland, or on organizing community activities that enhanced their social and economic incorporation into American society. Thus, whereas Salvadorans' networks primarily linked them to family, co-nationals, and the external Latino community, Peruvians' networks connected members to external Latino and North American communities and, less frequently, to co-nationals beyond kin.

Participants belonged to networks that substantially differed in their degree of internal class differentiation and density. Salvadoran networks encompassed a relatively homogeneous group of working class individuals, primarily from the same sending communities. Instead, Peruvians' included a more heterogeneous group of working and middle class business owners loosely connected along national lines. In fact, Peruvians' networks showed a higher degree of internal class differentiation than Salvadorans' with group members more adept at bridging to mainstream social circles. Nevertheless, their co-national networks failed to provide most members access to better opportunities because their connections were neither dense nor closely knit.

In contrast, Salvadorans' networks lacked internal class differentiation. Consequently, they did not allow co-nationals access to higher quality opportunity structures either. Despite their higher levels of ethnic solidarity, Salvadorans remained, with a couple of exceptions, constrained within a resource poorer community. The very few that broke away from it, resorted, invariably, to class endowments with which they too maximized potential opportunities. Therefore, the evidence suggests that weak and strong ties, class and ethnic based, are indeed necessary for immigrant economies to thrive.

Despite their weaker group cohesion and less favorable relational embeddedness, Washington Peruvians retained a more advantageous structural position than Salvadorans. This was due to their class-preponderant resources, higher levels of bridging social capital, and neutral reception levels. Yet, precisely because of their weaker relational embeddedness, Peruvians more closely typify Light's "individualist" entrepreneurs. Instead, Salvadorans' ethnic-preponderant networks granted them a better relational embeddedness, typifying them as "collectivist" entrepreneurs.

Salvadorans and Peruvians participated in gendered formal and informal networks that differentially mediated their access to opportunities. Salvadoran women had denser co-national and co-ethnic networks with lower levels of multiplexity relative to Peruvians. Thus, often times, they remained secluded within their closest circles, overwhelmed by demanding work schedules that absorbed their energy. Nevertheless, some participants managed to establish ties with women outside their inner circles. It was women's active participation in transnational, local, and women-exclusive networks what replenished their gender and ethnic-based social capital. In contrast, Peruvian women networks had higher levels of multiplexity, but lower levels of density and reactive ethnicity. Endowed with class-preponderant group resources relative to Salvadorans, Peruvian women's networks accrued more bridging than bonding social capital.

Salvadoran men's networks were dense, but, unlike their women's networks, they had lower levels of multiplexity as men had few ties to mainstream circles. Further, they were not as actively engaged in formal philanthropic circles mobilized around cultural, community, or commercial projects. Conversely,

Peruvian men's networks showed higher levels of internal class differentiation than Salvadorans, but less density and weaker cohesion. Like their women compatriots, Peruvian men's networks accrued bridging social capital best. Most notably, a sizable number of men-owned businesses operated in higher profit margin industries, such as information technology and telecommunications. Salvadoran and Peruvian men alike remained free from the unrelenting juggling of private and public duties common in women's routines. Moreover, patriarchal social mores did not restrict men's social interaction with members of the opposite sex, thus granting them access to wider range of financing and business ties.

9 Conclusion
The Social Bases and Consequences of Latino Entrepreneurship

This final chapter synthesizes the empirical and theoretical contributions of the book, reviewing main research findings and discussing the ways in which these contribute to existing knowledge. In broadening the Latino entrepreneurship theoretical framework, the chapter also identifies areas that might provide fertile terrain for future social inquiry. Finally, it considers policy implications of the study findings in the context of a politically contentious immigrant debate in post 9/11 America.

FINDINGS

Chapter one introduced a set of questions on the nature of Salvadoran and Peruvian immigrant mobilization strategies to develop business ventures. Further, it posed questions related to gatekeepers' and informants' perceptions of the Greater Washington area regulatory business environment for Latino business owners. The discussion of empirical findings that follows responds to these questions.

"Latino" Entrepreneurship, Panethnicity, and Resource Mobilization Strategies

Fictive panethnic labels such as "Latino" obscure important differences among the various national origin groups it categorizes. In the case of Washington Salvadorans and Peruvians, each immigrant group developed mobilization strategies that drew on differential resource bases. While both combined various types of resources in starting and developing small businesses, Peruvian group endowments were class-preponderant relative to Salvadorans. In contrast, Salvadoran collective practices were imbued with a strong ethnic flavor that counterbalanced their class resource deficiency.

Accordingly, such differential group endowments led to divergent business strategies. Whereas Peruvians' larger class resources enabled them to diversify their financing, labor, management, and marketing options, their lower ethnic-based endowments (class and racial cleavages, lower reactive ethnicity, and social cohesion) hampered their ability to solidify commercial ties with co-nationals. Most notably, only Peruvian participants experienced status incongruence and downward mobility upon immigration to the US, partly as a reflection of their higher skilled migration flow to the Washington area and their fragmented co-national community relative to Salvadorans. Washington Peruvians typify what Light calls "individualistic" entrepreneurs—that is entrepreneurs who "think and act independently, albeit in utilization of class-linked resources" (1984: 205). Yet, their class-preponderant resources equally pave the way for their faster economic and social incorporation into American society, including their breaking away from ethnic niches into mainstream markets.

Conversely, Washington Salvadorans' business strategies drew primarily from an ethnic resource base organized around extended kin and 'paisano' networks. Salvadorans' lower class endowments restricted their access to mainstream financing and marketing opportunities, slowing down their familiarization with the American regulatory business environment. Distinctly, Washington Salvadorans heavily relied on ethnic credit, ethnic markets, family businesses, family labor, informal business training, and cheap labor drawn from the informal economy. As discussed in chapter six, culturally specific factors such as Salvadorans' lingering distrust of financial institutions—rooted in a collective memory of previous malfeasance at the hands of ethnic banks—contributed to steer Salvadorans away from banking and borrowing practices. In all, Salvadorans closely embody Light's "collectivist" entrepreneur type—that is entrepreneurs who benefit from ethnic group resources by virtue, among other things, of their active participation in community life. As chapter seven examines, it is Salvadoran women, in particular, who most closely fit this description. Thus, Peruvian and Salvadoran narratives confirm theories that attribute individualistic qualities to entrepreneurial groups endowed with class-preponderant resources, and collectivist qualities to those with more predominant ethnic endowments.

Given scholars' contentions that ethnic entrepreneurship reaches its potential when immigrant groups are equally endowed with class as well as ethnic resources, findings from this study suggest that the Salvadoran and Peruvian economies have much room to grow. Whereas most Salvadorans remain secluded in ethnic niches, a few Peruvians manage to individually break away into mainstream markets. Yet, neither group manages to develop their immigrant economy into economic ethnic enclaves. Paradoxically, Peruvians' class-preponderant resources, including their concomitant higher levels of acculturation to American society, conspire to erode the ethnic sources of social capital crucial to develop thriving economic immigrant enclaves.

Whereas the use of fictive panethnic labels occasionally blurred informants' social boundaries, it often proved counterproductive as it created more cleavages than commonalties. Because of class and national rivalries among first generation Latino immigrants, panethnicity often turned into a liability rather than an asset. For example, as demonstrated in chapters five and six, Peruvians' labor business strategies often times concealed class interests behind a romanticized ideology of panethnic solidarity. As subsequent generations of Salvadorans and Peruvians further assimilate into American society and shed constraining social hierarchies brought from the ancestral homeland, they will more likely embrace a "Latino" panethnic identity. After all, panethnic identities are nothing but variants of American-ness, often not mutually exclusive to national origin identification (Portes and Rumbaut 1990; Fraga et al. 2007). Further empirical research on intergenerational identity formation among Latinos, both across national origin groups and immigrant generations, would provide valuable insights into the dynamics of segmented assimilation.

Overlapping Boundaries: Gender, Class, and Ethnicity in Entrepreneurial Strategies

Gender, as main organizer of social life, profoundly shapes aspirations, options, values, and the resource mobilization strategies of immigrant men and women. Salvadoran and Peruvian patriarchal ideology, including normatively prescribed behavior for men and women, conditions their differential access to information, knowledge, skills, values, social networks, and financial resources. Consequently, immigrants' class and ethnic-based endowments, including cultural and social sources of capital, are gendered. Most important, given that class and national origin play an equally instrumental role in granting uneven access to opportunity structures, gender inevitably becomes interwoven with class and ethnicity to mediate individuals' responses to social structure, constraining or otherwise.

Salvadoran and Peruvian stories in chapter seven eloquently described the ways in which gender patterned pre- and post-migration attitudes and behaviors. For example, men and women emphasized distinct motivations for migrating to the United States and to become self-employed. Whereas women stressed economic and family-related factors, men emphasized political circumstances fueling their decision to migrate. Notably, only women highlighted factors related to social control and gender oppression, such as the need to escape from domestic violence and patriarchal societies. Unlike men, most women described self-employment as a family strategy that conveniently allowed them to fulfill both private (social reproduction) and public (economic production) responsibilities. Quite poignantly, women's and men's narratives portrayed their entrepreneurial experience as a source of personal empowerment, both in the case of upwardly mobile as well as survivalist type entrepreneurs.

Corroborating existing studies, participants' experiences suggest that women deployed familial resources in their business operations to a larger extent than men (Martinez 2007; Robles and Cordero-Guzman 2007).

They staffed their businesses with kin and extended kin who provided paid or unpaid labor in various capacities. To this end, women brought infants, children, and teenagers to the workplace, often utilizing the latter's services as cultural brokers and/or in customer service roles. In contrast, whereas men leaned on their families for moral and, often, financial support, they preferred to keep family and business affairs separate. Both men and women justified their business preferences and practices with arguments informed by traditional gender role ideology, which assigns primacy to women's maternal responsibilities (Marianismo values) and to men's bread-winner roles as family heads and decision-makers (Machismo values). Most notably, gender ideology informed preferences in Salvadoran and Peruvian hiring practices, even with informants occasionally resorting to gender seg-regated co-ethnic pools of labor in the informal economy.

Furthermore, family loans remained the cornerstone of both men's and women's financing strategies. Several factors prevented full participa-tion in mainstream banking for many, including cultural aversion to debt among some participants, either because of the memory of bad experi-ences, or because debt carried a negative connotation in their homeland societies. Yet, whereas most women had access to ethnic credit, bor-rowed from family members and same sex friends, men had access to more diversified sources of start-up capital. In addition to their ethnic sources of credit, a few men accessed loans from commercial institutions and from friends and/or acquaintances of the opposite sex. Thus, patri-archal ideology and social stigmatization as forms of control restricted women's ability to diversify their ethnic credit portfolio beyond same sex co-nationals. To compensate for this, women resorted to ethnic and/or class-based resources. Whereas a few Peruvian women were able to lever-age their class advantage into commercial loans from mainstream insti-tutions, others simply financed their ventures through the liquidation of personal assets, home equity loans, or savings. In contrast, Salvadoran women compensated for limited financing alternatives through participa-tion in microcredit schemes and hard-earned savings, which they relied on for start-up capital. Remarkably, and to a larger extent than their Peruvian counterparts, Salvadoran women capitalized on membership in women-exclusive networks of co-ethnic business owners, with whom they shared information and strategic know-how early on.

In contrast, men enjoyed more freedom of action without the necessity to juggle private and public roles, or to adhere to stringent gender mores restricting exchanges with members of the opposite sex. Nevertheless, despite male privilege, not all men fared better than women insofar as business management practices. Whereas Peruvian men's class-preponder-ant resources often translated into their ability to diversify their financ-ing and marketing avenues, Salvadorans compensated for their deficient class endowments through ethnic-based social capital centered around kin and paisano loyalties. However, underscoring the intersectionality of gender, class, and ethnicity, Peruvian women commanding substantial class resources often had access to better financing and marketing opportunities than many Salvadoran men.

Social Networks, Social Capital, and Embeddedness

Chapter eight explored in detail Washington Salvadoran and Peruvian network features, including their participation in formal and informal networks of co-nationals, co-ethnics, and out-group members. Given that informants belonged to various class, ethnic, and gender-based networks, and that these differed in the extent to which they managed to develop bridging and bonding social capital, the embeddedness of their networks did not prove equally effective at acquiring new resources, maintaining existing assets and, ultimately, advancing entrepreneurial goals.

Salvadoran women's networks, with lower levels of multiplexity relative to Peruvians', were denser and tighter than those of their male counterparts, and of Peruvians in general. Although traditional gender ideology restricted Salvadoran women's social interaction with members of the opposite sex, many participants found alternative mechanisms to advance their commercial goals. Thus, some replenished their ethnic and gender-based social capital through active involvement in women-dominated local and transnational community networks. While such networks cemented women's co-national ties, significantly increasing their bonding social capital, some Salvadoran informants also managed to develop weak ties to American mainstream institutions. In this sense, they remained less marginalized, with networks better suited than their co-national men's at acquiring resources beyond immediate circles. To this extent, according to social network theory, Salvadoran women's networks were most effective at advancing members' instrumental and expressive goals.

In contrast, Salvadoran men's networks, while dense and rich in bonding social capital, did not present such incipient bridges to the mainstream. Nevertheless, traditional gender ideology granted them some advantages over women, as they were able to access a broader range of financial and marketing resources, and enjoyed unrestricted spatial mobility and social interaction, including assistance exchanges with members of the opposite sex. None of these actions entailed social stigmatization within the community. Therefore, Salvadoran men's networks were particularly efficient at maintaining network resources, but less so at acquiring new assets.

Inversely, Peruvian participants' networks were particularly effective at accruing bridging social capital, thus advancing their members' instrumental actions. Their ability to bridge to mainstream institutions was a manifestation of their larger class endowments and higher acculturation to American society. Therefore, their bridging social capital allowed those members best positioned within the network to take advantage of opportunities that enabled some of their businesses to develop faster and/ or to enter higher profit margin industries.

Notwithstanding, Peruvian men's and women's networks differed in important respects. Patriarchal gender ideology, although occasionally diluted by informants' class endowments, also granted Peruvian men better access to wider financing and marketing opportunities than women. Free from the need to reconcile private and public responsibilities, men were often able to find more space and time to network with fellow businessmen, although not necessarily co-ethnics. Unlike their Salvadoran counterparts, Peruvian women were not as actively engaged in community activities and, hence, their networks did not benefit from strong ties among co-ethnic women. In sum, the social embeddedness of Peruvian men's and women's networks seemed less effective at maintaining collective resources.

Accordingly, findings from this study suggest that the social embeddedness of Salvadoran and Peruvian networks advanced qualitatively distinct types of goals. Whereas most Salvadorans remained relatively satisfied with the idea of starting and maintaining small-scale businesses in the ethnic market, a few Peruvians aspired to develop their businesses to American-stardom standards of capital growth and accumulation. I believe this contrast in informants' aspirations and cultural definitions of commercial success is equally related to their differential levels of acculturation to American society.

As discussed in chapter four, the social embeddedness of immigrant networks is dramatically shaped by the demographic and institutional context of the receiving communities in which they operate. In the case of Washington Salvadoran and Peruvian participants, their entrepreneurial performance is similarly hampered by their geographic embeddedness in a metropolitan area where Latino collective interests need stronger representation, and where competition with other ethnic minorities is stiff. The post 9/11 environment has added complexity to this scenario as social tensions have, ironically, created the conditions for larger Latino mobilization and governance representation across the region.

Latino Entrepreneurs and the Washington Environment: Perceptions and Realities

Chapter four focused on the demand side of Washington Salvadoran and Peruvian entrepreneurship, including informants' and institutional gate-keepers' perception of the regulatory business environment for Latino small business development. The views expressed by institutional representatives to a large extent confirmed informants' perceptions of the Washington opportunity environment. Institutional gatekeepers largely agreed that inadequate federal support for minority small business development efforts adversely affected their programs. They emphasized that lack of funding curtailed their effectiveness as their organizations often found themselves competing for scarce funding rather than collaborating on developing a collective action agenda. Likewise, they explained that jurisdictional boundaries, with dissimilar governance structures across a multi-state metropolitan area, fragmented policy responses to the burgeoning presence of Latino small business owners. For some institutional gatekeepers, their deepest sense of frustration came with the dissonance between the legal status of potential program beneficiaries (many in legal limbo under temporary programs) and the eligibility criteria of their business assistance programs.

Related to the theme of competition within a resource deprived environment, many gatekeepers underscored a lack of effective leadership among Washington Latinos. In their view, this was a major hurdle that prevented their collective advancement, especially vis à vis the clout of more established ethnic minorities and immigrant groups in the region. More recently, the 9/11 terrorist attacks, the general slowdown of the economy, and the rapid demographic transformation of communities unprepared for such change have conspired to foster anti-immigrant sentiment across many suburban Washington localities. Such a hostile context has marginalized many Latino business owners, severely affecting their commercial interests. In fact, in Prince William County, Latino entrepreneurs have suffered as much as 50 to 90 per cent loss in sales after the County's Board of Supervisors passed anti-immigrant resolutions during the summer of 2007 (The Washington Post 2008). Examining the repercussions that such anti-immigrant backlash will have over time—both in terms of its impact on the mobility outcome of the second generation as well as on the economic well-being of receiving communities—would provide important insights into the symbiotic relationship between the immigrant and mainstream economies.

Coinciding with institutional gatekeepers, most Salvadoran and Peruvian study participants felt that small business assistance programs were ineffective at meeting their needs. Whereas most Peruvians perceived less discrimination from mainstream institutions, including less regulatory red tape and personal frictions with mainstream representatives, Salvadoran men, in particular, often felt unfairly targeted. They complained about being discriminated against when it came to filing paperwork or when their stores were inspected for regulatory compliance. As mentioned earlier, Salvadoran women did not share this perception. This might well be a reflection of their well-developed women networks and incipient linkages to mainstream microcredit and other social service agencies, which might assuage their sense of marginality and blocked mobility. Ultimately, participants' perceptions of the opportunities available to them naturally reflected their divergent class, ethnic, and gender-based endowments. This being the case, future research should look at the ways in which class and gender—as well as other stratifying forces—color individuals' perception of and resilience to prejudice, institutional discrimination and other forms of social exclusion.

RECONCEPTUALIZING IMMIGRANT ENTREPRENEURSHIP

So how do Salvadorans' and Peruvians' experiences provide insights into our understanding of immigrant economic incorporation processes in general, and Latino entrepreneurship in particular? In essence, participants' stories illustrate some of the mechanisms through which social structure maintains and reproduces social inequality. At the same time, however, these same stories underscore the role of agency at empowering individuals to reinvent their opportunity structure. While immigrants (and individuals in general) lead their lives within the contours of multidimensional hierarchies of difference (and power) that shape their identity and life chances in inextricable ways, agency empowers them through an increased sense of control over their own lives.

Whereas the new economic scholarship has tended to homogenize immigrant groups, conceived as genderless and without following class or territorial loyalties, findings from this study demonstrate significant variation between and within groups. As the narratives show, gender becomes inextricably interwoven with other structures of difference and the local opportunity structure to differentially position immigrants (men, women, Salvadoran, Peruvian, Salvadoran men, Peruvian women, etc.) along a hierarchy of social and economic locations. Therefore, to best capture nuances in immigrant mobility and opportunity structures, social embeddedness analysis needs to address the intersectionality of multidimensional hierarchies of power in people's lives. In fact, participants' experiences show that, even within the same immigrant group, networks can show uneven embeddedness along gender and/or other socially stratifying structures of difference.

Likewise, and at a broader scale, fictive panethnic labels conceal significant intra and inter group differences. While panethnic identities might be conducive to political mobilization and immigrant integration over time, they can also lead to misconceptions, stereotypes, and overgeneralizations. Recent Latino newcomers, such as participants in this study, tend to naturally reject panethnic identities since they arrive endowed with differing cultural, social, and class tool-kits, despite a common language or colonial ancestry. The shorter the time immigrant groups have had to acculturate to America, the more pronounced the sociodemographic variations within panethnic categories. The American experience would seem to be the ultimate equalizer over time. In fact, recent census data clearly show that in the case of Latin American recent newcomers, their sociodemographic characteristics differ widely according to country of origin (2006).

In examining within panethnic group variation, this book contributes to theorizing on the lesser known experiences of those labeled "Other" Latinos—that is Latinos other than Mexicans, Puerto Ricans, and Cubans. A better understanding of the wide diversity of Latino experiences has become a research imperative given the fast-paced influx of a greater mix of Latino newcomers over the past three decades (Singer et al. 2008). By current projections, if the Latino population continues to experience rapid growth, by 2030 they will constitute about one-fourth of the US population (Rodriguez, Saenz, and Menjivar 2008). In fact, it is within "Other" Latino immigrant groups that the fastest demographic growth is currently taking place (Rumbaut 2006). In sum, by comparing the experiences of Salvadorans and Peruvians, this book begins to address this knowledge gap, situating the entrepreneurial experiences of "Other" Latinos within concrete spaces (Greater Washington area) and historical settings (post-industrial America).

Throughout the book, participants' stories debunk the ethnic solidarity thesis, built upon the notion that social relations among co-ethnics and co-nationals are largely harmonious. Yet, there is clear empirical evidence that the solidarity of immigrant networks is not only contingent on structural forces in the context of reception (Menjivar 2000), but on specific pre-migration characteristics and demographic traits of particular immigrant communities. Thus, while some immigrant groups might show a higher incidence of social solidarity with co-nationals and co-ethnics, others will have fragmented co-national networks stratified along class and racial lines. In that sense, stories in this study bring to bear the limits of reactive ethnicity and social solidarity when class, racial, territorial, and gender hierarchies brought from the homeland shape immigrant identity formation in receiving communities (Paerregaard 2005).

Responding to the ethnic entrepreneurship literature, findings from this study support scholars' contentions that, to develop immigrant economies to their full potential, immigrant groups need to command (and combine) substantial class and ethnic-based resources. From participants' experiences, it is clear that entrepreneurial success can be relative and highly varied between and within ethnic groups. Neither Washington Salvadorans nor Peruvians manage to combine the magnitude of class and/or ethnic endowments necessary to develop their economies to ethnic enclave levels. Nevertheless, such assessment rests on scholars' traditional assumption that immigrant entrepreneurial success exclusively means superior economic performance. Given divergent cultural definitions of success (entrepreneurial and otherwise), it might be appropriate to broaden economic exclusive perspectives to account for the cultural, social, personal, family, and community aspects of business ownership. Therefore, this study moves away from an elitist entrepreneurial focus to provide a baseline of information on the lesser-known experiences of small-scale business owners. This is data that is critical given that Latino immigrant entrepreneurship is primarily a non-employer phenomenon (Robles and Cordero-Guzman 2007; Valdez 2008).

Equally important, in the process of unveiling within group variation, this study engenders the immigrant entrepreneurial experience. In so doing, it rectifies historical androcentric biases that have neglected gender as a main organizing category of social and economic life. Participants' narratives suggest that Salvadoran and Peruvian entrepreneurial options, practices, and decisions remain largely shaped by patriarchal gender relations within the family and immigrant community. Men's and women's access to capital, labor, and information, and their marketing and business styles, are regulated by varying degrees of patriarchal ideology, including the gendered division of labor within the immigrant family and economy. Social stigmatization, sexual predation, sexual harassment, and other forms of social control differentially affect men's and women's spatial mobility, options, aspirations, and value systems as they engage in economic life, including entrepreneurial activities. In other words, entrepreneurial practices are as gendered as any other type of human behavior.

Participants' stories also confirm that men and women participate in gendered networks. Whereas some immigrant women and men manage to effectively mobilize resources through same sex networks, others rely less on such connections, but draw larger benefits from class or ethnic-based resources. The experiences of Washington Salvadorans and Peruvians suggest that, for those immigrant women at the lower end of the social hierarchy, same sex and/or co-ethnic networks can often allow them to resist simultaneous forms of oppression in their new environment. For example, many immigrant women from lower socioeconomic background are forced to establish, and benefit from, connections to mainstream social institutions they resort to in their roles as family care providers. Others capitalize on the newfound camaraderie among co-ethnic women who serve as informal mentors, initiating newcomers into the retail trade business. Instead, some immigrant men coming from similar social circumstances become ghettoized in the ethnic community because of limited exposure to outside circles. Others, on the other hand, even suffer status loss and a profound sense of inadequacy, unable to fulfill masculine identity roles. In extreme cases, they even become marginalized from co-national friends and acquaintances. Thus, gender is intertwined with other structures of difference to condition men's and women's trajectories in multifaceted ways.

In a similar vein, participants' experiences confirm studies on the differential effects of gendered social capital among immigrants (Grasmuck and Grosfoguel 1997; Curran and Saguy 2001; Curran and Rivero-Fuentes 2003). But do gendered networks, and the social capital they accrue, empower or disempower participants in this study? Neither the literature nor findings from this study provide a straightforward answer, as the quality of social capital is contingent on the intersection of gender with other stratifying forces. For example, among female study participants, only Salvadoran entrepreneurs, not Peruvians, are able to cement strong ties with fellow co-national and co-ethnic women whom they initially rely on to get started on their own. In contrast, men's social capital tends to revolve around ties with fellow businessmen and acquaintances they resort to for advice and guidance. Whereas Salvadoran men's ties ghettoize them to the ethnic community, many Peruvians suffer significant status loss, becoming marginalized from co-national friends and acquaintances. Yet, other Peruvians manage to broaden their ties to prosperous external circles. Clearly, the evidence resists one-size-fits-all answers.

Remarkably, most Salvadoran and Peruvian participants describe entrepreneurship as a source of empowerment, which liberated them from constraining gender and/or economic oppression—even when entrepreneurship took the shape of an economic survival strategy. As seen in previous chapters, entrepreneurship granted immigrant women an escape route from patriarchal power relations. As women became engaged in the daily grind of running a business, they gained not only business knowledge, but also newfound freedoms and increased self-esteem. In fact, many talked about the power their entrepreneurial status had granted them to confront, control, and negotiate with their husbands, gaining the respect of their families as key decision-makers. Similarly, despite status incongruence for some, entrepreneurial ventures provided men a venue to compensate for status loss and lowered self-esteem. Although some entrepreneurial experiences provided significantly more social status and upward mobility than others, entrepreneurship allowed both men and women to recover a sense of autonomy and control over their new American lives.

Policy Implications

The development of Latino immigrant small businesses has far-reaching policy implications for immigrant integration, social welfare, and economic development strategies, including microenterprise and neighborhood revitalization approaches. The following discussion considers some of the concerns raised by findings from this study.

In America, immigrant entrepreneurship has long been an upward mobility strategy, providing newcomers and their children an alternative pathway towards economic integration into mainstream society. Focusing on entrepreneurship as a form of immigrant integration broadens the politically contentious immigrant debate beyond zero-sum conceptions of economic benefits; it also brings to the forefront the multiple contributions that immigrant groups stand to make to American society as they turn from immigrants to ethnic Americans. This is most clearly the case for Latino newcomers and their children, who comprise much of the current and future US population growth in years to come, and on whose economic productivity America's future aging, mostly white, baby-boomer population will need to rely on. Yet, because Latino immigrants comprise most of the undocumented, they have become increasingly vulnerable to intimidation tactics, exploitative working conditions, discrimination, and scapegoating. In fact, despite their well documented economic and civic contributions to America, the post 9/11 era seems to have exacerbated their vulnerability, further blocking their economic and social integration into mainstream society.

But effective immigrant integration goes beyond ensuring the future via-
bility of engaged citizens and a competitive workforce; it also serves to recreate a shared sense of national identity, a common sense of belonging that
benefits both newcomers as well as natives. In fact, the literature provides
substantive evidence that communities which provide all residents with
equal access to services and mainstream institutions are healthier, safer,
more prosperous, more inclusive, and richer in social capital than those that
do not. Integrated communities diffuse social tensions, reduce crime rates,
and offer broad financial access to all residents (Paulson et al. 2006).[12] Thus
framed, immigrant integration becomes salient and public policies informed
by a nuanced understanding of the complex forces shaping newcomers'
lives—especially their capacity to engage in productive activities that produce jobs, wealth, leadership opportunities, and tax revenue for state and
federal governments—become a demographic and moral imperative.

Almost exclusively, effective immigrant integration is predicated upon
the ability of newcomers to achieve economic prosperity and ensure, over
time, intergenerational mobility. Most importantly, collective wealth creation strategies can transcend the economic success of individual entrepreneurs, since they have valuable spillover effects on community-building and
social capital, conducive to the healthy adaptation of the second generation
and preventing the ghettoization of the dispossessed (Zhou 2004). Whether
through launching business start-ups, increasing homeownership rates, and/
or becoming engaged in asset building and alternative investment strategies,
immigrants mobilize resources to leverage wealth creation opportunities so
they can give their families a better life. For Latino business owners, entrepreneurship is not just as a strategy to overcome discrimination, but also a
means for intergenerational upward mobility (Raijiman and Tienda 2000).

Nonetheless, immigrant economic integration, including their engagement in entrepreneurial activities, is predicated on newcomer's ability to
access a wide range of financial products so they can benefit from those most
cost-effective. Yet, as illustrated through study participants' stories, Latino
immigrants remain a grossly untapped market for mainstream financial
institutions. According to recent studies, as many as 50 per cent of Latinos
are currently "unbanked," which means that half of them prefer to resort
to check cashing and wire transfer firms for banking and remittance needs,
despite paying inflated transaction fees (Fix, Zimmermann, and Passel 2001;
Martinez 2007). Once in the United States, many newcomers operate in a
"cash" economy that disadvantages them in a number of ways. It makes them
vulnerable to robbery; it prevents them from participating in credit and asset
building savings and investments programs; it forces them to pay exorbitant
fees for financial services and, ultimately, it slows down their integration
into the fabric of American society. Salvadorans, in particular, together with
other Central Americans and Mexicans, remain some of the most vulnerable
Latino newcomers. In fact, 44 per cent of all Salvadoran immigrants have
neither savings nor checking accounts (Paulson et al. 2006).

As stories in this book show, lack of trust in financial institutions, language, culture, education, gender, legal status, and other factors discourage immigrants from accessing services that provide a foundation for financial security, economic prosperity, and mobility. Chapters five and six show that small business owners primarily resort to personal assets—whether through savings or ethnic credit (personal loans)—for start-up capital. Only when these avenues had been fully explored were a few participants (especially Salvadoran women and Peruvian men) willing to resort to ethnic and/or mainstream banks. Such dissimilar borrowing practices underlines that Latino entrepreneurship encompasses a wide array of experiences: upwardly mobile business owners, survivalist entrepreneurs, immigrants with a college education, immigrants with limited financial and English language literacy, transnational or nationally-bound business owners, and second generation immigrant entrepreneurs. Further, whereas many Latino immigrants come from sending communities with weak financial institutions, others arrive with extraordinary financial sophistication.

Acknowledging this diversity, policymakers need to move away from one-size-fits-all policies for minority entrepreneurs and take into account differences in skills and needs of target sub-populations so as to develop the potentialities of those with higher human capital endowments, and of those who need assistance with basic entrepreneurial skills (Robles and Cordero-Guzman 2007). To eliminate barriers to Latino entrepreneurship, there are several actions that federal, state, and municipal governments might want to take. First, mainstream agencies and Latino community organizations could establish synergistic partnerships to facilitate the transitioning of Latino newcomers into mainstream banking. To this end, they could provide low-cost financial services, integrated to both asset building vehicles (IDA accounts, mortgage loans) and education programs, which would prepare Latinos to make more informed financial decisions, protect them from predatory lending practices, and provide them with necessary tools to navigate the US business regulatory environment.

Second, to further facilitate Latinos' financial integration, community development agencies could encourage the establishment of formally regulated Latino credit unions beyond ethnic banks. Staffed by bilingual and bicultural personnel, such institutions could make an important contribution towards increasing newcomers' consumer confidence in, and familiarization with, American mainstream banking. At the same time, alternative institutions, such as microenterprise programs, should continue to aid low-income immigrant entrepreneurs to build credit records that could eventually allow their graduation to mainstream banking.

Third, unequivocally, the evidence shows that training and technical assistance programs remain the most effective mechanism to reduce failure rates among nascent businesses. Yet, in the wake of the Bush administration's systematic dismantling of the PRIME budget—which went from 15 million in 2001 to two million in 2007—the institutional capacity of community and intermediary organizations offering such programs to low-income entrepreneurs has plummeted. Ironically, as findings from this study suggest, it is precisely technical assistance and training programs—and less so access to commercial credit—that the vast majority of junior entrepreneurs need most. Therefore, both aspiring and seasoned entrepreneurs would largely benefit from having access to adequately funded and culturally competent training and technical assistance programs.

Accordingly, to better address the needs of low-income Latino entrepreneurs, existing programs need to develop effective outreach strategies. These might include: 1) hiring bilingual personnel capable of both cementing personal relationships based on trust as well as of grasping Latino market dynamics; 2) producing informational materials in Spanish and English; 3) accepting alternative documentation for personal identification (such as Individual Taxpayer Identification Numbers); and 4) offering integrated education programs (i.e. financial literacy, basic entrepreneurship, homeownership) in Spanish, one-on-one counseling, and late and evening hours to accommodate work schedules of potential clients. Finally, policymakers and practitioners might want to review participant eligibility criteria to accommodate the unmet demand from those caught in between transitory and resident legal statuses.

As important, beyond its contribution to wealth creation and effective immigrant integration, Latino entrepreneurship serves community development goals in significant ways. This is particularly the case for businesses in ethnic niches ("tiendas," grocery stores, etc.), which provide a wide array of valuable services to recent newcomers, ranging from translation to notarized services, to community referrals to tax assistance (Levitt 1995). In the process of selling nostalgic clients commodities reminiscent of home, ethnic businesses (Latino and others) often cement community ties in the context of a familiar albeit new milieu. Therefore, in tangible ways, ethnic businesses lie at the intersection of the new and the old, literally connecting immigrants' worlds in a unified social space.

Ultimately, for most study participants, entrepreneurship unleashed a virtuous cycle of economic prosperity, community well-being, and inner sense of belonging to American society. Unequivocally, their ventures—small and large—provided a great source of personal motivation and empowerment, despite obstacles and frustrations along the way. In times of uncertainty and change, as growing socioeconomic inequality, nativism, and economic woes haunt America, immigrant entrepreneurship—in all its manifestations—merits a more nuanced examination given its function as a viable form of economic incorporation and mobility for those new Americans who might need it most. Thus, coming full circle, economic sociology remains, at the dawn of the twenty-first century, as intellectually relevant and vibrant a field as when it emerged over a century ago.

Appendix A
Research Instruments

[English version]
Contact Information_____ _Phone Survey_____Face to face_____
Respondent #_____Date_____

<u>Initial Survey Interview Questionnaire</u>

1) Sex:
   (a) Male
   (b) Female

2) Nationality
   (a) Salvadoran
   (b) Peruvian

3) How old are you?

4) What is the highest level of education you have completed?
   (a) Some primary school, no diploma
   (b) Primary school diploma
   (c) Some high school, no diploma
   (d) High school diploma
   (e) Some college but no degree
   (f) Bachelor's degree
   (g) Master's degree
   (h) Ph.D. degree
   (i) Professional degree
   (j) Vocational and technical degree

5) Other. Please specify: _____Where did you finish your education?
   (a) I finished my education in El Salvador/Peru
   (b) I finished my education in the United States
   (c)I completed my education in both countries
   (d)I finished my education in another country. Please specify_____

6) What is your marital status?
   (a) Single
   (b) Separated
   (c) Married
   (d) Divorced
   (e) Widowed

7) How many children do you have?
   (a) None
   (b) 1–2
   (c) 3–5
   (d) More than 6

8) Do you own a house or rent an apartment?
   (a) Own house/apartment
   (b) Rent apartment/house/room/mobile home
   (c) Other

9) Were you fluent in English upon your arrival to the US?
   (a) No
   (b) Very little
   (c) Somewhat
   (d) Considerably
   (e) Totally fluent

10) Are you fluent now?
    (a) No
    (b) Very little
    (c) Somewhat
    (d) Considerably
    (e) Totally Fluent

11) What year did you arrive in the US?

12) Did you come to this country alone or with your family?
    (a) Alone
    (b) With Wife
    (c) With wife and children
    (d) With wife, children and parents
    (e) With parents

13) What was the main reason you came to the US?

14) Are you planning to stay here or return to your home country?
    (a) Return home

(b) Establish here
(c) Don't Know
(d) Other

15) What was your occupation before you left your home country?

16) What were your parents' occupations?

17) Do you currently have a business in this area or are you planning to open one soon?
(a) I currently have a business.
(b) I don't have a business yet but would like to open one soon.
(c) I had a business but I had to close it.

18) What type of business do you have or would like to have one day?

19) Did you have a business in your country of origin or somewhere else?
(a) Yes
(b) No

20) What type of business did you have back home?

21) What is the zip code of your business?

22) How long have you had this business in the US?

23) How long did you have your business in your home country? (If Yes to 19)

24) Did you receive help from others when you started your business back home?
(a) Yes
(b) No
(c) N/A

25) How did those who helped you the most help you?
(a) They gave me information about the type and location of the businesses
(b) They lent me money
(c) They gave me training in their stores
(d) They put me in contact with their suppliers, distributors, or creditor
(e) They recommended me and increased my clientele.
(f) Other. Please specify
(g) N/A

26) Did you receive help from family, friends and acquaintances when you
    started your business in the US?
    (a) Yes
    (b) No
    (c) N/A

27) If you received help, which people helped you the most when starting
    your business?
    (a) Family
    (b) Friends
    (c) Institutions (i.e. banks, community organizations)
    (d) Acquaintances
    (e) Others. Please specify_____
    (f) N/A.

28) How did those who helped you the most help you here in the US?
    (a) They gave me information about the type and location of the busi-
        nesses
    (b) They lent me money
    (c) They gave me training in their stores
    (d) They put me in contact with their suppliers, distributors, or creditor
    (e) They recommended me and increased my clientele.
    (f) Other. Please specify:
    (g) N/A

29) Do you have any business partner(s)? If yes, how many?

30) Did you buy this business from somebody else or did you start it on
    your own?
    (a) I started it as a new business
    (b) I bought it from another Salvadoran man
    (c) I bought it from another Salvadoran woman
    (d) I bought it from another Peruvian man.
    (e) I bought it from another Peruvian woman.
    (f) I bought it from another Latino man.
    (g) I bought it from another Latina.
    (h) I bought it from a non-Latino man
    (i) I bought it from a non-Latino woman.
    (j) N/A

31) How long do you plan on being self-employed?

32) Before starting this business (either in your host country or the US), did
    you have the same work experience or any training or experiences in a
    business like you have now?

(a) Yes
(b) No
(c) N/A

33) Where is your business located (US)?
(a) Office building
(b) My house
(c) Shopping mall
(d) In the street
(e) In a store
(f) Other. Please specify_____

34) What type of neighborhood is your business located in?
(a) A predominant black neighborhood
(b) A predominant Hispanic neighborhood
(c) A predominant non-Hispanic white neighborhood
(d) A racially mixed neighborhood

35) What type of market do you target?
(a) Latin
(b) African-American
(c) Non Hispanic White
(d) Multicultural
(e) Don't know

36) Who is mainly in charge of your business?

37) Are many of your employees of your same nationality?
(a) Yes
(b) No
(c) Not necessarily
(d) N/A

38) And of Latino origin?
(a) Yes
(b) No
(c) Not necessarily
(d) N/A

39) How many people including yourself work in this business?

40) Of the people who work with you, how many work full-time and part-time?

41) Does your wife/husband work with you at your business?

    (a) Yes
    (b) No
    (c) N/A

42) Do your children work with you at this business?
    (a) Yes
    (b) No
    (c) N/A

43) Do other relatives help you in your business?
    (a) Yes
    (b) No
    (c) N/A

44) Please tell me about business regulations or business training opportunities targeted to entrepreneurs like you that have made it harder or easier for you to start your own business?

45) Which business regulations have affected you directly:
    (a) Zoning Laws
    (b) Labor standards
    (c) Licensing requirements
    (d) Types of loans and programs available/unavailable for entrepreneurs like you
    (e) Government sponsored business training courses and outreach programs
    (f) Tax Laws
    (g) Don't know
    (h) N/A
    (i) Other: _____

In-Depth Interview Protocol [English version]

Opening Questions

    a) Can you tell me about your business? For example, what exactly do you do here every day?
    b) How long have you been in this business?
    c) How many people do you employ?

Self-Employment Motive

    a) Can you tell me a little about yourself? For example, why did you decide to go into business?

b) And why did you choose this line of business?

c) I would like to ask your opinion: Some people prefer working for someone else because that way they know they get a check every week. Other people do not like to work for someone else because they want to be their own boss, or can make more money this way. What do you think?

Business Strategies

1. Labor

Hiring Practices and Ethnic Boundaries

a) Now I would like to ask some questions about the people who work for you. Are any of your employees of your same nationality and/or other Latinos? Are they related to you in some way?

Hiring Practices and Trust

b) Some owners say that they prefer to hire workers that they know. How do you feel about this?

Gender Preferences in Hiring Practices

c) Some owners say they prefer to hire women/men workers. How do you feel about this?

Labor-Management Relations

d) Can you tell me about some of the working arrangements you allow for your employees? For example, do you allow flexible working hours or do you allow employees to bring their children to the work site?

2. Financing

a) Some owners need help to get started in their business. For example, some owners get money by applying for a bank loan, or borrowing money from friends/relatives. Others use personal savings. Where did you get the capital to start this business?

b) How much money did you need to start your business?

3. Ethnic Boundaries, Gender and Commercial Solidarity

(a) Some business owners do business with members of other ethnic groups. Can you tell me about your clientele, vendors and distributors? Are they co-nationals, co-ethnics or from other ethnic groups?

b) Do you feel there is more solidarity and trust when you conduct business transactions with other Latinos? What about with other Salvadorans/Peruvians?
c) What about conducting business with women and/or men?

Social Networks

a) Do you have friends or relatives who work in this industry, outside of your business?
b) Can you tell me about them? For example, how did they get involved in the business and what do they do?
c) We all have friends, acquaintances and relatives we go for help when we need it. Can you list the persons (men and women) you would consult with if you had business problems and needed someone's advice?
d) Can you now list those other persons you know less well but who you might consider contacting because of their expertise or know-how in business?
e) Can you tell me about different ways in which your men and women friends/relatives and other compatriots or Latinos have helped you in starting your business?
f) Are you a member of any cultural, sports, religious, commercial or professional association? Are these women and men-dominated groups? Do you participate in these activities often?

Local Opportunity Structure

a) Can you tell me a little about the business regulations in your state?
b) Do you think they have helped you or that they had made it more difficult to start your own business? [if necessary probe with examples on specific regulations such as zoning laws, licenses required, insurance]
c) Are you aware of any business training opportunities available to you? If such exist, have you participated in any of these? If not, why not?

Closing

Is there anything else you would like to tell me about?

Appendix B
Study Participants Data

SALVADORAN AND PERUVIAN STUDY PARTICIPANTS

The 107 respondents to the initial survey interview and the 45 in-depth interviewees show similar sociodemographic profiles. Notwithstanding, there are important differences between the Salvadoran and Peruvian populations, as well as between the male and female populations in the sample. Fifty-three per cent of survey respondents were male and 47 per cent were female while, in the intensive interviews, 49 per cent of respondents were female and 51 per cent were male. On average, Salvadorans were younger than Peruvians and men were younger than women. Salvadoran men's and women's average age was 39 and 41 years respectively, whereas Peruvian men's and women's average age was 42 and 46 years respectively. Congruent with census data trends, most Peruvian and Salvadoran study participants arrived to the United States during the last three decades.

Salvadoran participants revealed lower levels of educational attainment than Peruvians, and women lower levels than men. Further, Salvadoran women were the only study participants reporting no formal education (four per cent). Nevertheless, to compensate, they were the sub-group with the strongest parental role models in the trade professions, and those with the longest self-employment history. Congruent with their higher self-employment rates, 31 per cent of Salvadoran women engaged in self-employment from the time of arrival to the US, whereas only eight per cent of Peruvian women engaged in similar activities. Yet, 46 per cent of Peruvian women study participants completed undergraduate education, and 21 per cent had attained graduate degrees.

Salvadoran men also showed lower educational levels than their Peruvian counterparts. Yet the gaps between male sub-populations were not as striking as that between both groups of women. Whereas 43 per cent of Salvadoran men reported having received or completed undergraduate education, 55 per cent of Peruvians did, and while four per cent of Salvadoran men indicated having completed post-graduate level work, 18 per cent of their Peruvian counterparts did. Likewise, Peruvians also reported higher levels of US education than Salvadorans. In fact, more of them studied both in the US and at home, with a fair amount having received education in as many as three countries.

Participants' backgrounds varied significantly, and included people who had been rural poor, small landowners, urban lower-middle class, middle-class, and a couple of upper middle class individuals. Before their migration, the occupation of the 107 survey respondents and of the 45 in-depth interviewees included medical doctors, nurses, accountants, teachers, small business owners, agricultural laborers, factory operators, soldiers, homemakers, professors, secretaries, and street vendors. Again, national origin was a strong determinant of participants' socioeconomic status, and while a large number of Peruvians reported prior professional and managerial occupations, Salvadorans reported occupations such as agricultural laborer, machinery operator, and small business owner. Overall, Salvadorans came from less service-oriented and more agricultural economies, with more women in the manual and factory-related occupations, and Peruvians from predominantly professional and managerial backgrounds in service oriented industries.

Unequivocally, Peruvian study participants arrived to the US with a higher command of the English language than Salvadorans. In fact, 77 per cent of Salvadoran women and 65 per cent of Salvadoran men reported no knowledge of the English language upon arrival, whereas only 29 per cent of Peruvian women and 26 per cent of Peruvian men did. Although Salvadoran participants showed a positive progression towards English language acquisition over time, Peruvians reported having achieved fluency faster, despite their large numbers of recent arrivals.

Both Salvadorans and Peruvians were predominantly in marital unions. Sixty-seven and 77 per cent of Peruvian and Salvadoran women, respectively, and 67 and 78 per cent of Peruvian and Salvadoran men were married. On average, Salvadorans had more children than Peruvians, and women had more children than men. Most study participants (70 per cent) lived in owned housing either with close relatives or extended kin. The remainder lived in rented rooms, by themselves, or with a spouse and/or children. They lived across various neighborhoods in the Washington metro area, and their businesses were located in urban and suburban neighborhoods such as Petworth, Columbia Heights, and Mount Pleasant in the District, Culmore and Arlandria in Northern Virginia, or Langley Park, Gaithersburg, and Wheaton in the Maryland suburbs.

In-Depth Interviewees

Respondent	Age	Sex	Nationality	Business Type
1. Reina	46	Female	Salvadoran	Restaurant
2. Blanca	47	Female	Salvadoran	Restaurant
3. Agustina	46	Female	Salvadoran	Apparel retail
4. Antonieta	48	Female	Salvadoran	Apparel retail
5. Ana Maria	38	Female	Salvadoran	Apparel retail
6. Sandra	33	Female	Salvadoran	Apparel retail
7. Rocibel	41	Female	Salvadoran	Beauty salon
8. Merci	39	Female	Salvadoran	Janitorial
9. Karla	29	Female	Salvadoran	Art/ Art retail
10. Mercedes	44	Female	Salvadoran	Home day care
11. Yolanda	33	Female	Salvadoran	Beauty salon
12. Haydee	30	Female	Salvadoran	Restaurant
13. Maria G.	50	Female	Peruvian	Restaurant
14. Grace	47	Female	Peruvian	Gourmet catering
15. Elsa	59	Female	Peruvian	Restaurant
16. Maria P.	42	Female	Peruvian	Carry-out
17. Silvia P.	37	Female	Peruvian	Retail
18. Gladys	41	Female	Peruvian	Party supplies
19. Carmen	51	Female	Peruvian	Bridal retail
20. Yanine	43	Female	Peruvian	Janitorial
21. Juana	47	Female	Peruvian	Catering
22. Clara	50	Female	Peruvian	Janitorial / Retail
23. Dori	52	Female	Peruvian	Entertainment /Marketing
24. Elizabeth	35	Female	Peruvian	Accounting
25. Silvia J.	42	Female	Peruvian	Wholesale jewelry
26. Samuel	30	Male	Salvadoran	Construction
27. Carlos R.	38	Male	Salvadoran	Home Improvement
28. Marlon B.	33	Male	Salvadoran	Home Improvement
29. Luis	40	Male	Salvadoran	Restaurant
30. Vidal	43	Male	Salvadoran	Restaurant
31. Carlos C.	45	Male	Salvadoran	Grocery Store
32. Henry	33	Male	Salvadoran	Accountant

continued

continued

33. Roberto H.	34	Male	Salvadoran	Newspaper/Press
34. Roberto J.	50	Male	Salvadoran	Multipurpose store
35. Salvador	30	Male	Salvadoran	Janitorial
36. Javier	27	Male	Peruvian	Painting
37. Roberto A.	50	Male	Peruvian	Painting
38. Fernando	43	Male	Peruvian	Carry-out
39. Esteban	46	Male	Peruvian	Marketing /Publisher
40. Carlos M.	48	Male	Peruvian	Transportation
41. Edi	26	Male	Peruvian	Grocery store
42. Ricardo	49	Male	Peruvian	Marketing / Communications
43. Arturo	52	Male	Peruvian	Janitorial
44. Maco	41	Male	Peruvian	Marketing / Communications
45. Jose	38	Male	Peruvian	Information Technology

Table 8   Appendix B: Survey Interviewees

Business Industries	Salvadorans		Peruvians	
	Women	Men	Women	Men
Food and Drink Retail				
Restaurant/Carry-out	5	7	4	2
Grocery Store	3	3	0	2
Bakery	1	1	0	0
Gourmet Coffee Distributor	0	0	1	0
Catering	0	0	1	0
Other Retail				
Apparel Retail (clothes, music & misc.)	8	1	1	0
Floors, Tiles and Carpet Retail	0	0	1	0
Printer and Party supplies	0	0	2	0
Jewelry, Gold & Watches	0	0	1	0
Travel Agency/International Courier	0	1	1	1
Bookstore and Other services (i.e. notary public, translations)	1	1	1	0
Atelier/Studio Painting/Portraits	1	0	0	0
Water Filters and Household Appliances	0	0	0	1
Car Dealership	0	0	0	1
Scientific Press	0	0	0	1
Wholesale Retail	0	0	1	0

continued

continued

Export/Import				
Export/Import of Crafts and Clothes	0	0	2	0
Export/Import of Defense Equipment	0	0	0	1
Services				
Beauty Salon	3	0	2	0
Childcare Services	2	0	1	0
Laundromat	0	0	0	1
Residential and Commercial Janitorial	2	1	4	3
Commercial and Residential Carpet Cleaning	0	0	0	1
Commercial and Residential Moving Services	0	0	0	3
Airport Transportation Franchise	0	0	0	1
Professional Accounting, Legal and Medical Services	0	2	1	3
Consulting Services	0	1	0	0
Communications & high-tech information technology	0	1	1	5
Marketing	0	0	0	1
Entertainment	0	0	1	1
Construction				
Home Remodeling	0	3	0	4
Commercial and Residential Painting	0	0	0	2
Aluminum Restoration	0	1	0	0
Manufacturing				
Tortilla Factory	0	0	0	1
Total	26	23	26	35

Notes

NOTES TO THE FOREWORD

1. McLoone, Sharon. *Small Business.* 2008. (http://voices.washingtonpost. com/small-business/2008/05/women). Retrieved on September 23, 2008.
2. Center for Women's Business Research. 2006. *Business Owned by Women of Color in the United States, 2004: A Fact Sheet,* http://www. womensbusinessresearch.org/minority/BusinessOwnedbyWomen of Color in the US.pdf) and National Women's Business Council. 2006. *Fact Sheet: Latinas and Entrepreneurship.* http://www.nwbc.gov. Retrieved on September 23, 2008.

NOTES TO CHAPTER 1

1. The Greater Washington region ranks high among Immigrant receiving destinations. According to Singer (2007), it ranks as the seventh largest metropolitan concentration of immigrants in the US. Likewise, the US Department of Homeland Security lists Washington-Arlington-Alexandria-Rockville, DC-VA-MD-WV, as the fourth most popular metropolitan destination for legal immigrants in 2007. Further, the Washington-Baltimore-Northern Virginia metropolitan area also ranks seventh among the top twelve combined metropolitan statistical areas with the largest numbers of Hispanic-owned firms in the US (US Census Bureau 2002).
2. For example, the Survey of Minority and Women-Owned Business Enterprises and the Characteristics of Business Owners' Survey compares selected socio-demographic characteristics among minority, women, non-minority male, and all business owners and businesses.
3. In-depth interviewees were offered $30 dollars for their participation.

NOTES TO CHAPTER 2

1. Centrality refers to the number of ties a particular member in a network has with other members of that same network. Size refers to the number of participants in a network and density to the distinct ties that bind together different members of a network such as family, religion, work, etc.
2. To a certain extent, Light acknowledges that ethnic economies are often fraught with within group variation. He terms this "internal ethnicity." See Light (1993).

3. Phizacklea defines "gendered economy" as a set of entrepreneurial activities inside the overall economy, characterized by family firms in which women's labor power provides the backbone of cheap labor costs and low wages.

NOTES TO CHAPTER 3

1. Central Americans constitute 8.2 per cent of the total US Hispanic population and Salvadorans make up 41 per cent of this share. Mexicans lead the way with 65.5 per cent of the total U.S. Hispanic population, Puerto Ricans make up 8.6 per cent, and South Americans make up 6.0 per cent, with Peruvians representing as much as 18 per cent of this share. Latest Census data show that Mexicans, Central and South Americans are gaining numerical dominance in detriment of Cubans and Puerto Ricans who are decreasing their share because of lower levels of new migrants.
2. Early queries on 2000 Census data showed that information on Latino populations was skewed. In fact, officials in various cities claimed the bureau had significantly underestimated the size of several groups, including Dominicans and Colombians. It seems that large numbers of Latinos failed to identify themselves as belonging to any specific Latino group. Demographers traced the problem to the rewording of a census question about Hispanic ethnicity.
3. Salvadorans use the term 'Department' to convey the idea of municipality or province.
4. Economic Census categories for Latino-owned small businesses have changed through the years. Whereas the 1997 Economic Census included Mexican, Hispanic Latin American (previously called Central or South American), Cuban, Puerto Rican, Other Spanish/Hispanic and Spaniard (previously European Spanish), the latest 2002 Census only distinguishes between four categories: 1) Mexican, Mexican-American, and Chicano; 2) Puerto Rican; 3) Cuban; and 4) Other Spanish/Hispanic/Latino.
5. Several changes to the economic census survey methodology make the data for 2002 not directly comparable to previous survey years, and thus exact estimates of change are not available. Yet, trends shown at the aggregate level seem reliable. Hispanic Latin American's share has grown from 21 to 24 per cent and Other Hispanics from 7 to 15 per cent respectively. Cubans', Mexicans', Puerto Ricans', and Spaniards' share has decreased, although such data should be used with caution because of the methodological limitations described before.
6. Based on 1990 Census data, Barkan estimates Salvadoran women and men's self-employment rate to be 5.9 and 3.8 per cent, respectively. In a different analysis, based on March 2000 CPS data, Camarota reports Salvadorans' self-employment rate to be as low as 2.4 per cent and Peruvians' as high as 13.5 per cent. Somewhat in the middle, based on 1990 Census data on the Foreign-Born population, Light and Gold estimate Salvadorans' self-employment rate at 4.9 per cent and Peruvians' at 6.9 per cent.
7. Self-employment rates depict self-employed individuals of a particular ethnic group as percentage of total employed. To calculate self-employment rates for particular ancestry groups, analysts divide the number of self-employed persons in the group by the total size of the group, and multiply it by 1,000. The total self-employment rate is partly a function of the sex ratio of the group and, therefore, it can be subject to slight variations. If the group were female-dominated, then it would have a slightly lower self-employment rate than if male-preponderant.
8. Even back in the early 1990s, Repak's research claimed that 200,000 Central Americans alone resided in the Washington DC area (Repak, 1995:33).

9. El Salvador, Mexico, and Peru are the leading Latin American source countries in the Washington metropolitan region. Further, El Salvador ranked number one among the top 10 immigrant-sending countries to the area. See Singer, A. et al. (2008).

10. Journalists brought Intipucá to public attention as early as 1979. In 1986, Salvadoran sociologist Segundo Montes conducted survey research in Intipucá and among Salvadorans in DC and, throughout the 1980s and 1990s, journalists from all over the world reported on Intipucá and its unique ties to DC.

11. The Washington Post, Harvard University, and the Kaiser Foundation conducted a phone survey of Washington Latinos between the months of June and August of 2000. 603 Latino adults were interviewed in either Spanish and/or English across the metro area and compared to a control group of 309 Washington non-Latinos and to a national sample of 1,814 Latinos and 1,888 non-Latinos. See the Washington Post, January 2000.

12. "Arlandria" is the geographical area where Alexandria and Arlington converge. This neighborhood is home to one of the Latino communities with highest density of Salvadoran residents and businesses.

13. Interstate 495 encircles Washington DC and is commonly referred to as the Capital Beltway.

14 In Virginia, Other Spanish/Hispanic Latinos own 67.3 per cent of all Latino businesses while in Maryland and in the District of Columbia they own 74.6 and 66.6 per cent, respectively (Economic Census, 2002).

15. In her research on Latino-owned businesses in the DC area, Pessar's ethnosurvey indicated that Salvadorans, Peruvians, and Bolivians remained the top three groups with higher representation in the area's small business community. El Salvador is the indisputable top country of birth for immigrants to the District of Columbia as well as to the Northern Virginia and Maryland suburbs. Peru figures as the only other South American nation among the top ten countries of birth for immigrants to Virginia, the District of Columbia, and Maryland.

16. South and Central Americans constitute 90 per cent of the Langley Park, 88 per cent of the Bailey Crossroads, 87 per cent of the Arlington County, 83 per cent of the Alexandria, 81 per cent of the Fairfax and Montgomery Counties, and 81 per cent of the District of Columbia Latino population (2000 Census).

NOTES TO CHAPTER 4

1. For a brief historical overview of US governmental policies towards minority businesses and a critical evaluation of its programs, see Aldrich et al, 1990.

2. Racial and ethnic minorities are presumed to be socially disadvantaged, and business owners' net worth should not exceed $250,000, not counting their equity in their home and business, to qualify as economically disadvantaged.

3. CARECEN also redefined its organizational purpose later on, expanding the array of social services it provided Central American immigrants and also broadening access to its services to non-FMLN members.

4. The riots spanned through three days of looting and violence sparked by the wounding of a Salvadoran man by a novice DC police officer. Subsequent inquiries by the Washington Lawyers' Committee, the US Civil Rights Commission, and the now-defunct Latino Civil Rights Task Force found that the community backlash was caused by frustration from years of harassment and discrimination. The Civil Rights Commission concluded that Latinos

in Washington were routinely abused by police and were denied "basic civil rights to an extent that was appalling." The panel said institutional obstacles in DC government denied Hispanics equal opportunities in employment, education, social services, and the criminal justice system.

5. The Latino Civil Rights Task Force was created to monitor allegations of abuse and to pressure city officials to hire more Spanish-speaking police officers, fund social programs and open DC government jobs to Hispanics.

6. The actual redefinition of "family" would make persons more than two generations removed from the head of the household eligible to be legally evicted from single-family homes. These attempts to address overcrowding in the city of Manassas have not been successful. The US department of Justice is investigating complaints by residents, civil right groups, and the US Department of Housing and Urban Development that the city illegally targeted Hispanic families in the enforcement of zoning laws. Complaints are also pending against the city with the US Department of Education from four Hispanic families who claim the Manassas public school system turned over students' records to zoning inspectors without notifying the children's parents, a violation of the Family Educational Rights and Privacy Act.

7. The Board consists of 21 citizen members appointed by the Governor, 15 of whom must be of Latino descent

8. There are many debates about the merits of microcredit programs and micro-entrepreneurship from an economic revitalization versus an economic development perspective. Community Development Corporations such as the LEDC and ECDC, for example, support community asset building through increased micro-entrepreneurship and homeownership, whereas former DC administrations have often sought to bring back large retailers to District neighborhoods.

9. In addition, informants' perceptions on the business regulatory environment varied according to specific industries they were in. Business owners of firms in service industries generally held a positive perception of regulations and their level of complexity while food and drink business owners had the worst outlook. This might be a function of the fact that the latter need to comply with an additional layer of municipal regulations in sanitation, zoning, and food and alcohol licenses.

10. SBA runs a volunteer program called SCORE that makes available to interested parties retired volunteers with some business expertise. These SCORE volunteers assist aspiring entrepreneurs as part of SBA services.

NOTES TO CHAPTER 5

1. Paisanaje is a term derived from 'paisano' which means fellow villager. Paisanaje, thus, signifies close social ties among country fellow villagers.

2. See Landolt's comparison of Salvadorans' labor market typification in Los Angeles and in Washington DC and her references to the distinct demographic dynamics in each community.

NOTES TO CHAPTER 6

1. I use participants' national origin as an imperfect measure of ethnicity. As discussed by Light, national origin conceals important regional, ethnoreligious, and other group variations. He has termed this "internal ethnicity" (1993).

2. This topic needs to be further explored since there is no systematic study of the differences between Latino immigrant congregations from various denominations and their role in facilitating economic incorporation of newcomers. Some anecdotal data from my fieldwork suggest that protestant denominations might further facilitate immigrants' aspirations for entrepreneurship, given their emphasis on individuals' prosperity and progress.

NOTES TO CHAPTER 7

1. Phizacklea defines "gendered economy" as a set of entrepreneurial activities inside the overall economy characterized by family firms in which women's labor power provides the backbone of cheap labor costs and low wages.
2. Peruvians show a slightly higher percentage of single parent households than Salvadorans. Whereas 33 per cent of Peruvian women were in non-marital unions, being either divorced, widowed, single, or separated, only 22 per cent of Salvadoran women were single heads of household. Although I did not observe differences in business strategies according to participants' marital status, women's accounts emphasized the strategic assistance provided by spouses' moral, financial, and logistical support. In fact, for many women, spousal financial support during the difficult start-up phase proved instrumental to get their businesses off the ground.
3. As anecdotal data, those Salvadoran men and women who emphasized the role religious beliefs had played in their self-employment motivation belonged to protestant denominations including Baptists, Evangelical, Pentecostal, and other Christian non-denominational traditions. Some of these informants even criticized the Catholic Church for failing to instill notions of progress and prosperity in individuals' lives.
4. There are far fewer day laborer sites where immigrant women can gather daily to seek employment. Many are in the New York and Los Angeles metropolitan area. Scholars claim this is a relatively novel phenomenon and that women day labor sites might be the beginning of a trend given the national economic slowdown in the aftermath of 9/11 and the ongoing war with Iraq. See Los Angeles Times, June 2007; The New York Times, August 2005; Newsday, July 14, 2002; Valenzuela and Meléndez, 2003.

NOTES TO CHAPTER 8

1. Whereas Salvadoran informants participated in Catholic or Evangelical congregations across the metropolitan area, Peruvians tended to congregate across Catholic worship communities.
2. Other negative effects of social capital include collective constraints on individual innovation and behavior, as noted by Nee and Nee in their study on San Francisco's Chinese community (1974).

NOTES TO CHAPTER 9

1. Paulson, Singer, Newberger, and Smith's study on immigrants' access to financial institutions provides a powerful argument about the strong linear relationship between income, employment, homeownership, crime rates, and the percentage of Metropolitan Statistical Area residents who have a bank account.

References

Abbott, C. 1990. Dimensions of Regional Change in Washington, DC. *American Historical Review* 95:1367–1393.

Aizenman, N. C. 2008. In N.Va., a Latino Community Unravels; Job Losses and Pr. William Law Hit Illegal Immigrants and Others. *Washington Post*, March 27.

Alba, R., and V. Nee. 1997. Rethinking Assimilation Theory for a New Era of Immigration. *International Migration Review* 31:826–876.

Aldrich, H., R. Ward, and R. Waldinger. 1990. *Ethnic Entrepreneurs: Immigrant Business in Industrial Societies*. London: Sage Publications.

Altamirano, T. 1992. *Exodo: Peruanos en el Exterior*. Lima: Pontificia Universidad Católica del Perú.

———. 2003. *El Perú y el Ecuador: Nuevos Paises de Emigración*. Universidad Andina Simón Bolivar 2003 [Accessed June 20 2008]. Available from http://www.uasb.edu.ec/padh/revista7/articulos/teofilo%20altamirano.htm.

Anthias, F. 1992. *Ethnicity, Class, Gender and Migration: Greek-Cypriots in Britain*. Aldershot: Avebury.

Auster, E., and H. Aldrich. 1984. Small Business Vulnerability, Ethnic Enclaves and Ethnic Enterprise. In *Ethnic Communities in Business: Strategies for Economic Survival*, edited by R. Ward and R. Jenkins. Cambridge, England: Cambridge University Press.

Bailey, C. 1996. *A Guide to Field Research*. Thousand Oaks, CA: Pine Forge Press.

Bailey, T., and R. Waldinger. 1991. Primary, Secondary and Enclave Labor Markets: A Training Systems Approach. *American Sociological Review* 56:432–445.

Barth, F., ed. 1963. *The Role of the Entrepreneur in Social Change in Northern Norway*. Bergen: Universitetsforlaget.

———. 1969. *Ethnic Groups and Boundaries: The Social Organization of Cultural Difference*. London: Allen and Unwin.

Basch, L., N. Glick Schiller, and C. Szanton Blanc. 1994. *Nations Unbound: Transnational Projects, Postcolonial Predicaments and Deterritorialized Nation-States*. Langhorne, PA: Gordon and Breach.

Bates, T. 1997. *Race, Self-Employment, and Upward Mobility: An Illusive American Dream*. Baltimore: John Hopkins University Press.

Becker, G. 1975. *Human Capital: A Theoretical and Empirical Analysis*. 2 ed. New York: National Bureau of Economic Research.

Bernard, J. 1995. The Good-Provider Role. In *Men's Lives*, edited by M. S. Kimmel and M. A. Messner. New York: Macmillan.

Bernard, R. H. 1988. *Research Methods in Cultural Anthropology*. Newbury Park, CA: Sage Publications.

Biggart, N. Woolsgold. 2002. *Readings in Economic Sociology*. Oxford: Blackwell.

Boissevain, J. 1974. *Friends of Friends: Networks, Manipulators and Coalitions*. New York: St. Martin's Press.

Bonacich, E. 1973. A Theory of Middleman Minorities. *American Sociological Review* 38:538–594.

———. 1993. The other side of ethnic entrepreneurship: A dialogue with Waldinger, Aldrich, Ward and Associates. *International Migration Review* 27 (3):685–692.

Bonacich, E., and I. Light. 1977. Koreans in Small Business. *Society* 14:54–59.

Bonacich, E., and J. Modell. 1980. *The Economic Basis of Ethnic Solidarity*. Los Angeles: University of California Press.

Borjas, G. J. 1990. *Friends or Strangers: The Impact of Immigrants on the American Economy*. New York: Basic Books.

Bott, E. 1957. *Family and Social Networks*. London: Tavistock Publications.

Bourdieu, P. 1977. Le Trois États du Capital Culturel. *Actes de la Recherche en Sciences Sociales* 30:3–5.

Boyd, M. 1989. Family and Personal Networks in International Migration: Recent Developments and New Agendas. *International Migration Review* 23:638–670.

Brennan, D. 2004. *What's love got to do with it? Transnational Desires and Sex Tourism in the Dominican Republic*. Durban and London: Duke University Press.

Browning, R., D. Marshall, and D. Tabb. 1984. *Protest Is Not Enough*. Berkeley: University of California Press.

Burt, R. 1992. *Structural Holes: The Social Structure of Competition*. Cambridge: Harvard University Press.

Camarota, S. 2000. *Reconsidering Immigrant Entrepreneurship: An Examination of Self-Employment among Natives and the Foreign Born*. Washington, DC: Center for Immigration Studies.

Cantú, L. Jr. 2002. De Ambiente: Queer Tourism and the Shifting Boundaries of Mexican Male Sexualities. *GLQ: Journal of Lesbian and Gay Studies* 8:139–166.

Censo Nacional del Perú. 1994. *Estadísticas Nacionales de Emigración al Exterior*. Lima: Imprenta Nacional.

Chavez, L. R. 1998. *Shadowed Lives: Undocumented Immigrants in American Society*. Fort Worth: Harcourt Brace College Publishers.

———. 1995. Understanding Knowledge and Attitudes about Breast Cancer: A Cultural Analysis. *Archives of Family Medicine* 4:145–152.

Chiswick, B. R. 1974. *Income Inequality: Regional Analysis Within A Human Capital Framework*. New York: National Bureau of Economic Research, Columbia University Press.

———. 1985. Differences in Education and Earnings Across Racial and Ethnic Groups: Tastes, Discrimination, and Investments in Child Quality. *Quarterly of Journal of Economics* CIII 3:590–591.

Chow, E. Ngan-ling. 1994. Asian American Women at Work: Survival, Resistance and Coping. In *Women of Color in US Society*, edited by M. B. Zinn and B. Thornton Dill. Philadelphia: Temple University Press.

———. 1996. Family, Economy, and the State: A Legacy of Struggle for Chinese American Women. In *Origins and Destinies: Immigration, Race and Ethnicity in America*, edited by S. Pedraza and R. Rumbaut. New York: Wadsworth Publishing Company.

———, ed. 2002. *Transforming Gender and Development in East Asia*. New York and London: Routledge.

————. 2003. Gender Matters: Studying Globalization and Social Change in the 21st Century. *International Sociology* 18 (3):443–460.

Chow, E. Ngan-ling, D. Wilkinson, and M. Baca Zim. 1996. *Race, Class and Gender: Common Bonds, Different Voices*. Newbury Park, CA: Sage Publications.

Coffey, A., and P. Atkinson. 1996. *Making Sense of Qualitative Data: Complementary Research Strategies*. Thousand Oaks, CA: Sage Publications.

Coleman, J. 1988. Social Capital in the Creation of Human Capital. *American Journal of Sociology* 94:S95-S121.

Cornelius, W. A. 1982. Interviewing Undocumented Immigrants: Methodological Reflections Based on Fieldwork in Mexico and the US. *International Migration Review* 16 (2):378–411.

Cornell, S. 1996. The Variable Ties that Bind: Content and Circumstance in Ethnic Processes. *Ethnic and Racial Studies* 19 (2):265–289.

Creswell, J. W. 1998. *Qualitative Inquiry and Research Design: Choosing Among Five Traditions*. Thousand Oaks, CA: Sage Publications.

Curran, S. R., K. Donato, F. Garip, and S Shafer. 2006. Mapping Gender and Migration in Sociological Scholarship: Is it Segregation or Integration? *International Migration Review* 40 (1):199–223.

Curran, S. R , and E. Rivero-Fuentes. 2003. Engendering Migrant Networks: The Case of Mexican Migration. *Demography* 40 (2):289–307

Curran, S. R., and A. C. Saguy. 2001. Migration and Cultural Change: A Role for Gender and Social Networks? *Journal for International Women's Studies* 2 (3):54–77.

Durand, J., and D. Massey. 1992. Mexican Migration to the United States: A Critical Review. *Latin American Research Review* 27:3–42.

Ebaugh, H. R., and J. S. Chafetz. 1999. Agents for Cultural Reproduction and Structural Change: The Ironic Role of Women in Immigrant Religious Institutions. *Social Forces* 78 (2):585–613.

Edwards, B., M. W. Foley, and M. Diani. 2001. *Beyond Tocqueville: Civil Society and the Social Capital Debate in Comparative Perspective*. Hanover, New Hampshire: Tufts University/University Press of New England.

Else, J., and C. Clay-Thomson. 1999. *Refugee Microenterprise Development: Achievements and Lessons Learned*. Washington, DC: Institute for Social and Economic Development.

Espiritu, Y. L. 1996. Panethnicity and US Racial Politics: The Asian American Case, edited by Calhoun and Ritzer. Columbus, OH: McGraw-Hill Primis.

————. 1997. *Asian American Women and Men: Labor, Laws and Love*. Thousand Oaks, CA: Sage Publications.

————. 2003. *Home Bound: Filipino American Lives Across Cultures, Communities and Countries*. Berkeley: University of California Press.

Fernández-Kelly, M. P. 1994. Towanda's Triumph: Social and Cultural Capital in the Transition to Adulthood in the Urban Ghetto. *International Journal of Urban and Regional Research* 18 (1):88–111.

————. 1995. Social and Cultural Capital in the Urban Ghetto: Implications for the Economic Sociology of Immigration. In *The Economic Sociology of Immigration*, edited by A. Portes. New York: Rusell Sage Foundation.

Fernández-Kelly, M. P., and A. M. García. 1990. Power Surrendered, Power Restored: The Politics of Home and Work among Hispanic Women in Southern California and Southern Florida. In *Women, Change, and Politics*, edited by L. A. Tilly and P. Gurin. New York: Rusell Sage Foundation.

Fernández-Kelly, M. P., and R. Schauffler. 1996. Divided Fates: Immigrant Children in a Restructured US Economy. *International Migration Review* 28 (4):662–689.

Ferree, M. 1979. Employment without Liberation: Cuban Women in the United States. *Social Science Quarterly* 60:35–50.

Fix, M., W. Zimmermann, and J. Passel. 2001. *The Integration of Immigrant Families in the United States.* Washington, DC: The Urban Institute.

Foley, M., J. McCarthy, and M. Chaves. 2001. Social Capital, Religious Institutions, and Poor Communities. In *Social Capital and Poor Communities*, edited by M. Warren, J. P. Thompson and S. Saegert. New York: Rusell Sage Foundation.

Fraga, L., J. Garcia, H. Rodney, M. Jones-Correa, V. Martinez-Ebers, and G. Segura. 2007. Redefining America: Key Findings from the 2006 Latino National Survey. *Presentation at the Woodrow Wilson Center.* Washington, DC.

Freeman, L. C., D. R. White, and A. K. Romney, eds. 1989. *Research Methods in Social Network Analysis.* Fairfax, VA: George Mason University Press.

Friedman, S. 2000. Behind the Monuments: Taking a Sociological Look at Life in the Nation's Capital. *Footnotes.*

Friedman, S., I. Cheung, M. Price, and A. Singer. 2001. *Washington's Newcomers: Mapping a New City of Immigration.* Washington, DC: Center for Washington Area Studies.

Funkhouser, E. 1992. Mass Emigration, Remittances, and Economic Adjustment: The Case of El Salvador in the 1980s. In *Immigration and the Workforce: Economic Consequences for the United States and Source Areas*, edited by G. Borjas and R. Freeman. Chicago: University of Chicago Press.

Gelles, P., and W. Martinez. 1992. Transnational Fiesta. Berkeley, CA: University of California Extension, Center for Media and Independent Learning.

Gilbertson, G. 1995. Women's Labor and Enclave Employment: The Case of Dominican and Colombian Women in New York City. *International Migration Review* 29 (3):657–671.

Glaser, B. G., and A. L. Strauss. 1967. *The Discovery of Grounded Theory: Strategies for Qualitative Research.* Chicago: Aldine.

Glazer, N., and D. P. Moynihan. 1970. *Beyond the Melting Pot: The Negroes, Puerto Ricans, Jews, Italians and Irish of New York City.* Cambridge, MA: The M.I.T Press.

Gordon, M. 1964. *Assimilation in American Life: The Role of Race, Religion, and National Origins.* New York: Oxford University Press.

Gorman, A. 2007. Day labor centers see some new faces: immigrant women. *Los Angeles Times*, June 11.

Granovetter, M. 1973. The Strength of Weak Ties. *American Journal of Sociology* 78:1360–1380.

———. 1974. *Getting A Job: A Study of Contacts and Careers.* Cambridge, MA: Harvard University Press.

———. 1985. Economic Action and Social Structure: The Problem of Embeddedness. *American Journal of Sociology* 91:481–510.

———. 1990. The Old and the New Economic Sociology: A History and an Agenda. In *Beyond the Marketplace: Rethinking Economy and Society*, edited by R. Friedland and A. F. Robertson. New York: Aldine de Gruyter.

———. 1995. The Economic Sociology of Firms and Entrepreneurs. In *The Economic Sociology of Immigration*, edited by A. Portes. New York: Russell Sage Foundation.

———. 2002. A Theoretical Agenda for Economic Sociology. In *The New Economic Sociology: Developments in an Emerging Field*, edited by M. Guillen, R. Collins, P. England and M. Meyer. New York: Russell Sage Foundation.

Grasmuck, S., and R. Grosfoguel. 1997. Geopolitics, Economic Niches, and Gendered Social Capital among Recent Caribbean Immigrants in New York City. *Sociological Perspectives* 40 (3):339–363.

Grasmuck, S., and P. Pessar. 1991. *Between Two Islands: Dominican International Migration*. Berkeley: University of California Press.

———. 1996. Dominicans in the United States: First and Second-Generation Settlement, 1960–1990. In *Origins and Destinies: Immigration, Race and Ethnicity in America*, edited by S. Pedraza and R. Rumbaut. Belmont: Wadsworth Publishing Company.

Guarnizo, L. E. 1992. One Country in Two: Dominican-owned Firms in New York and in the Dominican Republic. *Ph.D. diss.* Baltimore: Johns Hopkins University.

Guba, E. G., and Y. S. Lincoln. 1994. Competing Paradigms in Qualitative Research. In *Handbook of Qualitative Research*, edited by N. K. Denzin and Y. S. Lincoln. Thousand Oaks, CA: Sage Publications.

Guillen, M., R. Collins, P. England, and M. Meyer, eds. 2002. *The New Economic Sociology: Developments in an Emerging Field*. New York: Russell Sage Foundation.

Hagan, J. M. 1998. Social Networks, Gender and Immigrant Incorporation. *American Sociological Review* 63 (1):57–67.

Hamilton, N., and N. Stoltz Chinchilla. 1997. Central American Migration: A Framework for Analysis. In *Challenging Fronteras: Structuring Latina and Latino Lives in the US*, edited by M. Romero, P. Hondagneu-Sotelo and V. Ortiz. New York: Routledge

Hechter, M. 1987. *Principles of Group Solidarity*. Berkeley and Los Angeles: University of California Press.

Henry, S. 2000. Digital Capital: Bear this in Mind: Domain is Destiny. *Washington Post*, May 8.

Hondagneu-Sotelo, P. 1994. *Gendered Transitions: Mexican Experiences of Immigration*. Berkeley: University of California Press.

———. 2001 *Doméstica: Immigrant Workers Cleaning and Caring in the Shadows of Affluence*. Berkeley: University of California Press

Hondagneu-Sotelo, P., and E. Avila. 1999. I'm Here, But I'm There: The Meanings of Latina Transnational Motherhood. *Gender & Society* 11 (5):548–571.

Hoover, K. 2002. SBA's new chief operating officer to 'streamline' agency. *Washington Business Journal*, January 18.

Julca, A. 2001. Peruvian Networks for Migration in New York City's Labor Market, 1970–1996. In *Migration, Transnationalization, and Race in a Changing New York*, edited by H. Cordero-Guzmán, R. Smith and R. Grosfoguel. Philadelphia: Temple University Press.

Jurik, N. 2005. *Bootstrap Dreams: US Microenterprise Development in an Era of Welfare Reform*. Ithaca: Cornell University Press.

Kang, C. 2007. Prince William Crackdown Worries Some Merchants, Many Businesses Rely on Immigrants. *Washington Post*, October 27.

Kibria, N. 1993. *Family Tightrope: The Changing Lives of Vietnamese Americans*. Princeton, NJ: Princeton University Press.

Kimmel, M. S., and M. A. Messner, eds. 2001. *Men's Lives*. 5 ed. Boston: Allyn and Bacon.

Kingsley, T., K. S. Pettit, and C. Hayes. 1998. *Washington Baseline: Key Indicators for the Nation's Capital*. Washington, DC: The Urban Institute.

Kloosterman, R. 2000. Immigrant Entrepreneurship and the Institutional Context: A Theoretical Exploration. In *Immigrant Businesses: The Economic, Political and Social Environment*, edited by J. Rathe. New York: St. Martin's Press.

Klosterman, R., and J. Rath, eds. 2003. *Immigrant Entrepreneurs: Venturing Abroad in the Age of Globalization*. Oxford: Berg.

Latino Economic Development Center (LEDC). 2007. Annual Report.

Lee, E. S. 1966. A Theory of Migration. *Demography* 3 (47–57).

Levitt, P. 1995. A Todos Les Llamo Primo (I Call Everyone Cousin): The Social Basis for Latino Small Businesses. In *New Migrants in the Marketplace: Boston's Ethnic Entrepreneurs*, edited by M. Halter. Amherst, MA: University of Massachusetts Press.

———. 2001. *The Transnational Villagers*. Berkeley: University of California Press.

Light, I. 1972. *Ethnic Enterprise in America: Business and Welfare among Chinese, Japanese and Blacks*. Berkeley: University of California Press.

———. 1984. Immigrant and Ethnic Enterprise in North America. *Ethnic and Racial Studies* 7:195–216.

Light, I., and P. Bhachu, eds. 1993. *Immigration & Entrepreneurship: Culture, Capital and Ethnic Networks*. London: Transaction Publishers.

Light, I., and E. Bonacich. 1988. *Immigrant Entrepreneurs: Koreans in Los Angeles, 1965–1982*. Berkeley and Los Angeles: University of California Press.

Light, I., and S. Gold. 2000. *Ethnic Economies*. San Diego: Academic Press.

Light, I., and C. Rosenstein. 1995. Expanding the Interaction Theory of Entrepreneurship. In *The Economic Sociology of Immigration: Essays on Networks, Ethnicity and Entrepreneurship*, edited by A. Portes. New York: Rusell Sage Foundation.

———. 1995. *Race, Ethnicity and Entrepreneurship in Urban America*. New York: Aldine De Gruyter.

Light, I., G. Sabagh, M. Bozorgmehr, and C. Der-Martirosian. 1993. Internal Ethnicity in the Ethnic Economy. *Ethnic & Racial Studies* 16:125–146.

Lin, N. 2001. *Social Capital: A Theory of Social Structure and Action*. New York: Cambridge University Press.

Livingston, G. 2006. Gender, Job Searching and Employment Outcomes among Mexican Immigrants. *Population Research and Policy Review* 25 (1):43–66.

Logan, J. R., R. D. Alba, and W. Zhang. 2002. Immigrant Enclaves and Ethnic Communities in New York and Los Angeles. *American Sociological Review* 67 (2):299–322.

Lomnitz, L. 1977. *Networks and Marginality*. New York: Academic Press.

Lopez, D., and Y. L. Espiritu. 1990. Panethnicity in the United States: A Theoretical Framework. *Ethnic & Racial Studies* 13 (2):198–224.

Mahler, S. 1995. *American Dreaming: Immigrant Life on the Margins*. Princeton: Princeton University Press.

———. 1996. *Conflict and Symbiosis*. Needham Heights, MA: Allyn and Bacon.

———. 1999. Engendering Transnational Migration: A Case Study of Salvadorans. *American Behavioral Scientist* 42 (4):690–719.

Mahler, S., and P. R. Pessar. 2006. Gender Matters: Ethnographers Bring Gender from the Periphery towards the Core of Migration Studies. *International Migration Review* 40 (1):27–63.

Manning, R. D. 1998. Multicultural Washington, DC: The Changing Social and Economic Landscape of a Post-Industrial City. *Ethnic & Racial Studies* 21:328–355.

Marticorena, P. A. Landolt. 2001. The Causes and Consequences of Transnational Migration: Salvadorans in Los Angeles and Washington, DC. Ph.D. diss. Baltimore: Johns Hopkins University.

Martinez, M. A. 2008. *Promoting and Maintaining Household Ownership Among Latino Immigrants. Esperanza Hispanic Housing Studies* 2007 [accessed July 20 2008]. Available from http://www.esperanza.us.

Marx, K. 1956. *Selected Writings in Sociology and Social Philosophy, translated by T. B. Bottomore*. New York: McGraw-Hill.

———. 1965. *Capital*. Vol. 1. Moscow: Progress Publishers.

Massey, D. S. 1989. Hypersegregation in US Metropolitan Areas: Black and Hispanic Segregation along Five Dimensions. *Demography* 26:373–391.

Massey, D. S., R. Alarcon, J. Durand, and H. Gonzalez. 1987. *Return to Aztlan: The Social Process of International Migration from Western Mexico*. Berkeley: University of California Press.

Menjivar, C. 1997. Immigrant Kinship Networks and the Impact of the Receiving Context: Salvadorans in San Francisco in the Early 1990s. *Social Problems* 44 (1):104–123.

———. 2000. *Fragmented Ties: Salvadoran Immigrant Networks in America*. Berkeley: University of California Press.

Messner, M. A. 1990. Boyhood, Organized Sports, and the Construction of Masculinities. *Journal of Contemporary Ethnography* 18 (4):416–444.

Miles, M. B., and A. M. Huberman. 1994. *Qualitative Data Analysis: An Expanded Sourcebook*. Thousand Oaks, CA: Sage Publications.

Mobasher, M. 2003. Ethnic Resources and Ethnic Economy: The Case of Iranian Immigrants in Dallas. In *Migration, Globalization, and Ethnic Relations: An Interdisciplinary Approach*, edited by M. Mobasher and M. Sadri. Upper Saddle River, NJ: Prentice Hall.

Monaghan, J. 1973. *Chile, Peru, and the California Gold Rush of 1849*. Berkeley: University of California Press.

Montes, S., and J. García. 1988. *Salvadoran Migration to the United States: An Exploratory Study, Hemispheric Migration Project*. Washington DC: Center for Immigration Policy and Refugee Assistance, Georgetown University.

Morawska, E. 2004. Immigrant Transnational Entrepreneurs in New York: Three Varieties and Their Correlates. *International Journal of Entrepreneurial Behavior and Research* 10 (5):325–348.

Moreno, S. 2002. Prejudices Persist Against DC Latinos. *Washington Post*, May 2.

Morokvasic, M. 1983. Women in Migration: Beyond the Reductionist Outlook. In *One Way Ticket: Migration and Female Labor*, edited by A. Phizacklea. London: Routledge and Paul.

———. 1993. Immigrants in Garment Production in Paris and Berlin. In *Immigration and Entrepreneurship: Culture, Capital, and Ethnic Networks*, edited by I. Light and P. Bhachu. New Brunswick and London: Transaction Publishers.

Nee, V., and B. Nee. 1974. *Longtime Californ': A Study of an American Chinese Community*. Boston: Houghton Mifflin.

Nee, V., B. Nee, and J. Sanders. 2001. Understanding the Diversity of Modes of Incorporation: A Forms-of-Capital Model. *Ethnic & Racial Studies* 24:386–412.

Newsday. 2002. Changing Face of Labor: Immigrant women seek out daily work from street corners. *Newsday*, July 14.

Noon, T. 2001. Hitting Bottom: Homelessness, Poverty, and Masculinity. In *Men's Lives*, edited by M. S. Kimmel and M. A. Messner. Boston: Allyn and Bacon.

Olzak, S. 1983. Contemporary Ethnic Mobilization. *Annual Review of Sociology* 9:355–374.

Organización Internacional para las Migraciones. 2008. DIGEMIN. Perú: Estadísticas de la Migración Internacional de Peruanos, 1990—2007: Dirección General de Migraciones y Naturalización, Instituto Nacional de Estadísticas e Información, Lima.

Paerregaard, K. 2005. Inside the Hispanic Melting Pot: Negotiating National and Multicultural Identities among Peruvians in the United States. Special Feature: Los Que Llegaron: South American Immigrants in the United States. *Latino Studies* 3 (1):76–96.

Parreñas, R. 2000. *Servants of Globalization: Women, Migration and Domestic Work*. Stanford, CA: Stanford University Press.

————. 2003. *Children of Global Migration: Transnational Families and Gendered Woes*. Stanford, CA: Stanford University Press.

Paulson, A., A. Singer, R. Newberger, and J. Smith. 2008. *Financial Access for Immigrants: Lessons from Diverse Perspectives*. Federal Reserve Banks of Chicago and the Brookings Institution 2006 [accessed July 20 2008]. Available from http://media.brookings.edu/mediaarchive/pubs/metro/pubs/20060504_financialaccess.pdf

Pedersen, D. 2001. In Pursuit of American Value: Credibility, Credulity and Credit in El Salvador and the United States (Unpublished Manuscript).

Pedraza, S. 1991. Women and Migration: The Social Consequences of Gender. *Annual Review of Sociology* 17:303–325.

Pessar, P. 1986. The Role of Gender in Dominican Settlement Patterns in the United States. In *Women and Change in Latin America*, edited by J. Nash and H. Safa. South Hadley, MA: Bergin & Garvey Publishers.

————. 1995. The Elusive Enclave: Ethnicity, Class and Nationality among Latino Entrepreneurs in Greater Washington DC. *Human Organization* 54 (4):383–392.

————. 1999. Engendering Migration Studies: The Case of New Immigrants in the United States. *American Behavioral Scientist* 42 (2):577–600.

Pessar, P., and S. Mahler. 2003. Transnational Migration: Bringing Gender. *International Migration Review* 37 (3):812–846.

Phizacklea, A. 1983. In the Front Line. In *One Way Ticket: Migration and Female Labor*, edited by A. Phizacklea. London: Routledge and Kegan Paul.

————. 1988. Entrepreneurship, Ethnicity and Gender. In *Enterprising Women: Ethnicity, Economy and Gender Relations*, edited by S. Westwood and P. Bhachu. London and New York: Routledge.

Piore, M. J. 1979. *Birds of Passage: Migrant Labor and Industrial Societies*. Cambridge, UK: Cambridge University Press.

Polanyi, K. 1992 (1957). The Economy as Instituted Process. In *The Sociology of Economic Life*, edited by M. Granovetter and R. Swedberg. Boulder, Colorado: Westview Press.

————. 1944. *The Great Transformation*. Boston: Beacon Press.

Portes, A., ed. 1995. *The Economic Sociology of Immigration*. New York: Rusell Sage Foundation.

————. 1998. Social Capital: Its Origins and Applications in Modern Sociology. *Annual Review of Sociology* 24:1–24.

Portes, Alejandro, and Robert L. Bach. 1985. *Latin Journey: Cuban and Mexican Immigrants in the United States*. Berkeley: University of California Press.

Portes, A., and J. Borocz. 1988. Contemporary Immigration: Theoretical Perspectives On Its Determinants and Modes of Incorporation. *International Migration Review* 23:606–630.

Portes, A., J. M. Clark, and R. L. Bach. 1977. The New Wave: A Statistical Profile of Recent Cuban Exiles to the United States. *Cuban Studies* 7:1–32.

Portes, A., W. J. Halle, and L. E. Guarnizo. 2002. Transnational Entrepreneurs: An Alternative Form of Immigrant Economic Adaptation. *American Sociological Review* 67 (2):278–298.

Portes, A., and P. Landolt. 1996. The Downside of Social Capital. *The American Prospect* 26:18–22.

Portes, A., and R. D. Manning. 1986. The Immigrant Enclave: Theory and Empirical Examples. In *Competitive Ethnic Relations*, edited by S. Olzack and J. Nagel. FL: Academic Press.

Portes, A., and R. Rumbaut. 1996. *Immigrant America: A Portrait*. 2nd ed. Berkeley: University of California Press.

Portes, A., and J. Sensenbrenner. 1993. Embeddedness and Immigration: Notes on the Social Determinants of Economic Action. *American Journal of Sociology* 98:1320–1350.

Portes, A., and M. Zhou. 1992. Gaining the Upper Hand: Economic Mobility Among Immigrant and Domestic Minorities. *Ethnic & Racial Studies* 15 (4):491–522.

———. 1993. The New Second Generation: Segmented Assimilation and its Variants. *Annals of the American Academy of Political and Social Sciences* 530:74–96.

Price, M., and A. Singer. 2008. Edge Gateways: Immigrants, Suburbs, and the Politics of Reception in Metropolitan Washington. In *Twenty-First-Century Gateways: Immigrant Incorporation in Suburban America*, edited by A. Singer, S. W. Hardwick and C. B. Brettel. Washington, DC: Brookings Institution Press.

Putnam, R. 1993. The Prosperous Community: Social Capital and Public Life. *The American Prospect* 13:35–42.

Raijiman, R., and M. Tienda. 2000. Immigrants' Pathway to Business Ownership: A Comparative Ethnic Perspective. In *Immigration and Opportunity: Race, Ethnicity, and Employment in the United States*, edited by F. D. Bean and S. Bell-Rose. New York: Rusell Sage Foundation.

Rath, J. 2000. *Immigrant Businesses: The Economic, Political, and Social Environment*. New York: St. Martin's Press.

———. 2002. *Unraveling the Rag Trade: Immigrant Entrepreneurship in Seven World Cities*. Oxford: Berg Press.

Repak, T. 1995. *Waiting On Washington: Central American Workers in the Nation's Capital*. Philadelphia: Temple University Press.

Robles, B. J., and H. Cordero-Guzman. 2007. Latino Self-Employment and Entrepreneurship in the United States: An Overview of the Literature and Data Sources. *The ANNALS of the American Academy of Political and Social Science* 613 (1):18–31.

Rodriguez, H., R. Saenz, and C. Menjivar, eds. 2008. *Latinas/os in the United States: Changing the Face of America*. Secaucus, NJ: Springer.

Rouse, R. 1991. Mexican Migration and the Social Space of Postmodernism. *Diaspora: A Journal of Transnational Studies* 1 (1):8–23.

Roy, K., and H. McClure. 2002. *The State of Latinos in the District of Columbia: Trends, Consequences and Recommendations*. Washington, DC: Council of Latino Agencies.

Rumbaut, R., M. Tienda, and F. Mitchell. 2006. *Multiple Origins, Uncertain Destinies: Hispanics and the American future*. Washington, DC: National Academies Press.

Sanders, J. M., and V. Nee. 1987. Limits of Ethnic Solidarity in the Ethnic Economy. *American Sociological Review* 52:745–773.

———. 1996. Immigrant Self-Employment: The Family as Social Capital and the Value of Human Capital. *American Sociological Review* 61 (4):231–249.

Sassen-Koob, S. 1979. Formal and Informal Associations: Dominicans and Colombians in New York. In *Caribbean Life in New York City: Sociocultural Dimensions*, edited by C. Sutton and E. Chaney. New York: Center for Migration Studies of New York.

———. 1980. Immigrant and Minority Workers in the Organization of the Labor Process. *Journal of Ethnic Studies* 1:1–34.

———. 1984. Notes on the Incorporation of Third World Women into Wage Labor through Immigration and Off-shore Production. *International Migration Review* 18 (4):1144–1167.

———. 1994. *Cities in a World Economy, Sociology for a New Century*. Thousand Oaks, CA: Pine Forge Press.

Schiller, N. Glick, L. Bash, and C. Blanc-Szanton. 1992. *Towards a Transnational Perspective on Migration: Race, Class, Ethnicity and Nationalism Reconsidered.* New York: New York Academy of Sciences.

Schumpeter, J. A. 1934. *History of Economic Development, translated by Redvers Opie.* Cambridge, MA: Harvard University Press.

———. 1943. *Capitalism, Socialism, and Democracy.* London: Allen & Unwin.

———. 1988. *Essays: On Entrepreneurs, Innovations, Business Cycles, and the Evolution of Capitalism.* New Brunswick, NJ: Transaction Publishers.

Scott, J. 2001. A Census Query Is Said to Skew Data on Latinos. *New York Times,* June 27.

Shreiner, M., and J. Morduch. 2002. Opportunities and Challenges for Microfinance in the United States. In *Replicating Microfinance in the United States,* edited by J. Carr and Z. Y. Tong. Washington, DC: Woodrow Wilson Center Press.

Simmel, Georg. 1964. *The Sociology of Georg Simmel.* Glencoe, IL: Free Press.

Singer, A. 2007. Latin American Immigrants in the Washington, DC Metropolitan area. Washington, DC: Woodrow Wilson International Center for Scholars.

Singer, A., S. Friedman, I. Cheung, and M. Price. 2001. The World in a Zip Code: Greater Washington DC as a New Region of Immigration. In *The Brookings Institution Survey Series.* Washington, DC: Center on Urban & Metropolitan Policy, Brookings Greater Washington Research Program.

Singer, A., S. W. Hardwick, and C. B. Brettel, eds. 2008. *Twenty-First-Century Gateways: Immigrant Incorporation in Suburban America.* Washington, DC: Brookings Institution Press.

Singleton, R., B. C. Straits, and M. M. Straits. 1993. *Approaches to Social Research.* 2nd ed. New York: Oxford University Press.

Small Business Administration. 1998. The New American Evolution: The Role and Impact of Small Firms: SBA Office of Economic Research.

———. 2002. Tabulations of 1990–2000 Loans by Ethnicity. The Office of Advocacy, based on data from Office of Financial Assistance.

———. 2007. District Office Small Business Resource Guide. Washington, DC.

Smelser, N. J., and R. Swedberg, eds. 1994. *Handbook of Economic Sociology.* Princeton, NJ: Princeton University Press.

Sombart, W. 1951. *The Jews and Modern Capitalism.* Glencoe, IL: Free Press.

Stake, R. 1995. *The Art of Case Study Research.* Thousand Oaks, CA: Sage Publications.

Steinmetz, G., and E. O. Wright. 1989. The Fall and Rise of the Petty Bourgeoisie: Changing Patterns of Self-Employment in the Postwar United States. *American Journal of Sociology* 94:973–1018.

Stoller, P. 2002. *Money Has No Smell: The Africanization of New York City.* Chicago: University of Chicago Press.

Swedberg, R. 2000. The Social Science View of Entrepreneurship. In *Entrepreneurship: The Social Science View,* edited by R. Swedberg. Oxford: Oxford University Press.

———. 2003. *Principles of Economic Sociology.* Princeton, NJ: Princeton University Press.

Taylor, J. E. 1986. Differential Migration, Networks, Information and Risk. Migration and Development Program Discussion Paper No. 11. Cambridge, MA: Migration and Development Program, Harvard University.

Thornton, P. 1999. The Sociology of Entrepreneurship. *Annual Review of Sociology* 25:19–46.

Tilly, C., and C. H. Brown. 1967. On Uprooting, Kinship, and the Auspices of Migration. *International Journal of Comparative Sociology* 8:139–164.

Ulloa, R. E. 1998. *De indocumentados a ciudadanos: Características de los salva-doreños legalizados en Estados Unidos.* San Salvador: FLACSO.
US Bureau of the Census. 2007. The American Community—Hispanics: 2004. American Community Survey Reports: Washington DC: US Department of Commerce.
———. 2006. American Community Survey. Selected Population Profile in the United States. S0201 Washington, DC: US Government Printing Office.
———. 2000. Census of Population and Housing. United States: Summary Tape File 1 (SF1).
———. 1992, 1990. Census of Population, General Social and Economic Characteristics, DC Report: Washington, DC: US Government Printing Office.
———. 2003, 2000. Census of Population: The Foreign-Born Population in the United States. 2000 CP-3-1: Washington, DC: US Government Printing Office.
———. 2000. Current Population Report, March: Washington, DC: US Government Printing Office.
———. 1996, 1992. Survey of Minority and Women-Owned Business Enterprises, Hispanics: Washington, DC: US Government Printing Office.
———. 2001, 1997 Survey of Minority and Women-Owned Business Enterprises, Hispanics: Washington, DC: US Government Printing Office.
———. 2006, 2002 Survey of Minority and Women-Owned Business Enterprises, Hispanics: Washington, DC: US Government Printing Office.
US Dept. of Commerce, Bureau of the Census. *Census of Population and Housing, 1990.* United States: Summary Tape File 4B. Computer File. ICPSR version. Washington, DC: US Government Printing Office.
Valdez, Z. 2008. Latino/a Entrepreneurship in the United States: A Strategy of Survival and Economic Mobility. In *Latinas/os in the United States: Changing the Face of America,* edited by H. Rodriguez, R. Saenz and C. Menjivar. Secaucus, NJ: Springer.
Valenzuela, A. 1998. Gender Roles and Settlement Activities among Children and Their Immigrant Families. *American Behavioral Scientist* 42 (2):720–742.
———. 2000. Working on the Margins: Immigrant Day Labor Characteristics and Prospects for Employment. In *Working Paper No. 22:* The Center for Comparative Immigration Studies.
———. 2001. Day laborers as entrepreneurs? *Journal of Ethnic and Migration Studies* 27 (2):335–352.
Valenzuela, A., and E. Melendez. 2003. Day Labor in New York: Findings from the NYDL Survey. New York.
Vazquez, M. A., C. E. Seales, and M. Friedmann Marquardt. 2008. New Latino Destinations. In *Latinas/os in the United States: Changing the Face of America,* edited by H. Rodriguez, R. Saenz and C. Menjivar. Secaucus, NJ: Springer.
Verdaguer, M. E. 2001. Doctrinal Orientation, Social Networks and Immigrant Incorporation: Salvadoran Congregations in the Washington Metropolitan Area. *Annual Meeting of the Society for the Scientific Study of Religion.* Columbus, Ohio.
———. 2002. Gender, Congregational Learning Opportunities and Immigrant Incorporation. In *Religion and the New Immigrants. Working Paper No. 3.* Washington, DC: The Catholic University of America-The Pew Charitable Trusts as part of the Gateway Cities Project.
———. 2008. Virginia Latinos. In *Latino America: State-by-State,* edited by M. Overmeyer-Velazquez. Westport: Greenwood Press.
Villar, M. 1994. Hindrances to the Development of an Ethnic Economy among Mexican Migrants. *Human Organization* 53 (3):263–268.

Waldinger, R. 1985. Immigrant Enterprise and the Structure of the Labor Market. In *New Approaches to Economic Life: Economic Restructuring, Unemployment, and the Social Division of Labour*, edited by B. Roberts, R. Finnegan and D. Gallie. Manchester: Manchester University Press.

———. 1986. Immigrant Enterprise: A Critique and Reformulation. *Theory and Society* 15:249–285.

———. 1993. The Two Sides of Ethnic Entrepreneurship: Reply to Bonacich. *International Migration Review* 27 (3):692–701.

———. 1995. The 'Other Side' of Embeddedness: A Case Study of the Interplay of Economy and Ethnicity. *Ethnic & Racial Studies* 18:555–580.

———. 1996. *Still the Promised City: African-Americans and New Immigrants in Post-Industrial New York*. Cambridge, MA: Harvard University Press.

Ward, R. 1991. Economic Development and Ethnic Business. In *Paths of Enterprise*, edited by J. Curran and J. Blackburn. London: Routledge.

Ward, R., and R. Jenkins, eds. 1984. *Ethnic Communities in Business: Strategies for Economic Survival*. Cambridge: Cambridge University Press.

Watters, J. K., and P. Biernacki. 1989. Targeted Sampling: Options for the Study of Hidden Populations. *Social Problems* 36:416–430.

Weber, M. 1958. *The Protestant Ethic and the Spirit of Capitalism, translated by T. Parsons*. Boston: Unwin.

———. 1968. The Economic Relationships of Organized Groups. In *Economy and Society*. New York: Bedminster.

———. 1978. Anticritical Last Word on the Spirit of Capitalism by Max Weber, translated by W. M. Davis. *American Journal of Sociology* 83:1105–1135.

Wei, L., G. Dymski, M. Chee, H. Ahn, C. Aldana, and L. Zhou. 2006. How Ethnic Banks Matter: Banking and Community/Economic Development in Los Angeles. In *Landscapes of Ethnic Economy.*, edited by D. Kaplan and L. Wei. USA: Rowman and Littlefield.

Wellman, B. 1983. Network Analysis: Some Basic Principles. In *Sociological Theory*, edited by R. Collins. San Francisco: Jossey-Bass.

Wellman, B., and S. D. Berkowitz. 1988. *Social Structures: A Network Approach*. Cambridge: Cambridge University Press.

Young, G., and B. Dickerson. 1994. Introduction. In *Color, Class, and Country: Experiences of Gender*, edited by G. Young and B. Dickerson. London and New Jersey: Zed Books.

Young, G., V. Samarasinghe, and K. Kusterer. 1993. *Women at the Center: Development Issues and Practices for the 1990s*. West Hartford: Kumarian Press.

Zhou, M. 2004. Revisiting Ethnic Entrepreneurship: Convergencies, Controversies, and Conceptual Advancements. *International Migration Review* 38 (3):1040–1074.

Zhou, M., and J. Logan. 1989. Returns on Human Capital in Ethnic Chinese Enclaves: New York City's Chinatown. *American Sociological Review* 54 (5):809–820.

Zuiker, V. S., M. J. Katras, C. P. Montalto, and P. D. Olson. 2003. Hispanic Self-Employment: Does Gender Matter? *Hispanic Journal of Behavioral Sciences* 25:73–94.

Index